IRELAND

THE COMPLETE GUIDE

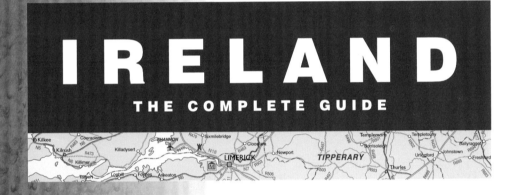

IRELAND

THE COMPLETE GUIDE

Appletree Press

First published in 1998 by The Appletree Press Ltd.
19-21 Alfred Street, Belfast BT2 8DL
Tel: +44 (0)1232 243074 Fax: +44 (0)1232 246756
E-mail: frontdesk@appletree.ie
Web Site: www.irelandseye.com

Text: Hugh Oram. Photographs: William Caddell,
Peter Zoller, John Murphy, Slide File, Belfast City Council,
Stock Pix and Northern Ireland Tourist Board.
Maps: Maps in Minutes and Engineering Surveys
Reproduction Ltd. Thanks also to Bord Fáilte,
Northern Ireland Tourist Board and
Belfast City Council for their assistance.
Design: Triplicate Isis, Belfast

First published in 1998 in the United States of America by
The Globe Pequot Press, Dept. Fil, PO Box 833,
Old Saybrook, CT 06475
Web Site: www.globe-pequot.com

ISBN 0-7627-0248-6

CONTENTS

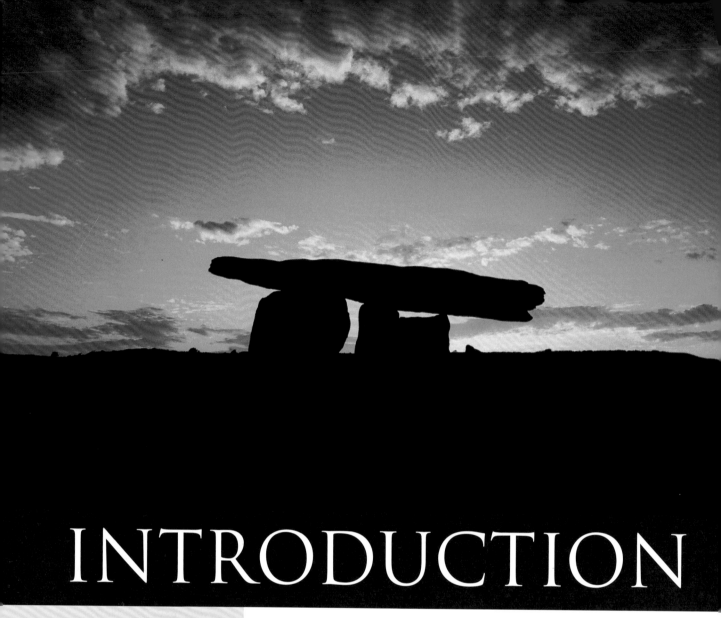

INTRODUCTION

Ireland has a wholly justifiable reputation as a desirable
destination for travellers and holiday-makers: the scenery
is spectacular and the roads are among the least crowded
in Europe; along its 5,600 km of coastline are some of
the best beaches to be encountered anywhere in the
world, while its interior, with some 800 rivers and lakes,
makes it a centre for anglers and naturalists. Its varied
landscapes and rugged, yet accessible, mountain ranges
are a walker's paradise and for those whose interests are
cultural or historical, Ireland has a wealth of fine
buildings, museums and galleries which help preserve
a fascinating if frequently turbulent past. Above all
the renowned welcome that Ireland affords its visitors
ensures that many return year after year.

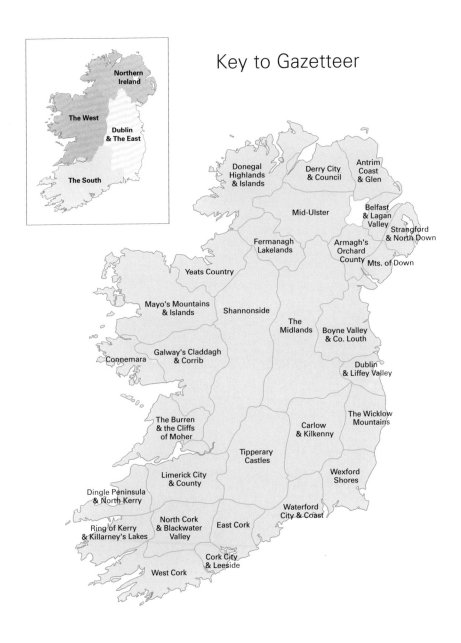

Key to Gazetteer

Northern Ireland

The West

Dublin & The East

The South

Donegal Highlands & Islands

Derry City & Council

Antrim Coast & Glen

Mid-Ulster

Belfast & Lagan Valley

Strangford & North Down

Fermanagh Lakelands

Armagh's Orchard County

Mts. of Down

Yeats Country

Mayo's Mountains & Islands

Shannonside

The Midlands

Boyne Valley & Co. Louth

Connemara

Galway's Claddagh & Corrib

Dublin & Liffey Valley

The Burren & the Cliffs of Moher

Carlow & Kilkenny

The Wicklow Mountains

Tipperary Castles

Wexford Shores

Limerick City & County

Dingle Peninsula & North Kerry

Waterford City & Coast

Ring of Kerry & Killarney's Lakes

North Cork & Blackwater Valley

East Cork

Cork City & Leeside

West Cork

Local Information

Tourists and other visitors are strongly advised to check opening times for buildings and sites before they set out. Quite often, opening times can vary slightly from those given although, especially with country locations, a certain flexibility is shown. Whenever possible, the telephone numbers of individual tourist attractions are listed; during the peak summer period most larger towns in Ireland have Tourist Information Offices (TIOs) in operation with full accesss to information on local opening times. If you are using boat facilities, it's worth checking with the local TIO that the boat operator is licensed. Local TIOs will also tell you which accommodation is registered, a useful consumer safeguard.

Telephones

The telephone systerm in both the Republic of Ireland and Northern Ireland are fully automatic for both national and international calls. In this book, area codes are given in brackets; they need only be dialled when phoning a number outside your own area.

Public Holidays

In the Republic the following are public holidays: 1 January, 17 March (St Patrick's Day), Easter Monday, first Monday in June, first Monday in August, last Monday in October, 25 and 26 December. In Northern Ireland the holidays differ slightly: 1 January, 17 March, Easter Monday, first and last Mondays in May, 12 July, last Monday in August, 25 and 26 December.

Currency

Northern Ireland uses the pound sterling (£) while the Republic uses the punt (IR£). Until 1979 the punt had parity with sterling but the two currencies are no longer interchangeable. The Euro (single European currency) is being introduced in the Republic on 1 January 1999. During the three year transition period, the euro and the punt will be shown side by side, although euro notes will not be introduced until 1 January 2002. Banking hours in the Republic are 10am-4pm Mon-Fri. In most towns there is opening until 5pm one day a week (Thursday in Dublin). In Northern

---

Ireland banks are open 9.30am-12.30pm, 1.30pm-3.30pm Mon-Fri. Some central Belfast banks now remain open over the lunchtime period.

Electric Current

In Ireland the usual voltage is 220v, AC current. Visitors should note that 13amp, square-pin plugs are generally used: adapters are readily available from shops if required.

HISTORY

The first people who settled in Ireland were hunters, probably from Scotland, who arrived in Co. Antrim c. 7000 BC. By 3000 BC tribes from the Mediterranean were building megalithic tombs all over Ireland which reveal a high degree of civilisation. The most spectacular are the passage graves at Newgrange in Co. Meath, Carrowmore and Lough Crew, all of which can be visited. The National Museum in Dublin has a collection of masterpieces from this period: gold collars, torcs, dress fasteners and hair ornaments.

The Celts arrived around 300 BC bringing their distinctive culture, laws and customs. The Irish language derives from a dialect of Celtic, and The Tain is an epic account of Celtic life at the time. In the fifth century St Patrick brought Christianity from Britain, establishing monasteries which became not only centres of learning but in effect small towns. Places associated with Patrick include Slane in Co. Meath where he lit the Paschal fire in defiance of the Druids, Tara, where he used the shamrock to convince the high king about the Trinity, and Downpatrick where a crude slab marks his grave. Irish monks produced a large number of beautifully illustrated manuscripts, among them the Books of Durrow, Armagh and Kells, which can be seen in Trinity College Dublin. The monasteries of Clonmacnoise, Glendalough and Kildare drew scholars from all over Europe. In turn Irish missionaries took education and religion to every corner of Europe. At the same time craftsmen were producing exquisite reliquaries, brooches, belts, and personal adornments made of gold and studded with precious stones (see the Ardagh Chalice and the Cross of Cong in the National Museum). This period is rightly known as the golden age.

The wealth of the monasteries and their towns attracted the Vikings, who swept in, burning and killing. Distinctive round towers and bell towers were built as a refuge fr them. Later the Vikings settled around the coast and founded towns such as Cork, Waterford, Limerick and Dublin. They were finally defeated by Brian Boru at the Battle of Clontarf in 1014. On his death, inter-kingdom rivalry led to a century of chaos until the Normans arrived from England and brought order and prosperity. They were so well assimilated into Irish society that the English crown decided a reconquest was needed. Ulster put up fierce resistance under Hugh O'Neill and Hugh O'Donnell but they were finally defeated at the Battle of Kinsale in 1601. Their exile and that of the Gaelic aristocracy is known as the "Flight of the Earls". The systematic dispossession of the natives and settlement of migrants from England and Scotland followed. This division of Protestant settler and native Catholic has had repercussions ever since.

The campaign of Oliver Cromwell in Ireland is infamous and lives on in folk memory as the "curse of Cromwell". His approach to the Irish problem was drastic: the remaining Irish land-owners were stripped of their property; those who could prove themselves loyal were exiled to Connacht, those who could not were put to death. The incompetent James II was deposed from the English throne (for trying to impose Catholicism on the English) by William of Orange in 1688. William then defeated him at the Battle of the Boyne on 12 July 1690. This battle is celebrated each year as Orangeman's Day, a public holiday in Northern Ireland.

James was replaced by Patrick Sarsfield, and the war dragged on until the signing of the Treaty of Limerick, which was accompanied by the imposition of harsh penal laws. This oppression, coupled with grinding poverty and recurring food shortages, continued for more than a century. A series of revolts at the end of the eighteenth century culminated in the French invasion of Killala, Co. Mayo. Although initially successful it was finally suppressed with great slaughter.

The Act of Union in 1800 abolished the Dublin parliament and removed power to London. Daniel O'Connell's election to Westminster (which, as a Catholic, he was forbidden to enter) led to the repeal of the more oppressive laws and to Catholic emancipation. A firm believer in non-violence, he came near to the repeal of the union but his final years were clouded by the Great Famine when nearly a million died and two million emigrated.

Parnell became leader of the Home Rule Party in 1877, and with Gladstone's support, a Home Rule Bill nearly succeeded. Other leaders followed: Arthur Griffith founded Sinn Fein as a non-violent movement and James Larkin and James Connolly became key people in the labour movement. In 1912

Sea Storm off Sybil Head, Dingle Peninsula

the Commons passed the Home Rule Bill. Ireland was to have self-government after World War I.

There was no rejoicing among the Protestants in Ulster. They quickly armed themselves to fight to maintain the link with Britain. In Dublin a group of volunteers decided they could not wait for the end of the war, and began the Easter Rising of 1916. Although unsuccessful and condemned by most Irish people, the execution of its leaders changed public opinion. The Anglo-Irish war lasted from 1919 to 1921.

The treaty of 1921 gave independence to 26 of the 32 counties; six of the Ulster counties remained under British rule with a parliament in Belfast. A sector of the Republican movement opposed this compromise and a bitter civil war followed, culminating in the death of Michael Collins, the brilliant young Corkman who masterminded the war of independence. World War II imposed great strains on the Free State (economically stagnant for many years) which stayed neutral. Sean Lemass later adopted a more vigorous, expansionist economic policy which brought new prosperity and paved the way for Ireland's entry to the European Economic Community (EEC) in 1972. The EEC has since become the European Union (EU).

Today the Republic of Ireland is a parliamentary democracy with a president as head of state. There are two houses of parliament, the Dail and the Seanad, and three major political parties, Fianna Fail, Fine Gael, and the smaller Labour Party. Northern Ireland has suffered some unrest since l921. In 1968 the Civil Rights movement called for power sharing and

equality in jobs and housing. Since then there has been an upsurge of extremist republican and loyalist paramilitary violence. However, despite its beleaguered image, it is quite safe to visit.

GEOGRAPHY

Ireland, an island in north-west Europe, has an area of 84,421 sq km (32,595 sq miles). At its greatest it is 486 km (302 miles) long and 275 km (171 miles) wide and consists of a central lowland surrounded by a broken range of hills and small mountains. The climate is mild on account of the Gulf Stream, without extremes of heat or cold. Average temperatures in January are 4-7°C and in July 14-16°C, rising occasionally as high as 25°C. May and June are often the sunniest months, and North American visitors in particular will notice that there are many more daylight hours in summer than in the US. Rainfall is heaviest in the mountainous west and lightest in the east but the weather is at all times very changeable. A day of prolonged drizzle can end with a clear sky, a spectacular sunset and the promise of a sunny day to follow. Even so it is wise to have a raincoat or umbrella to hand while touring.

There are thirty-two counties and four provinces: Connaught, Leinster, Munster and Ulster. Six of the nine Ulster counties are part of the United Kingdom and the other twenty-six form the Republic of Ireland. The population of the Republic is 3,500,000 and of Northern Ireland 1,580,000. Dublin is the capital of the former, with an urban population of about one million. The principal cities and towns are Dublin, Belfast, Cork, Derry, Limerick,

Waterford and Galway. Of these only the first three have a population in excess of 100,000.

Food, drink, tobacco, engineering, textiles, chemicals and electronics are the chief manufacturing industries. The recession has caused many redundancies but exports show a steady increase in real terms. The Industrial Development Authority (IDA Ireland) attracts foreign companies, except in food and timber which is the responsibility of Fobairt. Many firms from the USA, Britain, Germany, the Netherlands and France have located in Ireland. In the north the old reliance on linen and shipbuilding has been largely replaced now by light engineering and textiles, most of it from Britain and located in the east of the province.

Ireland does not have great mineral resources. There are some small coal deposits, cement is made at Limerick, Drogheda, Larne and Cookstown, and there is a large lead and zinc mine at Navan. Natural gas was discovered off the Cork coast and brought ashore in 1979. It now counts for 14 per cent of Ireland's primary energy. While oil exploration goes on there has not yet been a major find. Other minerals are dolomite, gypsum, barytes and salt. Turf is one natural fuel found in abundance. Bord na Mona, a state company, produces over 4 million tonnes of peat and 1 million tonnes of moss peat annually. Production is highly mechanised and much of the peat is used for electricity generation as well as by the domestic and industrial consumer. Other sources of electricity are oil, natural gas, hydroelectric systems and coal.

Farming is a major industry, being mainly of a mixed pastoral nature. Irish beef, lamb and pork, along with dairy products such as cheese, butter, yoghurt and cream, are famous. Output and profitability have greatly increased in recent years, largely as a result of Ireland's entry into the EU.

The main types of sea fish landed are herring, cod, mackerel and plaice. Shellfish include lobsters, mussels, periwinkles and oysters. Much of this is exported to Europe, where pollution-free Irish seafood is greatly prized. Salmon and trout are taken in large numbers, particularly from inland waters, and are also highly valued.

About 5 per cent of Irish land is under forest and coniferous trees grow particularly well in Irish soil. Over 350 forests are open to the public, and many are laid out with car parks, picnic areas, nature trails and walks. Among the loveliest are Glenveagh (Co. Donegal), Lough Key (Co. Roscommon), Connemara, Lough Navar (Co. Fermanagh) and the John F. Kennedy park (New Ross, Co. Wexford).

Provinces and Counties of Ireland

Ireland, as everyone knows, is very green. This is caused by the mild, damp climate which encourages growth. Two areas of great botanical interest may be cited. Around Glengariff, Co. Cork, which enjoys the full benefit of the Gulf Stream, there is a luxuriant growth of tropical flora such as arbutus, fuchsia and other delightful flowering plants. A trip to Garinish Island, just offshore from Glengarriff, with its beautiful plant collection is well worthwhile. By contrast the Burren is an area of Co. Clare which resembles a lunar-like landscape of bare, carboniferous limestone. It is 40 ha (100 sq miles) in size but in spring and early summer produces a host of exotic orchids, ferns and rare plants.

There are at least 380 wild birds to be seen in Ireland, for migration goes on all year. The most common species are blackbird, thrush, goldcrest, starling and curlew. Among the indigenous animal species are the Irish hare (once seen on the old three-pence coin), the Irish stoat, fox and red deer. Wild deer roam the Kerry and Wicklow mountains and are also to be seen in the Phoenix Park, Dublin. Irish horse breeding is world famous, being centred on counties Meath and Kildare. The national stud at Tully, Co. Kildare (near the Curragh) can be visited at certain times of the year. There are seven distinct breeds of Irish dog, the best known being the giant Irish wolfhound, the Irish setter and the Irish water spaniel. There is only one reptile, the common lizard, and, thanks to St Patrick, no snakes!

Ross Road, Killarney in autumn

9

ANCIENT MONUMENTS

All archaeological remains in Ireland are under state care and most can be easily visited, including those on private land. Please take care to close gates, not to disturb farm animals and to respect the landowner's property. A good detailed map, a pair of stout shoes or boots and occasionally a torch will be useful, especially for the more remote examples. Once you are in the area ask the locals for directions. They will tell you exactly where to find the monuments - and a lot more besides.

Jerpoint Abbey, Kilkenny

There are vast numbers of ancient monuments including dolmens, crannogs, forts, clochÁns, tumuli, cairns, passage graves, stone circles, round towers and high crosses. It is well worth visiting at least some of these, as they reveal much about how people have lived in Ireland over the last 5,000 years.

Forts were ramparts built of clay (raths) and stone (cahers or cashels). They have given their name to many Irish towns, for example Rathdrum, Rathfriland, Cahirsiveen and Cashel. Since there are said to be 40,000 forts it would be hard to miss them. This term was used for any strengthened structure including stockades and cattle enclosures. Staigue Fort in Kerry, Garranes in Cork, Grianan of Aileach in Donegal and Navan Fort near Armagh City are among the best. Tara, once the palace of the high kings of Ireland, has a number of raths.

Dolmens are tombs dating from about 2000 BC and consist of two or more unhewn stones supporting a flat capstone. There is a huge one at Kilternan, Co. Dublin. Others are at Proleek, Co. Louth, Knockeen, Co. Waterford and Legananny, Co. Down.

Passage graves are set in a mound of earth or stone with a passage leading to the central chamber, and often have side chambers. Many are 4,500 years old and show a sophisticated knowledge of construction, design and astronomy. They are often decorated with geometrical motifs, spirals, concentric circles, triangles, zigzags, the human face and of course, the sun. Their meaning has not yet been deciphered but presumably they are connected with the religion of the people who built them.

Passage graves often occur in groups and those found in the Boyne valley are superb: Newgrange, Knowth and Dowth. Newgrange is a vast earthen mound penetrated by a long narrow passage. Thc tumulus is surrounded by a ditch with a number of the original pillar stones in place. A kerb of 97 huge stones (many with spiral motifs) supports a dry wall. The threshold stone is carved with a triple spiral, circles and diamonds about whose meaning we can only speculate.

The passageway is narrow and low and the central chamber artificially lit. However, on one day of the year, the Winter Solstice (21 December), a shaft of light enters the passage at dawn and for a few minutes strikes the centre of the floor illuminating the chamber. It is by all accounts an extraordinary experience.

Stone circles (cromlechs) are quite rare but can be visited at Lough Gur, Co. Limerick, whose shores have a large number of ancient monuments including forts and tiny remains of stone-age dwellings. Pillar stones or gallans can often be seen in fields alongside the road. The most interesting are indicated by a signpost. Some have tracks of carving and many have inscriptions in ogham writing. The letters consist of up to five lines cut above, below or across the stem line and may record a name or event in Irish. They date from about AD 300 and are the earliest form of writing known in Ireland. While it is easy enough to transliterate ogham the meaning is often unclear because the Irish use is very obscure. Dunloe, Co. Kerry, has a number of ogham stones in good condition. One inscription reads 'Cunacena'- probably someone's name. There are many more in Kerry and Cork.

Crannogs are lake dwellings built on a small island, sometimes reached by a causeway. There are crannogs at Fair Head, Co. Antrim and a splendid reconstruction at Quin, near Shannon Airport in Co. Clare. There the Craggaunowen Project has recreated a number of ancient dwellings and ring forts which vividly show the lifestyle of people in Ireland 3,000 years ago.

Clochans are the distinctive beehive huts built of stone which were used as monk's cells. Many are on offshore islands such as Bishop's Island, Co. Clare, High Island, Co. Galway, Inishmurray, Co. Sligo, and the breathtakingly beautiful Skellig Michael, Co. Kerry. There are many more accessible ones on the Dingle peninsula, including the delightful Gallarus Oratory.

Round towers are spread evenly across the country, with about 65 examples to be seen. Many are still intact with the distinctive conical cap. They were used as places of refuge and as belfries, usually with the entrance high off the ground. Once the occupants were inside the ladder was drawn up. It is worth climbing at least one round tower just for the view of the surrounding countryside. Among the best are those at Glendalough. Co. Wicklow, Ardmore, Co. Waterford, Devenish, Co. Fermanagh, Clonmacnois, Co. Offaly and that beside St. Canice's Cathedral, Kilkenny.

High crosses vary from small inscribed stones to massive free-standing sculptures with beautifully detailed carvings and a celtic circle around the head of the cross. Good examples are Muiredach's Cross at Monasterboice, Co. Louth and Clonmacnois, where a number of inscribed crosses are individually displayed. Both sites have round towers and extensive monastic remains. Another high cross and the stump of a round tower are located at Drumcliff, Co. Sligo, the burial place of the poet William Butler Yeats.

ARCHITECTURE

The Rock of Cashel, once the palace of the kings of Munster, dominates the surrounding plain and has a fine collection of early Irish buildings. The 13th-century cathedral, although a ruin, is a most impressive edifice. Nearby there is a round tower and the delightful 11th-century Cormac's Chapel built in Irish-Romanesque style. It is similar to Clonfert Cathedral with its ornate yet delicate doorway.

Gothic architecture was brought to Ireland by the Normans and the expanding monastic orders. The ruined Mellifont Abbey which still has part of its cloister and octagonal lavabo is an early example. Boyle Abbey, also built around 1200, retains its solid arcade but St. Patrick's Cathedral, Dublin, and St. Canice's, Kilkenny, are perhaps the finest examples of gothic architecture intact today. Also worth a visit is Jerpoint Abbey which has a 15th-century tower and an elaborately decorated cloister. Nearby is the restored Duiske Abbey at Grainguenamanagh with its outstanding processional doorway and delightful medieval tiles (ask to see them).

Castles or fortified houses are found in great numbers in Ireland. One of the largest is Trim Castle, whose extensive ruins cover several acres. It was built in 1170 by Hugh de Lacy. Reginald's Tower in Waterford pre-dates Trim by nearly two centuries and is a circular building with a conical roof and

The Four Courts in Dublin

One of Ireland's many castles

walls 3m (10 ft) thick. Once used as a prison, it now houses a small museum. Blarney Castle is a large tower with a parapet 25 m (83 ft) from the ground and houses the famous Blarney Stone, which promises eloquence to all who kiss it. The 15th-century Bunratty Castle near Shannon Airport has been carefully restored and holds a good collection of old Irish furniture and tapestries. In the grounds is the Folk Park where typical thatched farmhouses, fishermen's and labourers' cottages have been reconstructed. The park also includes shops and workshops.

Kilkenny city has a number of first rate buildings. The medieval castle of the Dukes of Ormonde stands on a commanding site above the River Nore. Rothe House dates from the 16th-century and is built around a cobbled courtyard. Other noteworthy buildings are the Black Abbey, the Tholsel and St. Canice's Cathedral.

Among other superb castles worth visiting are Carrickfergus, Cahir, Malahide, Dunguaire, Thoor Ballylee (once home of W.B. Yeats) and Dublin Castle. An outstanding unfortified 16th-century house is that of the Ormondes at Carrick-on-Suir. Town walls have survived in part at Limerick, Dublin, Clonmel, Fethard (near Clonmel), Youghal, Wexford and Kilmallock. The walls of Derry are complete and give an excellent view over the whole city.

Dating from the late 17th-century is one of Ireland's prize buildings, the Royal Hospital, Kilmainham. Originally an old soldiers' home, it is in the form of an arcaded quadrangle with dormer windows on its two stories. It also has a spacious hall and a beautiful clock tower. The Irish Museum of Modern Art has been added.

Classical architecture came to Ireland in the early 18th-century when Castletown House was built for William Connolly, speaker of the Irish House of Commons. Many of Dublin's finest buildings, including Trinity College, the Bank of Ireland (old Parliament House), Leinster House, the Rotunda, the Custom House, Powerscourt House, the Four Courts, the Marino Casino, Carton House, the King's Inns and the City Hall

were built in the Palladian style. They are the supreme jewels of Irish architecture. This was also the period when the gracious Georgian squares of Dublin were laid out - Merrion Square, Fitzwilliam Square, Parnell Square, Mountjoy Square and St Stephen's Green. The interior of many of these buildings are equally beautiful. Visit Russborough House, Castletown, Powerscourt Town House, 85-86 St Stephen's Green, and you will appreciate the exquisite plasterwork, carving and decor of these magnificent houses. Outside Dublin several towns were built along classical lines, for example Tyrellspass, Hillsborough, Birr, Armagh, Portarlington and Westport.

The l9th-century saw an upsurge in church building. Noted examples are Killarney and Enniscorthy cathedrals both by Pugin the gothic revivalist - St Finbarre's, Cork and St Saviour's, Dublin. The railway companies have also left a valuable heritage in the large number of elegant stations. In Dublin the terminal of Heuston, Connolly, the Broadstone and Harcourt Street are gracious buildings. When travelling by train it is also worth noting the many excellent country stations, especially en route to Galway/Sligo and Kilkenny. Their structure has, for the most part, scarcely altered since the day they opened. From the same period are the sturdy coastal forts known as Martello towers, built to counter the threat of a French invasion. The best known is probably James Joyce's tower at Sandycove, south of Dublin.

Not all interesting buildings were designed for the wealthy. All over Ireland the traditional thatched cottage may be seen, especially in the, west and in Adare. There are also elaborate, brightly painted shop fronts in every town along with neat little churches and simple public houses that have escaped 'modernisation'. The local Protestant church is usually older and of more interest than its Catholic counterpart, but, except for Sunday services, they are normally closed to the public.

Twentieth-century architecture is the subject of some controversy. Most towns have undergone ribbon housing development, and modern rural bungalows sometimes show a depressing sameness with unimaginative sitting. The population of inner cities has fallen as people move to the suburbs, and a number of architectural horrors have been inflicted on Dublin notably O'Connell Bridge House and the ESB headquarters in Lower Fitzwilliam Street. However, some new buildings blend happily into their background, such as the Irish Life Centre in Abbey Street and the corporation housing schemes in Ringsend, the Coombe and along the south quays of the Liffey. A great addition to the Smithfield area is the attractive Irish Distillers' building, while

the Central Bank, the Arts Block in Trinity College and the Abbey Theatre with its fine new facade, deserve favourable mention.

LITERATURE AND THEATRE

From the 6th to the 17th century most literature was composed in Irish. Some has been lost but a good deal is still available in the original and in translation. The early monks produced a large body of poetry, much of it religious, but they also recorded a great deal of pre-Christian material. Perhaps the best known of these is The Tain Bo Cuailnge (The Cattle Raid of Cooley). This is the epic account of the raid of the men of Connaught led by Queen Maeve to capture the marvellous bull owned by the men of Ulster. It has been beautifully translated by Thomas Kinsella, among others. The Navigatio Brendani (Voyage of St Brendan) is another example of this type of writing.

Later classics include The Book of the Dun Cow and The Book of Leinster which date from the 12th-century and feature the adventures of Cuchulain, Finn McCool, Oisin, the Fianna and other legendary heroes who succumbed to Patrick's crozier. These works provided great inspiration for writers such as Yeats and James Stephens.

Unto Rome thou woulds't attain?
Great the toil is, small the gain,
If the King thou seek'st therein,
Travel not with thee from Erin

An extract from *A Little Book of Celtic Verse* published by Appletree Press

Also dating from this period are the Annals of the Four Masters, a magnificent historical record of events in Ireland from the earliest times. Much of our knowledge of Irish history comes from the work of these Donegal scholars. In the 18th-century a schoolmaster from Clare, Brian Merriman, composed The Midnight Court (Cuirt an Mhean Oiche), a witty satire on the reluctance of Irishmen to marry. Writing later in the same century Jonathan Swift was the first Irish author to win international acclaim. He lampooned social and political mores at the time and the English attitude to Ireland in A Tale of a Tub, A Modest Proposal and Gulliver's Travels. Contemporary with him was George Berkeley, the noted philosopher and author of Principles of Human Knowledge. Other outstanding figures of this period are Edmund Burke, the philosopher and orator whose statue stands outside Trinity College and Oliver Goldsmith, the gentle author of The Vicar of Wakefield, The Deserted Village and She Stoops to Conquer. Richard Brinsley Sheridan is remembered for his dramatic works including The Rivals and The School for Scandal while Thomas Moore gained a reputation as a poet, author and musician. The brilliant wit and bohemian lifestyle of Oscar Wilde, coupled with his novel The Picture of Dorian Gray and comic plays such as Lady Windermere's Fan and The Importance of Being Earnest, have made his name immortal.

George Bernard Shaw had no doubt of his ability and compared his best works, Arms and the Man, Saint Joan and Candida, to those of Shakespeare; his play Pygmalion was the basis for the musical My Fair Lady. In 1925 he won the Nobel Prize for literature. William Butler Yeats is probably Ireland's best known poet and has had an immense influence on Irish letters. He won the Nobel Prize in 1923. Collections of his poetry and plays are now available in many languages. In celebration of life on the western seaboard J.M. Synge wrote Riders to the Sea and The Playboy of the Western World. The Irish-speaking Blasket Islands off the Kerry coast have produced three great writers: Peig Sayers (An Old Woman's Reflections) Tomas O Criomhtain (An tOileanach) and Muiris O Suilleabhain (Fiche Blian ag Fas). They lyrically portrayed the hard but contented life of the islanders at the turn of the century. Irish Fairy Tales and the exquisitely written The Crock of Gold are the fanciful work of James Stephens while Sean O'Casey is remembered for his tragicomedies The Shadow of a Gunman, Juno and the Paycock and The Plough and the Stars. James Joyce, the author of Ulysses and Dubliners, now has a worldwide following. Samuel Beckett (another Nobel Prize winner), was a magnificent novelist as well as playwright, who first achieved fame with his play Waiting for Godot.

Among the leading contemporary poets are Patrick Kavanagh, Louis MacNeice, Thomas Kinsella, Seamus Heaney, John Montague, Richard Murphy and Derek Mahon. Prominent prose writers include masters of the short story such as Sean O'Faolain, Frank O'Connor, Liam O'Flaherty, Bryan McMahon, Benedict Kiely, Mary Lavin and James Plunkett. Brian Moore, Francis Stuart, Flann O'Brien and Edna O'Brien have also been widely praised. Of the major living Irish playwrights mention must be made of Brian Friel, Tom Murphy, Billy Roche and Hugh Leonard.

The founding of the Abbey Theatre in 1904 by Lady Gregory, Edward Martyn and WB

Yeats marks a turning point for Irish drama. The early years of the Abbey were marked by great controversy. One of the first productions was The Playboy of the Western World and it caused a small riot when members of the audience disrupted the performance, saying it was an attack on rural life. This was the occasion on which Yeats delivered his famous rebuttal of the audience's narrow-mindedness. Such protests occurred from time to time when any works considered remotely salacious or critical of the old Gaelic-Catholic way of life were performed. Indeed at one point such a disrupted performance became the guarantee of a work's success.

These events marked the growing pains of the literary movements as Irish writers fought to free themselves from the suffocating constraints of a narrow nationalist philosophy. It was a time when any foreign work of art was considered suspect and led to the vicious and absurd censorship laws which plagued Irish writing for half a century, driving many of the finest authors into exile. Happily times have changed and there is now a diverse richness in the literary and theatrical diet which is unsurpassed. Modern farce, Shakespeare, classical pieces and modern Irish plays can now be seen happily co-existing. Every large town has its own amateur drama group which puts on at least one production a year. Ask at the Tourist Office for details of amateur dramatics in your area.

As the National Theatre, the Abbey is dedicated to producing the best works of Irish and international playwrights. Michael MacLiammoir and Hilton Edwards set up the Gate Theatre in 1928 to produce a broad range of plays while the Project Arts Centre is an experimental theatre. In addition there are a large number of repertory groups, amateur enthusiasts, lunchtime plays and pub theatres offering a rich programme of drama throughout Ireland. Among them is Siamsa Tire, the National Folk Theatre established in Tralee, which presents authentic folk productions in the Kerry area.

FOLKLORE

Ireland has a vast heritage of folklore going back to pre-Christian times. The sagas, epics, legends, stories, poems, proverbs, riddles, sayings, curses and prayers are all part of that tradition. Much of it comes by way of the seanachie, the storyteller who sat beside the fire and enchanted his audience with tales of times past. Often he was a nomad and moved from house to house earning his bed and board by storytelling.

The Department of Irish Folklore at University College, Dublin, has recorded and preserved a great part of the country's

An Té ná gabhann comhairle gabhadh sé comhrac

Let him who will not take advice have conflict

Bíonn grásta Dé idir an diallait agus an talamh.

The grace of God is found between the saddle and the ground.

An extract from *Classic Irish Proverbs* published by Appletree Press

heritage, and almost every sizeable town in Ireland has a small museum where the life and history of the local community is documented in antiquities and relics of the past. A good place to start is the National Museum in Dublin which has a large collection dating from pre-history to the recent past. Also in Dublin are the Civic Museum for items relating to the capital, the Heraldic Museum where you can trace your ancestors, the Guinness Museum, dedicated to Dublin's famous brew. Other recommended museums are the Ulster Museum in Belfast, the Ulster Folk and Transport Museum, Co. Down, Rothe House in Kilkenny, the James Joyce Museum at Sandycove, Enniscorthy Museum, Co. Wexford, Limerick and Galway Museums, and Kinsale Museum, in Co. Cork, which displays mementoes of the ill-fated Lusitania sunk off Kinsale in 1915. A number of towns have developed heritage centres and folk parks where the richness of local life is displayed in a less formal setting. Fine examples are located at Damer House, Roscrea (Co. Tipperary), Glencolumbkille (Co. Donegal), Bunratty (Co. Clare), Cultra (Co. Down) and theUlster American Folk Park near Omagh (Co. Tyrone).

A delightful way to see a collection of old furniture, farming implements and kitchenware is to visit one of the many pubs displaying such items and imbibe a pint and some culture at the same time. Among them are The Seanachie (Dungarvan, Co. Waterford), Durty Nelly's (Bunratty, Co. Clare), the Asgard (Westport, Co. Mayo) and The Hideout (Kilcullen, Co. Kildare).

Craftworkers now produce a wide range of first-class products such as pottery, ceramics, leatherwork, wood carving, jewellery, weaving, basketry, linen, lace, crystal, tweed, pewter and other quality souvenirs. Almost everywhere you will find a shop selling the products of local craftworkers, many of whom employ techniques handed from one generation to the next. Craft centres where these skills can be seen in practice will be found at Marlay Grange and Powerscourt Town House in Dublin and at Muckross House, Killarney (see also 'Shopping').

FESTIVALS

Wherever you go in Ireland you can't avoid coming across a festival. Some of the best known are the Rose of Tralee Festival, a week-long Irish beauty contest which draws the comely daughters of exiles from as far afield as Australia and the USA. The Galway Oyster Festival offers the chance of sampling delicious Irish shellfish in the pleasant city of Galway, washed down with Guinness, of course, while the Yeats Summer School in Sligo is a gathering of the followers of Ireland's foremost poet. The Wexford Opera Festival has international status and attracts world stars but you need to book months in advance.

There are many more which take in dancing, traditional music, drama, steam traction, boating, agricultural shows and sports of all kinds. In fact there are very few you need to book beforehand so look through the list and plan your vacation to take in those that interest you most. Dates and venues may change so check with the tourist office on arrival.

Calender of Events

JANUARY
- National Crafts Trade Fair, Royal Dublin Society (RDS), Ballsbridge, Dublin.
- Esat Telecom Young Scientist Exhibition, RDS, Dublin.

FEBRUARY
- Ulster Motor Show, King's Hall. Belfast.
- Cavan International Song Contest.
- Dublin Film Festival.
- Kate O'Brien Weekend, Limerick.

MARCH
- St Patrick's Day, 17 March: national holiday with parades in Dublin and many other centres.
- Arklow Music Festival, Arklow, Co. Wicklow.
- Celtic Spring Festival, Derry.
- Heritage Festival, Donegal town.
- Connemara Walking Festival.
- International Marching Band Festival, Limerick.
- Galway International Set Dancing Festival, Salthill, Co. Galway.
- West Cork Drama Festival, Clonakilty, Co. Cork.
- Guiness Roaring 1920s Festival, Killarney.

APRIL
- Killarney Easter Folk Festival.
- Sligo Feis Ceoil, Sligo.
- West of Ireland Golf Championships, Rosses Point, Co. Sligo.
- World Championships in Irish Dancing, Dublin.
- Feis Ceoil, Dublin.
- Cork International Choral Festival, City Hall, Cork.
- Circuit of Ireland motor rally.

MAY
- All-Ireland Amateur Drama Festival, Athlone. Co. Westmeath.
- Dundalk International Maytime and Drama Festival, Dundalk.
- Birr Castle Exhibition, Birr, Co. Offaly.
- Dublin Grand Opera season, Dublin and Cork.
- International 3-day event, Punchestown Racecourse.
- Mussel Fair, Bantry, Co. Cork.
- Leixlip Festival, Co Kildare.
- Surfing Association contest, Bundoran, Co. Donegal.
- Cat's Laugh Comedy Festival, Kilkenny.
- Royal Ulster Agricultural Show, Belfast.
- Listowel Writers Week.
- Belfast City Marathon.

JUNE
- Bloomsday, 16 June, Dublin.
- Eigse, Carlow Arts Festival.
- Proms, Belfast.
- Ulster Air Show, Newtownards, Co Down.
- Kinsale Arts Week.
- Ardara Weavers' Fair, Co. Donegal.
- Kenmare Walking Festival, Co. Kerry.
- Dublin International Organ Festival.
- Walter Raleigh potato festival, Youghal, Co. Cork.
- Murphy's Irish Open Golf Championship.
- Music Festival in Great Irish Houses: recitals by world famous artists in lovely 18th century mansions.
- Glengariff Festival.

- Spancilhill Horse Fair, Ennis.
- Ballybunion Bachelor Festival.
- Goldsmith Summer School, Longford.
- International Cartoon Festival, Rathdrum, Co. Wicklow.
- An Tostal Traditional Pageant, Drumshanbo, Co. Leitrim.
- Budweiser Irish Derby, The Curragh.

JULY
- Dun Laoghaire Summer Festival.
- Clones Agricultural Show, Co. Monaghan.
- West Cork Festival, Clonakilty.
- North of Ireland Amateur Golf Championship, Portrush.
- Willie Clancy Summer School, Miltown Malbay.
- Schull Festival.
- Cobh International Folk Dance Festival.
- Glens of Antrim Feis, Glenariff: music, dancing, sports.
- Skibbereen Annual Show.
- Orangeman's Day, 12th July: parades throughout Ulster.
- Mary from Dungloe Festival, Dungloe.
- Sham Fight, Scarva: re-enacts Battle of the Boyne.
- Ulster Steam Traction Rally, Shane's Castle. Antrim.
- South Sligo Summer School of Traditional Irish Music, Song and Dance.
- Mullingar Festival.
- Ballina Salmon Festival.
- Galway Arts Festival.
- French Festival, Portarlington.
- Ballyshannon International Folk Festival, Co. Donegal.
- Rose of Arranmore Festival, Co. Donegal.
- Wexford Strawberry Festival, Enniscorthy.
- Kells Heritage Festival, Co Down.
- Wicklow Regatta Festival.
- Boyle Arts Festival, Co Roscommon.
- Lewidge Day, Slane, Co Meath.
- Buncrana Music Festival, Co Donegal.
- Rose Trials, Belfast.
- Ford Cork yacht week, Crosshaven, Co Cork.
- International Music Festival, Coalisland, Co Tyrone.
- Tour de France, Dublin and south east, 12-13 July 1998.

AUGUST
- Gorey Arts Week.
- Humbert Summer School, Killala, Co. Mayo.
- Kinsale Regatta.
- Ballyshannon Music Festival, Co. Donegal.
- O'Carolan Harp and Traditional Irish Music Festival, Keadue, Co Roscommon.
- Powers Irish Whiskey Festival, Foynes, Co Limerick.
- Ancient Order of Hibernians parades, 15 August.
- Feile an Phobail, West Belfast.
- 1798 commemoration, Co Wexford and elsewhere.
- Tall Ships Race, Dublin, 22-25 August 1998.
- Stradbally Steam Rally.
- Claddagh Festival, Galway.
- Yeats International Summer School, Sligo.
- Irish Antique Dealers' Fair, Dublin.
- Kerrygold Horse Show, RDS, Dublin.
- Granard Harp Festival.

- John Millington Synge Summer School, Co Wicklow.
- Puck Fair, Killorglin.
- Percy French Festival, Newcastle, Co. Down.
- Oul' Lammas Fair, Ballycastle: one of the oldest fairs in Ireland.
- Connemara Pony Show, Clifden.
- Ulster Grand Prix (motorcycling), Belfast.
- Schull Regatta.
- Birr Vintage Week.
- Merriman Summer School, Lahinch.
- Limerick Show.
- Carlingford Oyster Festival.
- Letterkenny International Folk Festival.
- Fleadh Cheoil na hEireann: top festival for traditional music, song, dance; location changes each year.
- Kilkenny Arts Week.
- Galway Races: more than just horse racing.
- Rose of Tralee Festival.
- Wexford Mussel Festival.
- All-Ireland Road Bowls Final, Armagh.
- Abbeyshrule Fly-in Festival (Air Show), Co. Longford.
- Moynalty Steam Threshing, Co. Meath.
- Parnell Summer School, Avondale.
- Rathdrum, Co. Wicklow.

SEPTEMBER
- Autumn Fair, RDS, Dublin.
- Clifden Arts Week, Co. Galway.
- Dromore Horse Fair, Co. Down.
- Cape Clear Island Storytelling Festival, Co. Cork.
- Waterford International Festival of Light Opera.
- Listowel Harvest Festival and Races.
- Lisdoonvarna Folk Festival.
- All-Ireland Hurling and Football Finals, Dublin.
- Galway Oyster Festival.
- Clarinbridge Oyster Festival, Co. Galway.

OCTOBER
- Kinsale Gourmet Festival.
- Flower Festival, St Nicholas, Galway.
- Ballinasloe October Horse Fair.
- Cork Film Festival.
- Wexford Opera Festival.
- Guinness Jazz Festival, Cork.
- Queen of the Burren Autumn Festival, Lisdoonvarna.
- Dublin Theatre Festival.
- Dublin City Marathon.
- International Horse Show, Millstreet, Co. Cork.

NOVEMBER
- Belfast Festival at Queen's.
- Dublin Indoor International Showjumping. RDS, Dublin.
- Sligo International Choral Festival.
- Allingham Arts Festival, Ballyshannon, Co. Donegal.

DECEMBER
- Grand Opera International Season, Dublin.
- Irish Craft Fair, RDS, Dublin.
- Christmas Crafts Fair, Mansion House, Dublin.
- Moving Crib, Dublin.
- Christmas Races, Leopardstown.
- New Year's Eve Celebrations, Dublin and regional centres.

MUSIC

Like the seanachie, the music teacher of old once wandered the country, playing an instrument and teaching music and dance to his pupils. The best known is probably Turlough O'Carolan, the blind harpist and composer of the late 1600s. His beautiful lifting airs are now available on record. Two l9th century composers are particularly outstanding: John Field, the inventor of the nocturne, and Thomas Moore, whose famous Irish Melodies includes the "Last Rose of Summer" and "The Vale of Avoca". There is a monument to Moore at the Meeting of the Waters near Avoca, in Co. Wicklow, where he is said to have composed this song, and it is a magical spot. Notable among modern composers are A.J. Potter, Gerard Victory, Seoirse Bodley and Sean O Riada, who wrote the haunting Mise Eire.

Bíonn dhá insint ar scéal agus dhá leagan déag ar amhrán.

There are two versions of every story and twelve versions of every song.

An extract from *Classic Irish Proverbs* published by Appletree Press

Traditional music and dance is jealously guarded by Comhaltas Ceoltoiri Eireann which organises music festivals all over the country and has regular sessions at its Monkstown headquarters in south Dublin. Many pubs also hold impromptu ballad evenings. In Dublin they occur regularly at O'Donoghue's, the Abbey Tavern, the Chariot Inn, Slattery's, the Stag's Head, and the Old Shieling. Irish cabaret can be seen at Jury's, the Burlington and Clontarf Castle. There are nightly sessions also at the Granary in Limerick, McCann's and O'Connor's in Doolin, near Ennis, Co. Clare, Duchas in Tralee, Teach Beg in Cork and O'Flaherty's in Dingle, but every town has at least one pub with music. All you have to do is stroll around until you hear singing or the sound of an accordian, tin whistle or the wail of uileann pipes.

The National Concert Hall in Dublin has become the centre for music in Ireland. There is a musical event there every day of the year ranging from classical to jazz, traditional, folk music, piano recitals and pop concerts. There are two principal orchestras, the National Symphony Orchestra in the Republic and the Ulster Orchestra in Northern Ireland. Both can be heard throughout the year at the National Concert Hall in Dublin and the Ulster Hall in Belfast respectively, with occasional performances in other centres. The Dublin Grand Opera Society has one or two seasons in the Gaiety Theatre, Dublin and at the Opera House, Cork. In Dublin, other concerts and recitals take place in the Royal Dublin Society, Ballsbridge, the National Stadium and the Examination Hall of Trinity College. In Belfast the recently refurbished Opera House provides an impressive venue for concerts, plays and musicals. The new Waterfront Hall in Belfast is a glitzy, ultra-modern venue for concerts and other events. During the winter months musicals and light opera are performed in many provincial towns by amateur groups, culminating in the Waterford Festival of Light Opera.

Discos and night clubs will be found in the major cities, sometimes attached to hotels. In Dublin the area around Leeson Street and Baggot Street has a number of such places, while in Belfast try the famous "Golden Mile" - a mile long strip of pubs, clubs and restaurants.

SPORT AND RECREATION

The traditional Irish games are known as gaelic games and include the ancient game of hurling, plus football, handball and camogie. The Gaelic Athletic Association (GAA) organises hundreds of local clubs, and county teams compete in hurling and gaelic football at the All-Ireland finals each year in Croke Park, Dublin. Hurling is a fast game played with wooden hurley sticks while gaelic football resembles Australian rules football.

Ireland offers many opportunties for recreational sport, in unspoiled landscapes and waters. Angling is a popular visitors' pastime. Coarse fishing, for such species as bream, carp, dace, eel, pike, perch and rudd, is abundant in the Grand and Royal Canal systems and in the Shannon system. In the North, the River Erne and its tributaries are good coarse fishing grounds, while the lakes of counties Cavan, Meath and Monaghan are excellent for such species as pike.

Ireland is often described as the best game fishing location in Europe, with brown trout widely distributed in parts of the north, the midlands and the south-east. The north-west, west and the south-west are salmon territory. Controversy rages over the extent to which fish farming may have affected salmon fishing in the west. Sea-angling, too, is good, with many fine catches possible from beaches and boats. Species range from the mundane to the exotic, cod to shark, the latter caught off the south coast.

Ireland has innumerable locations for water sports in their many facets, canoeing, cruising, rowing, sailing and windsurfing. Golf is the most popular sport for visitors to Ireland, with most clubs welcoming guests for modest entrance fees. In Ireland as a whole there are over 300 courses. The North has some truly spectacular courses, like those at Newcastle and Portrush and some old established clubs within the city itself. In the south, many of the most prestigious courses, the likes of Portmarnock, Co. Dublin, Lahinch, Co. Clare and Waterville, Co. Kerry are long established. Numerous new courses are equally spectacular in their settings and their golfing challenges. The Dublin area has some magnificent new courses, including the Kildare Country Club at Straffan, St Margaret's near Dublin Airport and Luttrellstown, just west of the city. Some of the finest new courses are located by the coast, including the Carn course at Belmullet, Co. Mayo, St Helen's Bay near Rosslare and Charlesland near Greystones, Co. Wicklow.

The horse, that quintessential animal in Ireland, provides many sporting opportunities including trail riding and hunting. Ireland, north and south has an excellent selection of racecourses, the most prestigious of which include the Curragh, Leopardstown, Mallow, Down Royal and Downpatrick. The Irish Grand National is run at Fairyhouse on Easter Monday and the Irish Sweeps Derby at the Curragh in June. At certain races, as with the Galway Races at the end of July and again in September, the social content is every bit as important as the racing.

The hills, mountains and uplands of Ireland give ample opportunity to those in search of physical exercise, whether hill walking, orienteering or mountain climbing. Walking has been developed substantially over the last few years, with over thirty long distance walking ways provided throughout Ireland, including the Ulster Way in Northern Ireland, the Western Way, Dingle Way, the Kerry Way and the Wicklow Way. The towpaths of the Grand Canal and Royal Canal have been developed into long distance walking ways.

SPECIALIST HOLIDAYS

With many kinds of recreational sports, including cycling, walking, water sports and equestrian sports, numerous specialist companies provide all-in holidays geared specifically to one sport. In addition, with water-based and equestrian sports, many centres provide full tuition and accommodation in package deals. The tourist boards will have full details of recommended specialist holiday providers in the sport of your choice.

FOOD AND EATING OUT

Four thousand years ago the Irish cooked enormous joints of meat by filling a ditch with water and dropping in heated stones to keep the water boiling. Recent duplicate experiments proved that this method works perfectly although it seems rather troublesome! In pre-Christian times the feasts at Tara and other royal palaces were known to go on for several weeks without a break. Since then the Irish have lost little of their enthusiasm for food although appetites are now more moderate!

A unique pleasure of a stay in Ireland is enjoying the unpretentious but delicious cooking. Fresh ingredients simply prepared and served without fuss make eating in Ireland a real pleasure. The rich pastures produce meat of the highest quality so that beef, lamb and dairy products like cream, cheese and butter are second to none. Among the tempting dishes on offer are Limerick ham, Irish stew, bacon and cabbage, Galway oysters, sirloin steak and onions, game of all sorts , smoked salmon, Dublin Bay prawns, spring lamb, grilled trout, fresh farm eggs and delicious brown soda bread.

In Irish cooking the basic ingredients are so good that elaborate sauces are unnecessary to bring out the flavour of the food. The humble potato is appreciated as nowhere else and a plate of steaming, floury 'spuds' with butter, salt and a glass of milk is a meal in itself. Indeed potatoes are the principal ingredients of several dishes which once formed the bulk of the countryman's diet. Colcannon is mashed potato with butter and onions. Boxty is grated potato fried in bacon fat. Potato cakes are often served at breakfast but are delicious anytime.

It is difficult to suggest food items to take home as dairy products and the like do not travel well. However no-one should leave Ireland without at least one side of smoked salmon which keeps fresh for up to ten days. Whiskey cake, brack and soda bread can also be carried easily.

An Irish breakfast is a substantial affair: fruit juice, cereals, bacon, egg, sausage, tomato, mushrooms, (plus soda farls and potato bread in the North!), wheaten bread, toast, tea or coffee. Many pubs serve tasty lunches ranging from a simple sandwich to a full meal and this is a pleasant way to break up a day's sightseeing. Visit Bewley's in Grafton St or Westmoreland St, if in Dublin, for excellent tea, coffee and cakes, or one of the tea rooms attached to many of the stately homes. For dinner eat in your hotel or choose a restaurant to suit your taste and pocket from the list provided by the tourist board or from the booklet of the Irish Country houses and Restaurants Association. Some people prefer to go out to a hotel to eat and this is quite acceptable.

International cooking is available in Ireland and includes Italian, French, Spanish, Indian, Chinese, Greek, Russian and Japanese. There is also a wide price range form a simple one-course meal to haute cuisine. It is worth looking for restaurants which have the Bord Failte award for excellence, an independent commendation of good and reasonable value. In addition to table d'hote and a la carte menus many restaurants also participate in the special value tourist menu scheme. This involves offering a three-course meal at a fixed price and is usually excellent value. Look for the symbol or ask Bord Failte for a list of participating restaurants. In Northern Ireland the Tourist Board publishes a useful book Let's Eat Out.

Recommending restaurants is a highly risky business, however the following Dublin restaurants have been highly praised. For a tasty lunch try the Kilkenny Shop (Nassau St), the National Gallery (Merrion Square), the Municipal Gallery (Parnell Square), or any of the very pleasant Bewley's cafes in Grafton St, Westmoreland St and South Great George's St. You could also drop into one of the many pubs serving lunch such as the Stag's head (Dame court), Henry Grattan (Lr Baggot St), Kitty O'Shea's (Upr Grand Canal St), R Foley's (Merrion Row). For dinner try Brasserie Na Mara (Dun Laoghaire), Le Coq Hardi (Pembroke Rd), Patrick Guilbaud (Merrion Hotel), King Sitric (Howth), Le Coquillage (Blackrock), Locks (Portobello), Nico's (Dame St), Trocadero (Andrews St) or Digby's (Dun Laoghaire). The Powerscourt Town House Centre (South William St) also has several excellent restaurants and coffee bars. Outside Dublin the Cork/Kerry region is

DUBLIN CODDLE
A popular dish, especially in Dublin…

1 lb / 500g best sausages, 8 oz / 250g streaky bacon, ¹/₂ pt / 300ml / 1 cup stock or water, 6 medium potatoes, 2 medium onions, salt and pepper, serves four.

Cut the bacon into squares. Bring the stock to the boil in a medium saucepan with a well-fitting lid, add the sausages and bacon and simmer for 5 minutes. Remove the sausages and bacon and save the liguid. Cut each sausage into four or five pieces; peel potatoes and cut into slices; skin onions and slice them. Assemble a layer of potatoes, followed by a layer of onions and then half the sausages and bacon. Repeat once and finish with a layer of potatoes. Pour the stock over and season. Cover and simmer gently for 1 hour. Adjust seasoning and serve piping hot .

An extract from *A Little Irish Cook Book* published by Appletree Press

excellent for eating out, with Kinsale the gourmet capital of Ireland.

Other recommended restaurants include Ballymaloe House (near Cork), the Arbutus Lodge (Cork City), Aherne's (Youghal), Doyle's Seafood Bar (Dingle), the Park Hotel (Kenmare), Ballylickey House (Bantry), Renvyle House Hotel (Connemara), the Galley Floating Restaurant (New Ross), Durty Nelly's (Bunratty), Restaurant St John's (Fahan), and Dunraven Arms Hotel (Adare). In Northern Ireland try Balloo House (Killinchy, Co. Down), The Nutgrove (Downpatrick), Nick's (Belfast), Roscoff (Belfast), The Grange (Waringstown), The Ramore (Portrush), Portaferry Hotel (Portaferry).

PUBS & DRINK

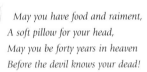

May you have food and raiment,
A soft pillow for your head,
May you be forty years in heaven
Before the devil knows your dead!

An extract from *Irish Toasts*
published by Appletree Press

The Irish have always had a close relationship with drink. Public houses began as illicit drink shops or shebeens where people met to exchange news and drink the raw fiery spirit, poitín. Pubs are still very much a social centre and a convivial meeting place where you can chat to local people in informal surroundings.

Opening hours are 11am-11/11.30pm on weekdays and 12.30pm-2pm and 4pm-10pm on Sundays. In Northern Ireland most pubs are open between 11am and 11pm on weekdays and between 12.30pm-2.30pm and 7pm-10pm on Sundays. Many pubs have preserved their original decor with features such as solid mahogany bar furniture, brass lamps, lovely old mirrors and stained glass. To experience a traditional Irish session it is best to head for one of these pubs and avoid the more modern places. There are some 900 pubs in Dublin alone and many are excellent. The following is just a representative sample of the best but there are lots more worth exploring.

Doheny and Nesbitt's (Lwr Baggot St) has kept the original interior and has a delightful little snug. This is a small enclosed room with a hatch opening directly on to the bar for discreet imbibing and is found in many pubs. Toner's (Lwr Baggot St) has lots of atmosphere and traditional music and so has O'Donoghue's nearby. Neary's (Chatham St) is a pleasant watering hole with an attractive old bar while the Stag's Head (Dame Court) is noted for its beautiful stained glass and highly ornate snug.

There is a fine collection of cartoons, photographs and drawings of noted customers in the Palace Bar (Fleet St) and Mulligan's (Poolbeg St) has a low beam inscribed 'John Mulligan estd. 1782'. Ryan's (Parkgate St) is perfectly preserved and has lovely old bar furniture.

Other traditional pubs worth visiting on a pub crawl are McDaid's, Bowe's, Davy Byrne's, the Long Hall, the Auld Dubliner, Kitty O'Shea's, Conway's, Keogh's, Mulligan's (Stoneybatter), The Brazen Head, O'Brien's and the International. Outside the capital you will find every Irish town is well endowed with pubs. You should have no trouble finding a welcoming hearth, a blazing turf fire and a cheering glass. But just in case you're stuck head for one of the following: Kate O'Brien's (Fermoy), the Breffni Inn (Dromod), Dan Lowry's, Teach Beag or the Vineyard in Cork, the Seanachie, Dungarvan and Kate Kearney's (Killarney), Taylor's (Moyasta), O'Shea's (Borris), The Thatch (Ballysodare), Crown Liquor Saloon (Belfast), The Spaniard (Kinsale), Durty Nelly's (Bunratty), The Abbey Tavern (Howth), Morrissey's (Abbeyleix), the Granary, South's and Hogan's (Limerick), and O'Flaherty's (Dingle).

When someone asks for a pint they usually mean Guinness, the dark stout with a white head which is synonymous with Ireland. There is hardly a pub in the country that does not stock Guinness on draught or in bottles. Try it on its own or with some oysters. Other top quality beers are Murphy's, Macardle's, Smithwick's, Bass, Harp and Beamish.

Visitors are welcome at the Guinness brewery in Dublin, Smithwick's in Kilkenny, Beamish in Cork and Harp and Macardle's in Dundalk and will be invited to taste the product. Guinness is the oldest brewery; Arthur Guinness (Uncle Arthur as he is affectionately known) began brewing at St James's Gate in 1759. Telephone in each

case before you go. Equally famous is Irish whiskey (spelt with an 'e'). The word comes from the Irish uisce beatha meaning water of life and there is an old saying "There's more friendship in a glass of spirit than in a barrel of buttermilk!" The whiskey is matured for 7 to 12 years and has a mellow distinct flavour. It is made from malted and unmalted barley, yeast and pure spring water. The oldest (legal) distillery is at Bushmill's near the Giant's Causeway, dating from 1609, and it welcomes visitors by appointment. At Irish Distillers' head office in Smithfield, Dublin, there is an excellent display of models, kits and tools showing the history of whiskey and how it is made. The new Jameson whiskey heritage centre is also in Smithfield. Midleton, Co. Cork has a fine new whiskey heritage centre, so has Kilbeggan, Co Westmeath. A comparatively recent development is the number of cream liqueurs which are made from a blend of whiskey and cream. These include Bailey's, Carolans and Waterford Cream.

Irish people often drink their whiskey diluted with water. So if you order "a ball of malt" you will usually get a jug of water with it. Try it on its own first. Some of the 12-year-old whiskeys are like nectar and are as good as a fine brandy.

Irish coffee is now world famous and often drunk at the end of a meal or on a cold day. Another warming drink is a hot whiskey which is simply whiskey with hot water, sugar, lemon and cloves. Black Velvet is a potent mixture of Guinness and champagne.

May the strength of three be
in your journey.

An extract from *Irish Toasts*
published by Appletree Press

GENEALOGY

Many people visiting Ireland would like to find out more about their family history. What makes ancestor research so fascinating is that it increases your knowledge of yourself; who you are and where you come from. You would expect to find Christian names recurring in a family but you might be surprised to see the same occupation held by members of the family over several generations or even spot similarities between your handwriting and theirs! You can engage a professional to do the research work or you can have a go yourself. There are many sources of information although some records have been lost in the various upheavals of Irish history.

Whether the offspring of Kings, warriors, poets, workers in wood or stone, or tillers of the soil, a son or daughter shall follow the career of his or her parents.

An extract from *Traditional Irish Laws* published by Appletree Press

It will make things much easier if you do some simple research before you leave home. Try to find out: the full name of your emigrant ancestor; where he came from in Ireland; dates of birth, marriage and death; occupation and background (rich, poor, farmer, tradesman, professional, etc.); religion; date of emigration from Ireland. The more details you have the greater the chance of success. Sources are old letters and diaries, family bibles, military service records, emigrant ship lists, newspapers, local church and state records. Ask the oldest member of your family about their earliest memories too.

Armed with as much information as you can muster, you can then visit the following places in Ireland: The Registrar General in Joyce House, 8-11 Lombard Street East, Dublin 2 holds the general civil registration of births, marriages and deaths from 1864. Non-catholic marriages are listed from 1845. You can make the search yourself or have it done for you. A small fee is payable. The Public Record Office (now The National Archive), Four Courts, Dublin 7, although badly damaged in 1922 has many valuable records including tithes dating from 1800 (the first valuation records), wills and extracts of wills and marriage licences for some families. The returns for the extensive 1901 census may be seen here. The Registry of Deeds, Henrietta Street,

Dublin 2 has documents from 1708 relating to property such as leases, mortgages and settlements. You make the search yourself and a small fee is due.

The National Library, Kildare Street, Dublin 2 has an enormous collection of useful sources including historical journals, directories, topographical works, private papers and letters and local and national newspapers from the earliest times. It is necessary to contact the Library for a reader's ticket in advance. Catholic Parish Records can now be consulted in the National Library on microfilm. The staff are helpful and there is no charge. The Genealogical Office, Kildare Street, Dublin 2 records official pedigrees, coats of arms and will extracts of the more well-to-do families. Staff will conduct a search on your behalf for a fee.

The detailed full-colour brochure published by Bord Failte, Tracing Your Ancestors, has useful information on the subject, including a full listing of all heritage centres now in operation throughout the Republic. Information on the 243 Irish clans researched to date from the Clans of Ireland Office, c/o Genealogical Office, 2 Eldare Street, Dublin 2, tel. (01) 618811. The Public Record Office, Four Courts, Dublin 1 has the excellent and comprehensive Griffith's Valuation. This was a national survey of land ownership and leases made in the 1850s. There is an immense amount of detail in it. The Valuation Office, 6 Ely Place, Dublin 2 has records of subsequent alterations in land ownership.

If your ancestors came from Northern Ireland the Public Record Office of Northern Ireland at 66 Balmoral Avenue, Belfast BT9 6NY will help. It has tithe appointment books and other valuable sources. Linked to it is the Ulster Historical Foundation which will carry out a search for you. The Presbyterian Historical Society at Church House, Fisherwick Place, Belfast 1 also has various records of its members. You might also contact the Registrar General's Office, Oxford House, 49 Chichester Street, Belfast BT1 4HL. If you know the parish where your ancestor came from, then start there. Every parish keeps records of the baptisms performed in it giving details of the child's parents and sometimes their date of birth and domicile. Many go back 150 years and some over 200 years. Some Church of Ireland registers go back to the 1700s. To see them apply to the parish priest or minister. Study the baptismal and marriage registers for five years before and after the date you have. Jot down each name that seems likely. Remember too that there is another useful source nearby - the graveyard. Note the details of each gravestone bearing your family name, rubbing away the moss and using a piece of chalk to bring up faint lettering.

Contact the local historical society. Their journal may well have interesting information and perhaps articles on the history of the parish. They will put you in touch with any genealogist specialising in the families of that district. If there is a parish newsletter ask the editor if he would insert an item on your search: 'Information sought about Sean Murphy, believed born in this parish about 18-, emigrated 18-. Please contact...' A similar letter should be sent to the local newspaper; every county has at least one. Lastly, before you leave the area ask to speak to the person who knows most about local history. Even if he or she can't shed light on your elusive ancestor you will learn a great deal about the place where your family originated and that alone should make the trip worthwhile. If you are unsuccessful or don't want to do a search you can employ a professional to do it for you. Results cannot be guaranteed but for a modest sum they will complete an initial search and let you know the likelihood of success. Try one of the following: Irish Genealogical Office, Kildare Street, Dublin 2; Heraldic Artists, 3 Nassau Street, Dublin 2: Hibernian Research, Windsor Road, Dublin 6. For coats of arms, plaques, parchments and the full range of heraldic goods mail order from Mullins, North Great George's Street, or visit Heraldic Artists (see above) or Historic Families, 8 Fleet Street, Dublin 2.

SHOPPING

Shopping in Ireland is leisurely and while the choice may not be as wide as London or New York you will discover lots which cannot be found elsewhere. Opening hours are usually 9am-5.30pm Monday to Saturday. Most shops, including department stores are open on Sunday. However, in smaller towns many shops close for lunch and on one afternoon a week. The larger shops will change currency and traveller's cheques but you will get a better rate in a bank. There is a value added tax (VAT) refund scheme for goods taken out of the Republic. You must have the invoice stamped by customs at the exit point before returning it to the shop for refund. Ask Bord Failte or the Tourist Information office for a leaflet explaining how the system works and the allowances.

Visitors to Ireland will want to take home some gifts or mementoes of their stay and there is a wide choice of quality Irish-made goods available. Avoid those displaying an excessive amount of shamrocks, leprechauns, etc. they probably came from the Far East! If it is not marked ask the assistant where the item was made and look for the 'Guaranteed Irish' symbol, an assurance that the product is quality Irish-made. Many of the larger shops will pack,

insure and mail goods home for you and don't forget to visit the enormous Duty Free Shop if passing through Shannon Airport where you can save a lot of money on the full price.

In Dublin the main shopping areas are all within easy walking distance: Grafton Street, Wicklow Street, O'Connell Street and Henry Street. The Powerscourt Town House in South William Street has a large assortment of shops, boutiques, restaurants and a craft centre all housed within a carefully restored 18th-century mansion. There are more shopping complexes in the ILAC Centre off Henry Street, St Stephen's Green Centre, Grafton Street, and the Irish Life Centre, Talbot Street. The principal department stores are Clery's (O'Connell St), Switzer's and Brown Thomas's (Grafton St), Arnott's, Dunne's and Roche's (Henry St). There are several large, out of town shopping centres in Dublin, including The Square, Tallaght and Blanchardstown. The Quarryvale shopping centre off the main road to the west is due to open in 1998. Not to be missed at any cost is the Kilkenny Shop in Nassau Street which displays and sells only the best designed Irish goods such as clothing, pottery, jewellery, glass

and furniture. It is also a pleasant spot for lunch or afternoon tea.

In Belfast the principal shops are located in Donegall Place and Royal Avenue and the streets nearby. Cork, the Munster capital, has Patrick Street and Grand Parade as the main shopping thoroughfare. In Galway the aptly named Shop Street has a good selection of stores, especially for clothes and crafts. In fact every town, no matter how small, is usually amply catered for by its retail trade. Watch out for the combined grocery shop and bar where you can order your rashers and have a pint under the same roof.

What to buy
Waterford is almost synonymous with crystal and the factory just outside the town welcomes visitors by appointment. There you can see the ancient skill of moulding, blowing and cutting glass. The factory does not sell direct to the public but the glass is available in outlets everywhere. Less well-known but equally beautiful crystal is made in Tyrone, Galway, Dublin, Cavan, Kilkenny, Cork and Sligo, and many have shops attached where you can pick up first-rate bargains.

Tweed is a strong woollen fabric used in making suits, skirts, curtains, jackets, ties, hats and carpets. It comes in many beautiful designs, much of it from Donegal and Connemara where the rugged landscape provides the colour and texture of this versatile cloth. You can buy tweed garments made up or choose a pattern and order a length of fabric to be made up at home. A tweed hat or cap is a useful precaution against unpredictable Irish weather.

Aran sweaters have been worn by west coast fishermen for generations. The patterns are so varied and intricate that it is said a drowned man could be recognised by his pullover alone. The bainin

or undyed wool came originally from the Aran Islands and makes the garment warm and rain resistant. You can buy sweaters, cardigans, dresses, caps and mitts in Aran patterns. Ask for a card explaining the meaning of the pattern. A hand-knitted Aran sweater (more expensive than handloomed) will last for more than 15 years if looked after.

The north has a long tradition of weaving linen for tablecloths, sheets, handkerchiefs and garments, and Irish poplin is now woven in Cork. Locally-made pottery is on sale in most towns although Kilkenny is now the mecca for potters (and most other crafts). The tiny village of Belleek in Fermanagh is the home of delicate, almost transparent porcelain. Other well-known potteries are Wicklow Vale Pottery, Stephen Pearce (Shanagarry, Co. Cork) and Royal Tara. In these you can buy anything from an egg cup to a full dinner service.

Claddagh rings, celtic design plaques and jewellery in gold and silver are popular souvenirs and you can have a pendant engraved with your name in ogham (ancient Irish lettering). Every record shop stocks a selection of traditional Irish music. Among the well-known performers are the Chieftains, Clannad, The Dubliners, Paddy Reilly, the Furey Brothers and the Clancy Brothers. Irish publishers produce an enormous range of books on every aspect of Irish life and there are bookshops in every large town.

PUBLIC TRANSPORT

Rail
All train services in the Republic are operated by Iarnrod Eireann-Irish Rail. Fast trains operate from Dublin to the main centres of population, namely Cork, Belfast, Sligo, Westport, Ballina, Galway, Limerick, Tralee, Waterford and Wexford. There are two main-line stations in Dublin: Connolly Station (Amiens St) runs services to Belfast, Sligo and Wexford/Rosslare. All other long distance trains depart from Heuston (Kingsbridge). The number 24 bus runs at regular intervals between the two stations.

Train frequency varies according to the route and time of year but there are at least three or four trains in each direction daily, and more to Cork and Belfast. The service is sparse on Sundays and public holidays. The suburban rail lines in Dublin stretch from Drogheda to Greystones and westwards to Maynooth. There is also a new fast commuter train service on the east coast line between Dundalk and Arklow, and from Dublin to Maynooth and Kildare. The three city centre stations are Connolly, Tara Street and Pearse. The DART (Dublin Area Rapid Transit) electric service is a marvellous way to get about on the 32 km (20 mile) coastal line. Trains run from early morning to late at night at 5 minute intervals during peak hours and every 15 minutes at other times.

There are many kinds of tickets available for use on Dublin public transport. Weekly and monthly commuter tickets are valid on suburban rail and all city bus services. Ten journey tickets can be bought for a specific journey and used without a time limit. Reduced fares at off-peak periods apply for journeys within the city centre.

Northern Ireland Railways (NIR) operate trains within Northern Ireland and run the Belfast-Dublin service jointly with Iarnrod Eireann. From Belfast Central Station, trains run to Derry, Portrush, Bangor and Dublin. York Street (connecting bus from Central via the city centre) is the station for the ferryport of Larne. Local trains to Bangor, Portadown, Ballymena and Larne are frequent, with fare reductions for travel at certain times. The Enterprise high speed service runs several trains daily between Dublin and Belfast with carriages modelled on those used on the Eurostar service.

When travelling by train at peak times it may be worthwhile reserving a seat for a small charge. In addition, restaurant and buffet cars are provided on the main services where you can enjoy a drink, a snack or a full meal (served at your seat in first class). The food is in the main excellent and the service courteous. It is a very pleasant way to travel. Check that the train that you are aiming for has a restaurant car.

Bus

Dublin has an extensive bus network, operated by Bus Atha Cliath/Dublin Bus. On weekdays, main services start just after 7am and run until just before midnight. Some all-night services run from the city centre to certain suburbs. An extensive feeder service links in to stations on the DART line, while Imp services and CitySwift services are new variations designed to be quicker. CitySwift services have a very limited number of stops. All main bus routes either traverse the city centre, going through O'Connell Street, or have their termini in the city centre, either along the quays or in adjacent streets, especially College Street, Fleet Street and Middle Abbey Street.

A regular express bus service connects Dublin airport, Heuston station, Connolly station and Bus Áras, the main provincial bus station. For the Stena Line ferry terminal at Dun Laoghaire, the 46A bus from Fleet Street has its Dun Laoghaire terminus near the ferry terminal. A special

bus service connects the ferry terminal and Heuston station. For the B&I ferry terminal in Dublin, a bus service runs from Bus Aras, the city centre bus staion in Store Street. The 53 and 53A bus routes can also be used. A wide variety of commuter tickets is available, for different periods of bus use, from one day to one month, or even a year if you wish. Some tickets combine DART and suburban rail travel. These tickets offer reasonable savings, of about 10 per cent, on the cash price of bus tickets. These pre-paid tickets can be bought either at Dublin Bus headquarters, 59 Upper O'Connell Street, Dublin 1 or at a wide variety of shops in the greater Dublin area. They can also be bought at the CIE desk in Dublin airport. For full details of timetables, fares, etc. call Dublin Bus at 873 4222, Monday to Saturday, 9am-7pm. Cash fares range from about 60 pence for the shortest distance, to about £1.20 for the longest. Fares are subject to price increases.

The only privately-owned, scheduled bus service in the greater Dublin area is the St Kevin's service, which starts outside the College of Surgeons at St Stephen's Green, Dublin, and runs regular daily services to and from Glendalough, Co Wicklow. Telephone 281 8119 for details.

Belfast bus routes radiate out from the city centre and operate from about 6am until just before midnight. Buses from the city centre depart mostly from the City Hall area and pick up and set down passengers from clearly marked stops along the route. You can either pay the driver upon boarding or present an 8-journey ticket. The latter may be purchased from the Citybus kiosks at Donegall Square West and Castle Place, and at a wide variety of shops throughout the city and represent a saving of about 20 per cent on the cash fare. A number of other discounted tickets are available. For full details of these and other bus information, telephone 246485.

All Ulsterbus (out of town) scheduled services will pick up and set down passengers within the city on Sundays only (on Lisburn and Falls Road every day). The Rail-Link bus (No. 100), a regular bus service connecting the city's two train stations and the city centre, departs approximately every 15 minutes between 7.18am and 8.25pm (Monday to Saturday, no Sunday service) from both stations with stops at Royal Avenue, Donegall Place and Chichester Street in the city centre. The airport bus runs every half hour from the Europa bus centre in Glengall Street to Belfast International Airport from Monday - Saturday and approximately every 45 minutes on Sundays, between 6am and 9.30pm.

The provincial bus network in Ireland is extensive; many private operators run

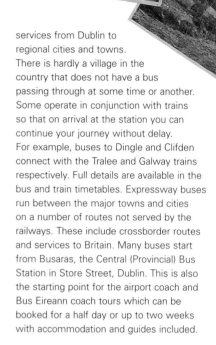

services from Dublin to regional cities and towns. There is hardly a village in the country that does not have a bus passing through at some time or another. Some operate in conjunction with trains so that on arrival at the station you can continue your journey without delay. For example, buses to Dingle and Clifden connect with the Tralee and Galway trains respectively. Full details are available in the bus and train timetables. Expressway buses run between the major towns and cities on a number of routes not served by the railways. These include crossborder routes and services to Britain. Many buses start from Busaras, the Central (Provincial) Bus Station in Store Street, Dublin. This is also the starting point for the airport coach and Bus Eireann coach tours which can be booked for a half day or up to two weeks with accommodation and guides included.

Ulsterbus has a similar itinerary of provincial routes and express buses. These normally depart from two points in Belfast, The Europa Bus Centre in Glengall Street and Oxford Street. Tourist excursions run during the summer to the main beauty spots of Ulster. If you plan to use public transport a lot enquire about Rambler and Overlander tickets. These are valid for 8 or 15 days and give unlimited travel by rail or rail and bus. For a supplement you can include both Northern Ireland and the Republic in your itinerary. They are very good value indeed and cost no more than the price of two or three ordinary return tickets. While timetables are issued for all services, it is worth enquiring locally before setting out, especially in rural areas. Expressway buses are usually reliable but in remote areas the local bus may not adhere so painstakingly to the schedule.

WHERE TO STAY

Before departure contact Bord Failte or the NITB in your own country for full information on the range of accommodation available in Ireland. You can stay in anything from a hostel to a luxurious castle. In tourist board approved premises the rates are fixed and if you wish you can make your booking through the tourist office (see Useful

Iveragh Peninsula, St. Finian's Bay Looking out towards Puffin Island

Addresses). During the summer it is advisable to book well in advance and remember that some places close for part of the winter. Tourist staff will help you choose accommodation and give advice on eating out, excursions, sightseeing, shopping, public transport, etc. Each year Bord Failte and the NITB assess and grade hotels and guesthouses listed in their brochures, based on the overall standard of accommodation and service. Grading also establishes the maximum price which may be charged:

Hotels

Five star. Ireland's most luxurious hotels,with high international standards. These hotels have some of the country's finest restaurants.

Four star. Contemporary hotels of excellent quality and charming period houses renovated to high standards. Excellent restaurant cuisine.

Three star. These range from small, family operated premises to larger, modern hotels. All rooms have private bathroom. Restaurants offer high standard of cuisine.

Two star. Usually family operated premises, with all guest rooms having a telephone and most with a private bathroom. Dining facilities offer wholesome food.

One star. Simple hotels where mandatory services are to a satisfactory standard. Some guest rooms have a private bathroom.

Guesthouses

- Four star. Accommodation includes half suites and all guest rooms have private bathroom and direct dial telephone. Many provide dinner.
- Three star. All guest rooms have private bathrooms and direct dial telephones. Restaurant facilities in some guesthouses.

- Two star. Half or more of the guest rooms have private bathrooms. Facilities include reading/writing room or lounge area. Some have restaurant facilities.
- One star. These premises meet the mandatory requirements for guesthouses and offer simple accommodation. Some have restaurant facilities.

Town and Country Homes

A large number of houses in urban and rural areas ranging from period style houses to modern bungalows; evening meals by arrangement.

Farmhouses

Many farming families offer accommodation in a unique rural setting where fresh farm produce and tranquillity are guaranteed. Ideal for children; evening meals by arrangement.

Self-Catering

Houses, cottages and apartments can be rented at numerous locations across the country with sleeping accommodation for up to 10 people. These are very popular and should be booked well in advance. Contact the Regional Tourism Organisation in the area of your choice for a list of such places (see Useful Addresses).

Camping and Caravanning

With quiet country roads and approved sites this can be a perfect holiday for those who don't want to rush. Many sites have shops, laundry, cafes and play areas for children.

Boating

Ireland's waterways are beautiful, uncrowded and clean and you can hire a fully equipped 2-8 berth cruiser. Cruisers are fitted with a fridge, cooker, central heating,

hot water, shower, charts, dinghy, bed linen, crockery, etc. They are easy to handle and the inexperienced sailor can receive instruction before casting off. The River Shannon is the most popular cruising waterway but equally attractive are the Grand Canal, the River Barrow, the River Erne and the new Shannon-Erne Link. Hire companies are located at Carrick-on-Shannon, Co. Leitrim; Whitegate, Co. Clare; Portumna, Co. Galway; Tullamore, Co. Offaly; Athlone, Co Westmeath; Belturbet, Co. Cavan, Kesh, Enniskillen, Killadeas, Lisbellaw, Bellanaleck, Co. Fermanagh.

Rates

The current brochures from Bord Failte and the NITB contain the rates for all approved accommodation in Ireland. Check that these apply when booking. Reductions are usually available for children under 12 and those under 4 are free if they share their parents' bedroom. Special rates apply for full board and a stay for a week or longer; ask for details. Generally you will pay less and have greater choice outside the high season (July and August).

Please contact the tourist boards if you are particularly pleased with your accommodation. Any complaints should be taken up with the manager in the first instance. Failing satisfaction, contact the Regional Tourism Organisation who will investigate the matter and if appropriate refer it to Bord Failte or the NITB. Every effort will be made to satisfy the complainant.

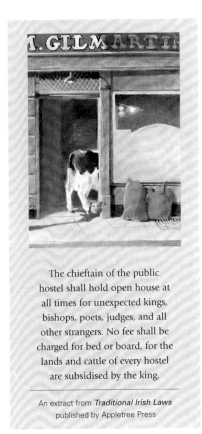

The chieftain of the public hostel shall hold open house at all times for unexpected kings, bishops, poets, judges, and all other strangers. No fee shall be charged for bed or board, for the lands and cattle of every hostel are subsidised by the king.

An extract from *Traditional Irish Laws* published by Appletree Press

USEFUL INFORMATION

Bord Fáilte

The Irish Tourist Board
PO Box 273, Dublin 8 (postal enquiries).

The following offices are open all year round or for most of the year. About fifty others are open only in the summer (details from Bord Failte).

- Athlone, The Castle,
  ☎ (0902) 96430/92856
- Belfast, 53 Castle Street, Belfast
  BT1 1GH ☎ (01232) 240201
- Cashel, Town Hall, Cashel
  ☎ (062) 61333
- Cork, Tourist House, Grand Parade, Cork
  ☎ (021) 273251 Fax. (021) 273504
- Derry, Foyle Street, Derry
  ☎ / Fax. (01504) 369501
- Dublin, Suffolk Street, Dublin 2
  ☎ (01) 605 7700
- Dundalk, Market Square, Dundalk
  ☎ (042) 35484 Fax. (042) 38070
- Dun Laoghaire, St Michael's Wharf,
  Dun Laoghaire ☎ (01) 550 112233
- Ennis, Bank Place, Ennis ☎ (065) 28366
- Galway, Eyre Square, Galway
  ☎ (091) 583081 Fax. (091) 585201
- Kilkenny, Rose Inn Street, Kilkenny
  ☎ (056) 51500 Fax. (056) 63955
- Killarney, Town Hall, Killarney
  ☎ (064) 31633 Fax. (064) 34506
- Letterkenny, Derry Road, Letterkenny
  ☎ (074) 21160 Fax. (074) 25180
- Limerick, Arthur's Quay, Limerick
  ☎ (061) 317522 Fax. (061) 317939
- Mullingar, Dublin Road, Mullingar
  ☎ (044) 48650 Fax. (044) 40413
- Nenagh, Kickham Road, Nenagh
  ☎ (067) 31610
- Rosslare Harbour, Co Wexford
  ☎ (053) 33622 Fax. (053) 33421
- Shannon Airport ☎ (061) 471664
- Skibbereen, North Street, Skibbereen
  ☎ (028) 21766 Fax. (028) 21353
- Sligo, Temple Street, Sligo
  ☎ (071) 61201 Fax. (071) 60360
- Tralee, Godfrey Place, Tralee
  ☎ (066) 21288
- Waterford, 41 The Mall, Tralee
  ☎ (051) 75788 Fax. (051) 77388
- Westport, The Mall, Westport
  ☎ (098) 25711 Fax. (098) 26709
- Wexford, Crescent Quay, Wexford
  ☎ (053) 23111 Fax. (053) 41743
- Wicklow Town, Fitzwilliam Square,
  Wicklow ☎ (0404) 69117

Regional Tourism Organisations

- Cork/Kerry, Tourist House, Grand Parade,
  Cork ☎ (021) 273251 Fax. (021) 273504
- Donegal/ Leitrim/ Sligo, Temple Street,
  Sligo ☎ (071) 61201 Fax. (071) 60360
- Dublin, Suffolk Street, Dublin 2
  ☎ (01) 605 7700
- Dun Laoghaire, Co Dublin
  ☎ (01) 280 8571 Fax. (01) 280 2641
- Midland East Tourism (Kildare, Louth,
  Wicklow, Meath, Cavan, Laois, Longford,
  Monaghan, Offaly, Roscommon,
  Westmeath) Dublin Road, Mullingar
  ☎ (044) 48650 Fax. (044) 40413
- Shannon Development (Clare, Limerick,
  North Tipperary, South East Offaly, North
  Kerry) Shannon, Co Clare
  ☎ (061) 361555 (061) 361903
- South Eastern (Carlow, Kilkenny,
  South Tipperary, Waterford, Wexford),
  41 The Quay, Waterford
  ☎ (051) 75788 Fax. (051) 77388
- Ireland West (Galway, Mayo) Victoria
  Place, Eyre Square, Galway
  ☎ (091) 583081 Fax. (091) 585201

N I Tourist Offices (all year)

A number of office open summer only;
details from NITB.

- Armagh, 40 English Street
  ☎ (01861) 521800
- Ballycastle, 7 Mary Street
  ☎ (012657) 62024
- Banbridge, Newry Road
  ☎ (018206) 23322
- Bangor, 34 Quay Street
  ☎ (01247) 270069
- Belfast, 59 North Street
  ☎ (01232) 246609
- Cookstown, 48 Molesworth Street
  ☎ (016487) 66727
- Derry, 8 Bishop Street ☎ (01504) 267284
- Dungannon, Ballygawley Road
  ☎ (01868) 767269
- Enniskillen, Wellington Road
  ☎ (01365) 323110
- Larne, Narrow Gauge Road
  ☎ (01574) 270517
- Limavady, Benevenagh Drive
  ☎ (015047) 22226
- Omagh, 1 Market Street
  ☎ (01662) 247831/2

Travel

Air

- Belfast City Airport ☎ (01232) 457745
- Belfast International Airport
  ☎ (018494) 22888
- Cork Airport ☎ (021) 313131
- Derry Airport ☎ (01504) 810784
- Dublin Airport ☎ (01) 844 4900
- Shannon Airport ☎ (061) 471444

Rail

- Connolly Station, Amiens Street, Dublin
  ☎ (01) 836 3333
- Heuston Station, Dublin ☎ (01) 836 3333
  Passenger enquiries
  ☎ (01) 836 6222
- Belfast Central Station
  ☎ (01232) 899400
- Yorkgate Station, Belfast
  ☎ (01232) 899400
  Passenger enquires ☎ (01232) 230310

Bus

- Bus Éireann, Bus Áras central bus station,
  Dublin ☎ (01) 836 6111
- Dublin Bus, Dublin ☎ (01) 873 4222
- CIE Tours International, Lower Abbey
  Street, Dublin 1 ☎ (01) 703 1888
- Citybus, Belfast ☎ (01232) 246485
- Ulsterbus, Belfast ☎ (01232) 333000
  Europa Bus Station, Glengall Street,
  Belfast ☎ (01232) 320574
- Oxford Street Bus Station, Belfast
  ☎ (01232) 232356

Embassies

- Australia, 6th Floor, Fitzwilton House,
  Wilton Terrace, Dublin 2 ☎ (01) 676 1517
- Belgium, 2 Shrewsbury Road, Dublin 4
  ☎ (01) 269 2082
- Canada, 65 St Stephen's Green, Dublin 2
  ☎ (01) 478 1988
- France, 36 Ailesbury Road, Dublin 4
  ☎ (01) 260 1666
- Germany, 31 Trimleston Avenue,
  Booterstown, Co Dublin ☎ (01) 269 3011
- Italy, 63 Northumberland Road, Dublin 4
  ☎ (01) 660 1744
- Netherlands, 160 Merrion Road, Dublin 4
  ☎ (01) 269 3444
- Spain, 17a Merlyn Park, Dublin 4
  ☎ (01) 269 1640
- Switzerland, 6 Ailesbury Road, Dublin 4
  ☎ (01) 269 2515
- United Kingdom, 31 Merrion Road,
  Dublin 4 ☎ (01) 205 3700
- United States of America, 42 Elgin Road,
  Dublin 4 ☎ (01) 668 8777

Cultural Institutes

- Goethe Institut, 37 Merrion Square,
  Dublin 2 ☎ (01) 661 1155
- Alliance Française, 1 Kildare Street,
  Dublin 2 ☎ (01) 676 1732
- Instituto Cervantes (Spanish), 58
  Northumberland Road, Dublin 4
  ☎ (01) 668 2024

Government Offices

- Department of Foreign Affairs,
  80 St Stephen's Green, Dublin 2
  ☎ (01) 478 0822
- Government Information Services, Upper
  Merrion Street, Dublin 2 ☎ (01) 662 4422
- European Commission Press &
  Information Office, 39 Molesworth Street
  ☎ (01) 662 5113
- National Library, Kildare Street, Dublin 2
  ☎ (01) 603 0200
- National Museum, Kildare Street, Dublin 2
  ☎ (01) 667 7444
- Northern Ireland Information Office,
  Stormont Castle, Belfast BT4 3ST
  ☎ (01232) 763255

TOURING IN IRELAND

If you ride your chariot to the great assembly and it is damaged, you may not claim compensation unless it was broken through furious driving.

An extract from *Traditional Irish Laws*
published by Appletree Press

If you plan a touring holiday it is worth contacting your local automobile association and the tourist board beforehand. They will supply you with full details of the rules of the road, insurance, breakdown services, petrol, road signs, etc. Most of this information can be had in Ireland but it is better to find out before you arrive. Bring your driving licence and insurance certificate, and display a nationality plate if bringing your car into Ireland.

There are lots of sea routes to choose from.
- *B&I Line* operate car ferries from Holyhead-Dublin, Liverpool-Dublin, Pembroke-Rosslare;
- *Stena Line:* Holyhead - Dun Laoghaire, Fishguard-Rosslare; Stranraer-Belfast;
- *Norse Irish Car Ferries:* Liverpool-Belfast;
- *Townsend Thoresen:* Cairnryan-Larne;
- *Irish Continental Line:* Le Havre-Rosslare, Le Havre-Cork;
- *Brittany Ferries:* Roscoff-Cork; Swansea-Cork ferry;
- *Seacat:* Stranraer-Belfast.

There are also regular summer sailings from the Isle of Man to Belfast and Dublin.

Cars can be hired from a number of companies in Ireland. Bord Failte and the NITB will supply you with a list of authorised car hire firms and you can pick up your chauffeured or self-drive car at the port or airport. If you plan to cross the border check with the hire company that your insurance is valid north and south. Rates vary according to the model, time of year and hire period. Weekend rates are good value especially in the off-season. Make sure you know whether the rate is for limited or unlimited mileage. You can also save money by transferring you own insurance to the hire car. You can avail of numerous packages involving travel by sea or air and a self-drive car for the duration of your holiday. Hotel or farmhouse accommodation can be included. If you choose to stay in one area you can arrange your holiday through CIE, travelling by train to Galway or Killarney, for example, and picking up a car at the station. For full details of all these combinations and special offers contact your local tourist board, Aer Lingus, B&I or CIE (see Useful Addresses).

Ireland has the lowest population density in Europe so there is lots of room on the roads, which makes driving a pleasure. The speed limit is 96 kmph (60 mph) and 48 kmph (30 mph) in towns. On motorways and dual carriage-ways in Northern Ireland the speed limit is 112 kmph (70 mph); otherwise the limits are as in the Republic. In the Republic roads are classed as motorway (M7), national primary (N5), secondary (N71) and regional (R691). In the north you will find motorways (M1), class A (A5) and class B (B52) roads. However, when seeking directions it is more common to refer to "the Longford Road" than "the N4". The road network is very extensive and while the principal highways are good those in more remote areas will vary. In the country watch out for cows, sheep and other animals being herded along the road.

You will find most routes well signposted although there may not be much advance warning. It's hard to get really lost and in any case it is a pleasure to drift along a country road admiring the countryside. Ask someone on the road or stop at a country pub or shop and you'll get all the directions you need and a great deal more besides. Placenames are written in Irish and English in the Republic and signposts increasingly give distances in kilometres. Motorists should take care when reading roadsigns since at present some distances are given in miles and some in kilometres. In Ireland drive on the left and yield to traffic from the right. All drivers and front-seat passengers must wear a seat belt at all times; the gardai (police) are likely to stop you for not wearing one. Children under twelve are not allowed on front seats. While in Dublin you would be advised to park your car in an attended car park, place all valuables in the boot and lock the car securely. Parking is unrestricted in country towns and there are many lay-bys, picnic sites and beauty spots where you can pull in to take a break from driving. You must not park in town centres in Northern Ireland. For security reasons these are classed as control zones and unattended cars will be removed. Watch out also for ramps and be prepared to stop for security checks.

Roadsigns of various kinds are in operation. Hazards are indicated by black and yellow symbols on a diamond shaped board. Speed limits and parking restrictions are shown by black spots which are clearly marked. These often indicate dangerous junctions or very sharp bends and can be deceptive, especially at night. An unbroken white line in the centre of the road indicates that overtaking is forbidden.

Parking meters are common in cities although you can park at one after 6pm without charge. The meter works by

clocking up one or two hours according to the number of coins inserted. A single yellow line next to the kerb allows parking for a short period only. A double yellow line forbids parking at any time. In Cork you must display a parking disc inside the car indicating the time of day. These may be bought from newsagents and tobacconists. Bus lanes operate in cities and are reserved for buses and cyclists at certain times of the day. Watch out for the signs. Although some leniency is extended to visitors it is worthwhile observing the traffic regulations otherwise you risk being fined or having your car towed away!

TEN TOURING IDEAS

These ten scenic tours are designed to help you get the most from your motoring holiday in Ireland - to show you the most beautiful scenery, and to introduce you to Ireland's many interesting cities and towns. As all ten tours are circular you can commence at any point of the given routes. The daily distance covered is shown with each tour, in miles and kilometres. Included are maps of the ten tours, with alternative routes indicated by broken lines.

Tour of Ireland
A ten-day tour over 1,600 kilometres (1,000 miles), suggested starting point - Dublin.

Day 1: *Dublin-Tramore 190 km (118 miles).*
Having seen Dublin's historic buildings and Georgian squares and having sampled its lively cosmopolitan atmosphere, you're on your way to Enniskerry, a pretty hillside village just twelve miles south of the city. Nearby you can visit the splendid Powerscourt Estate, with its gardens, deer

One of Ireland's many beautiful beaches

Tour of Ireland

Day 4: *Killarney*
It's worth spending a day in Killarney, setting out the next day for Galway.

Day 5: *Killarney-Galway 251km (156 miles).* On the fifth day your drive takes you through Abbeyfeale, Newcastle West, the lovely village of Adare, and into Limerick, 25 km (16 miles) from Shannon Airport on the River Shannon, a graceful and historic city, featuring King John's Castle, Hunt Museum, the Treaty Stone and St Mary's Cathedral. Traditional medieval banquets can be enjoyed at Bunratty Castle (13 km (8 miles) from Limerick) and Knappogue Castle (13 km (8 miles) from Ennis). Continuing on you reach Ennis with its old abbey and the seaside resort of Lahinch, featuring excellent golf courses. You should make your next stop by the breathtaking Cliffs of Moher, before driving to Lisdoonvarna, Ireland's premier spa. Drive through the bare limestone hills of the Burren to Ballyvaughan, to Kinvara (mediaeval banquets at Dunguaire Castle), Clarinbridge and into Galway. Galway is the capital of the 'Western World' with its famous Spanish Arch and Church of St Nicholas, where, tradition holds, Columbus prayed before sailing to America.

Day 6: *Galway-Westport 138 km (86 miles).* The next day your route through Connemara takes you to Moycullen, Oughterard, Recess, Clifden capital of Connemara), Leenane and Westport-on ClewBay, with over 100 islands.

Day 7: *Westport-Bundoran 154 km (96 miles).* Head north next day to Castlebar, Pontoon, Ballina and the family resort of Inniscrone. Enjoy a swim before driving on to Sligo, where you can look around the 13th c. Franciscan Friary and the museum, situated in the county library. Head on to Drumcliff (burial place of W.B. Yeats) to complete your day's driving at Bundoran.

Day 8: *Bundoran-Dunfanaghy 193 km (120 miles).* On the following day head further up the Atlantic Coast through Ballyshannon to Donegal town, visiting the Franciscan Friary and castle. Drive through Dunkineely, Ardara, Glenties, Maas and

herd and waterfall. Continue on through Roundwood to Glendalough and see the ruins of an early-Christian settlement in a beautiful wild setting of mountains and lakes. Your next stop, via Rathdrum, is Avoca, made famous by Thomas Moore's song "The Meeting of the Waters". Southwards is the prominent holiday resort of Arklow, overlooking the sea. Onwards to Enniscorthy, with its old-world charm - just 53 km (33 miles) from the car ferry port of Rosslare Harbour - and then by New Ross, with its twisting lanes and Dutchtype houses, to Waterford. Or visit Wexford and on to Waterford by the Ballyhack Passage East car ferry. Spend your first night at Tramore, a family resort with 4 km (3 miles) of sandy beaches.

Day 2: *Tramore-Cork 117 km (73 miles).* After lunch leave for Cork, via Dungarvan and Youghal, a popular holiday resort. Continue through the market town of Midleton to Cork. Enjoy the friendly atmosphere of Cork, built on the banks of the River Lee. Visit St Mary's Shandon, where the famous Shandon Bells can be played by visitors, and admire the many fine public buildings.

Day 3: *Cork-Killarney 151 km (94 miles).* Leaving Cork on the third day your first stop

is Blarney Castle with its famous stone, said to impart the gift of eloquence to all who kiss it! Continue through Macroom, Ballingeary, Pass of Keimaneigh - 3 km (2 miles) from Gougane Barra Forest Park Ballylickey, and into the beautiful holiday resort of Glengarriff. Then in a northerly direction you drive through Kenmare into Killarney, enjoying one of the finest scenic drives on the way. You'll find plenty to do in Killarney - pony riding, boating and visiting islands and ancient abbeys. Drive around the 'Ring of Kerry', a brilliant 174 km (109 mile) scenic drive bringing you to Killorglin, Cahirsiveen, Waterville, Sneem, Parknasilla, Kenmare and back to Killarney.

Killarney / Kemare, Black Valley Gap of Dunloe, Tomies Mountain

Dingle Peninsula, Kenmare (Ring of Kerry)

Kinscasslagh noted for their cottage industries and Donegal tweed. Then by Annagry, Crolly, Bunbeg, Bloody Foreland, Gortahork into Dunfanaghy, nestling in the cosy inlet of Sheephaven Bay.

Day 9: *Dunfanaghy-Carrick-On-Shannon 177 km (110 miles).* Next day your tour takes you south via Portnablagh to Letterkenny-Donegal's chief town. This is an excellent point from which to extend your drive, by taking the 'Inishowen 100' an extremely scenic trip around the Inishowen Peninsula, to Buncrana, Malin Head and Moville. Return to Letterkenny by Bloody Foreland, Co. Donegal Manorcunningham. Total mileage for the trip is 193 km (120 miles). Continue south through the picturesque Finn Valley to the twin towns of Stranorlar and Ballybofey, completing your round trip of County Donegal in Donegal town. The next stage takes you to Ballyshannon and Bundoran in a southerly direction to Manorhamilton. Overlooking the town you'll see the picturesque ruin of Sir Frederick Hamilton's castle - built in 1638. Continue south through Drumkeeran along the beautiful shores of Lough Allen into Drumshanbo. Drive on through Leitrim into Carrick-on- Shannon, an important cruising and angling centre.

Day 10: *Carrick-on-Shannon-Dublin 240 km (150 miles).* On the final day head for Cavan, travelling by Mohill, Carrigallen, Killeshandra and Crossdoney, enjoying the lake scenery on the way. Continue to Bailieborough -14 km (9 miles) from the

important angling centre of Virginia) and into the attractive town of Carrickmacross. The last stage of your trip takes you to Drogheda - a historic town in Co. Louth. From Drogheda visit the prehistoric tombs at Newgrange, Knowth and Dowth. Drive on by Slane into Navan. 10 km (6 miles) from here see the Hill of Tara, a former residence of Irish High Kings. Complete your tour of the Boyne Valley in Trim, rich in historical associations and ancient monuments, before returning to Dublin, via Black Bull, Clonlee, Blanchardstown and the Phoenix Park.

The following alternative two-day route from Dunfanaghy to Dublin takes in the Antrim Coast and the Mourne Mountains.

Day 9: *Dunfanaghy-Belfast 240 km (150 miles).* Take the road from Dunfanaghy to Letterkenny, travelling north-east from here to Derry (you will cross the border into Northern Ireland at Bridgend). Stop to explore this historic city on the banks of the River Foyle, whose walls (the only remaining unbroken fortifications in either Britain or Ireland) afford superb views of the surrounding countryside and of the city itself. Continue north-east to Limavady, Downhill, Castlerock and Coleraine and on to the bracing seaside resort of Portrush. Then follow the coastal road eastwards to see the famous Giant's Causeway, the beautiful beaches at White Park Bay and the Carrick-a-Rede Rope Bridge (not for the faint-hearted). The steep, winding road around Torr Head and down to picturesque

Cushendun is worth the slight detour - views are breathtaking. From Cushendun head for Larne, departure point for ferries Scotland. The final stage of your journey takes you to Belfast via Carrickfergus, where you can visit the country's best-preserved Norman castle.

Day 10: *Belfast-Dublin 192 km (120 miles)* The last day of your tour takes you south out of Belfast through the heart of County Down towards the spectacular Mourne Mountains. Stop at Downpatrick en route to see Down Cathedral, in whose churchyard you will find St Patrick's grave marked by a crude slab. Continue towards Newcastle, County Down's most popular holiday resort, where, in the words of the song, "The Mountains of Mourne sweep down to the sea". Stroll along the beach at Dundrum or, if you're feeling energetic, make an assault on Slieve Donard (the Mournes' highest peak), which can be reached either through Donard Park or from Bloody Bridge (just outside Newcastle). Follow the road from Newcastle via Kilkeel and Warrenpoint to Newry, cross the border into the Republic, then continue to Dundalk whose surrounding hills and forests are full of history and charm. Then make your way south to Drogheda (stopping at Monasterboice on the way to admire one of the most magnificent High Crosses in the country). From Drogheda, the mysterious passage tomb of Newgrange is easily accessible and well worth a visit. The last stretch of road takes you south into Dublin city.

27

East Coast Tour

Two circular tours - one north, the other south of Dublin.

Day 1: *Northern tour 306 km (190 miles)*. Take the Navan road out of Dublin to Tara site of a former royal acropolis, situated in an area rich in ancient monuments and historical associations. Continue north to Navan, Donaghmore and Slane. Visit the Bronze Age cemeteries at Brugh na Boinne, King William's Glen, Mellifont Abbey and Monasterboice, before heading for Dunleer, Castlebellingham and Dundalk - an ideal base for exploring the surrounding countryside. If you wish you can travel further north to see the delightfully rugged Carlingford Peninsula, taking you through Ballymascanlon, Carlingford, Omeath and back into Dundalk.

Heading south you reach Castlebellingham, Clogher, Termonfeckin, Baltray, with its fine beach and golf course and on into Drogheda, on the River Boyne. In Bettystown, further south, there's a long sandy beach linking up with Laytown, while further on is Julianstown. Following the coast enjoy a pleasant drive through Balbriggan, Skerries, Rush, Lusk, Swords and Howth, stopping to admire the magnificent views from the rocky Hill of Howth. Return to Dublin via Sutton.

Day 2: *Southern Tour 467 km (290 miles)*. Next day the southern tour takes you through Dun Laoghaire, Dalkey and Killiney - with its magnificent view over the bay from the Vico Road - into Bray, one of Ireland's premier seaside resorts. Continuing on you reach Enniskerry, a pretty village beneath the Sugarloaf Mountain and near the beautiful Powerscourt Estate. The scenic mountain drive takes you to Glendalough, with its ancient ruins and picturesque lakes, passing through Glencree, Glenmacnass and Laragh. If you wish you can return to Dublin by Blessington, making a short but enjoyable trip - or keep south to Rathdrum, Avoca and Woodenbridge into Arklow, where you can enjoy a swim or go sea fishing. Driving on through County Wexford takes you to

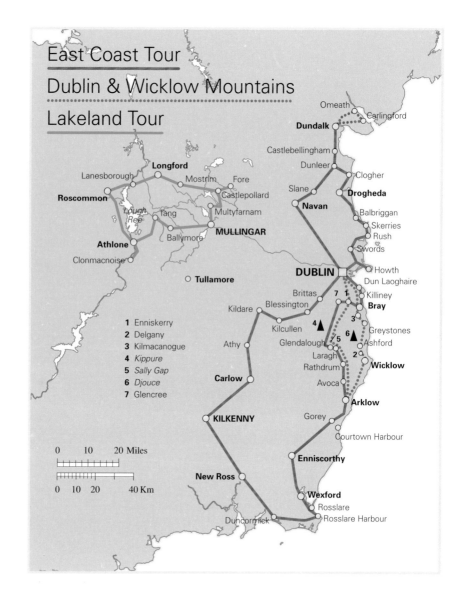

Thatched cottage Mooncoin Village, Kilkenny

Gorey, Courtown Harbour (seaside resort), Ferns, Enniscorthy and Wexford, which is within easy reach of Rosslare Harbour. These charming old towns are well worth a visit. Follow the coast through Rosslare, Duncormick, Arthurstown and into New Ross. From here take the road to Kilkenny, a cheerful city steeped in history. Visit the Kilkenny Design Workshops, Rothe House and Kilkenny Castle. Return to Dublin through Carlow and County Kildare towns of Athy, Kildare, Kilcullen, and Ballymore Eustace, taking in the lake drive near Blessington and reaching the city via Brittas.

Lakeland Tour

This is a two-day circular drive of about 240 km (150 miles). This tour of Ireland's quiet heart offers a charm of a different kind from the coastal tours.

Day 1: *Athlone-Mullingar 135 km (84 miles)*. The starting point is Athlone - capital of the midlands. From here drive to Roscommon visiting Hodson Bay and Rinndown Castle en route. Have a look around Roscommon Abbey. North-east of Roscommon is Lanesborough, a popular angling centre at the head of Lough Ree. Then visit the busy market town of Longford with its nineteenth-century cathedral. Move on to Edgeworthstown, which gets its name from the remarkable literary family. Continue to Castlepollard, a good angling centre near Lough Derravaragh featured in a tragic myth "The Children of Lir". See nearby Tullynally Castle. Drive to Fore, with its ancient crosses and Benedictine Abbey, returning to Castlepollard and south via Multyfarnham to Mullingar - an important town and noted angling centre. Spend the night there.

Day 2: *Mullingar-Athlone 105 km (65 miles)*. Next day a westward drive takes you to Ballymore and to the Goldsmith country via Tang. Visit Lissoy and The Pigeons on the road to the pretty village of Glasson, passing the tower-like structure marking the geographical centre of Ireland. Return to Athlone. From Athlone make an excursion to Coosan Point for a good view of Lough Ree, one of the largest Shannon lakes. Going downriver it's worth a visit to Clonmacnoise, one of the country's most celebrated holy places, completing your tour in Athlone.

Dublin and Wicklow Mountains

This is a one-day scenic tour of about 177 km (110 miles). Leave Dublin by the suburb of Rathfarnham, four miles south of the city. The ruined building known as "The Hell Fire Club" forms a prominent landmark to the summit of Mount Pelier, 6 km (4 miles) south of Rathfarnham. Drive via Glencullen, Kilternan and the Scalp into Enniskerry - one of the prettiest villages in Ireland. From here you can visit the Powerscourt Estate and Gardens, which include the highest waterfall in these islands. Continue to Sally Gap, a notable crossroads situated between Kippure Mountain and the Djouce Mountain, where the road leads to Glendalough, by Glenmacnass and Laragh. Have a look around Glendalough - one of the most picturesque glens of County Wicklow with extensive ruins of the 6th c. Irish monastery of St. Kevin. Drive on through Laragh by the Military Road to Rathdrum. Head south by the Vale of Avoca into Arklow, a popular holiday centre. From Arklow drive north to Wicklow where you can admire the view over the bay. Ashford is the next village on your route close by the beautiful Mount Usher Gardens with countless varieties of trees, plants and shrubs. Move on through the rugged Devil's Glen to Newtown Mount Kennedy, Delgany and into the attractive resort of Greystones, which retains the atmosphere of the former quiet fishing village. Head back through Delgany to the Glen of the Downs, Kilmacanogue (from where you can climb the great Sugar Loaf) into Bray. From this fine resort at the base of Bray Head take the route to Killiney and the Vico Road to Dalkey, enjoying the superb views of Killiney Bay. Follow the coast road to Dun Laoghaire into Dublin.

South-West Tour

This is a two-day circular tour of about 700 km (440 miles) on main route.

Day 1: *Cork-Killarney 359 km (223 miles).* The suggested starting point is Cork - a charming city on the River Lee, excellent for shopping and offering first-class pubs and restaurants with entertainment for every member of the family. Blarney Castle, with its famous Stone of Eloquence is 8 km (5 miles) away. Visit there to kiss the stone, before continuing to the old-world town of Kinsale. Drive on to Timoleague - where you'll see the remains of the once largest friary in Ireland - to Clonakilty, Rosscarbery, Glandore, Union Hall and Skibbereen. Continue this exceptionally beautiful drive through Ballydehob, Schull, Toormore, Durrus and Bantry into Glengarriff - visiting the Forest Park and Garinish Island, with its ornate gardens. Afterwards take the "Tunnel Road" to Kenmare or head west over the Healy Pass. Some of the finest sea and mountain scenery in Ireland can be enjoyed on the next stage of the tour, around the 'Ring of Kerry' through Sneem, Castlegrove, Derrynane, Waterville,

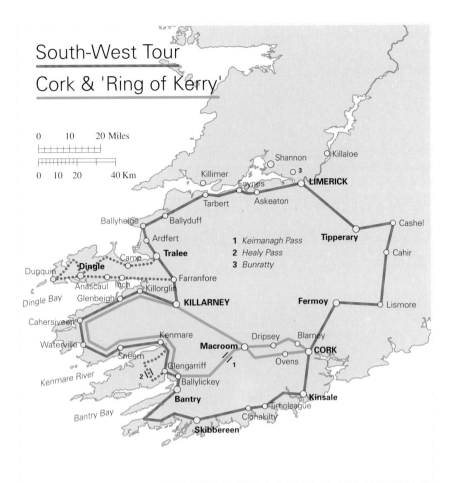

Ballyheig Bay / Tralee Bay with Dingle Peninsula in the background

Cahirsiveen, Glenbeigh and Killorglin into Killarney. There are some lovely quiet beaches in this region for example Rossbeigh near Glenbeigh. Spend the night in Killarney.

Day 2: *Killarney-Cork 352 km (220 miles).* From Killarney drive direct to Tralee or alternatively explore the Dingle Peninsula,

the heart of Ryan's Daughter country. Places along the route are: Inch, Annascaul, Dingle, Ventry, Slea Head, Dunquin, Ballyferriter, Murreagh, back to Dingle and on through Stradbally and Camp to Tralee. An unforgettable drive of breathtaking beauty. Follow the coast from Tralee to Ardfert, Ballyheigue, Causeway, Ballyduff, Lisselton Cross Roads, Ballylongford, and

Tarbert, where a car ferry operates to Killimer, County Clare. Drive through Foynes along the Shannon Estuary via Askeaton to Limerick - an old and historic city, not far from Bunratty Castle, with its medieval-style banquets.

Having spent some time looking around Limerick head back to Cork through Tipperary and Cashel, visiting the magnificent ruins of the Rock of Cashel - including a cathedral, castle, chapel and round tower. Enjoy the mountain views on the way to historic Cahirtown and into Cork by Clogheen, Lismore and Fermoy, providing a splendid trip through the Knockmealdown Mountains.

Cork and 'Ring of Kerry'

A one-day tour about 354 km (220 miles).

Travel west from Cork via Ovens to Macroom. Turn off for Toon Bridge and Inchigeelagh through the wild mountain scenery of the Pass of Keimaneigh into Ballylickey. Along the way you could visit Gougane Barra Forest Park which is just north of your route. From Ballylickey enjoy the superb views of Bantry Bay en route to Glengarriff, from where you can visit the beautiful Italian gardens of Garinish Island. Head north to Kenmare through rugged mountains. Here your trip around the 'Ring of Kerry' begins encircling the Iveragh Peninsula, which features Ireland's highest mountains, the Macgillycuddy's Reeks. Excellent views are provided over Dingle Bay to the north and the estuary of the Kenmare River to the south. Travel south-west through Parknasilla and Sneem, into Caherdaniel, where you'll find excellent swimming and diving along the fine beach. Go north to the well-known resort of Waterville, continuing your tour by Cahirciveen, Glenbeigh and Killorglin, completing this exceptionally scenic trip to Killarney. Your route back to Cork takes your through the Derrynasaggart Mountains to Macroom, turning off the main road for Dripsey and Blarney Castle, where you can stop to kiss the famous Blarney Stone.

Camp Caherconree, Dingle Peninsula

West Coast Tour

This is a four-day circular tour of about 842 km (523 miles).

Day 1: *Athlone-Limerick 151 km (94 miles).* Athlone is the suggested starting point for a tour of this richly varied region. From this impressive town south of Lough Ree you pass the early-Christian site of Clonmacnois to the south and on to Birr, where the gardens of Birr Castle are open to visitors. Driving in a southerly direction you come to Nenagh with its fine castle, built about 1200. Continue via Portroe with fine views over Lough Derg into Killaloe, a popular water-skiing centre. From here drive

to O'Brien's Bridge, Ardnacrusha and on to Limerick for the night.

Day 2: *Limerick-Galway 232 km (144 miles).* Having seen the sights of Limerick head for Bunratty Castle where mediaeval banquets are held, and visit the Bunratty Folk Park. Drive south-west from Ennis to the resorts of Kilrush and Kilkee, going north to Lahinch and around Liscannor Bay to the magnificent ruggedness of the Cliffs of Moher, reaching up to 213 m (700 ft). Move on to Ireland's premier spa, Lisdoonvarna, enjoying the remarkable "Burren Country", consisting of a desert of bare limestone hills which are a botanist's paradise in the spring. Take the road from Lisdoonvarna through Black Head, Ballyvaughan, Kinvara and Clarinbridge into Galway. Discover Galway for yourself - its Church of St Nicholas, the Spanish Arch and the gathering of salmon (in season) under the Salmon Weir Bridge.

Day 3: *Galway-Westport 196 km (122 miles).* Next day start your tour of Connemara by Spiddal, Costelloe, Screeb, Gortmore, Carna, Toombeola, Ballynahinch and Glendalough. From Clifden you head northwards to Tullycross and on to Leenane, on the corner of picturesque

West Coast Tour
Galway & Connemara
Donegal & Yeats Country

1 Oughterard
2 *Rosguill Peninsula*
3 *L. Glencar*
4 *L. Mask*
5 *Croagh Patrick*
6 Bunratty

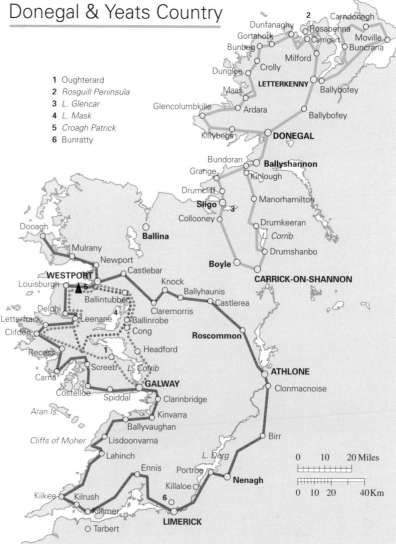

Thatched Cottage, Bunratty Folk Park

31

Near Recess, Co. Galway

Killary Harbour. Drive northwards through the mountains to Louisburgh, in the shadow of Croagh Patrick. Stop in Westport, an important sea angling centre. Alternatively you can get from Leenane to Westport through Joyce Country, taking you to Maam, Cong, Ballinrobe, Partry Mountains, Ballintubber with its famous abbey and into Westport.

Day 4: *Westport-Athlone 262 km (163 miles)*. The following day explore the beauties of Achill Island, taking the road to

Newport, Mulrany, through Curraun Peninsula, Achill Sound and on to Keel and Dooagh. Return via Newport to Castlebar, visiting Clonalis House. Then on to Claremorris, Ballyhaunis, Castlerea, Roscommon and back to Athlone.

Galway and Connemara

This is a one-day tour of about 257 km (160 miles)

Travel north-west of Galway to the pretty village of Oughterard, with views of Lough

Corrib along the way. Continue through the rugged countryside of Connemara, dominated by the craggy peaks of the Twelve Bens, via Maam Cross and Recess into Clifden - the capital of Connemara. From Clifden drive to Letterfrack and on to Leenane, at the head of picturesque Killary Harbour. Along the way you'll see the magnificent Kylemore Abbey. Having left Leenane turn off the main road for Louisburgh and Westport, passing Doo Lough and the lofty Croagh Patrick. The town of Westport was designed by James Wyatt - an architect of the Georgian period. Castlebar, principal town of County Mayo, is the next on your route offering you a charming old-world atmosphere. Of particular note is the pleasant tree-lined Mall. Return to Galway by Ballintubber, with its impressive abbey, Ballinrobe and Headford.

Donegal and Yeats Country

This is a two-day circular tour over 515 km (320 miles) on main route.

Day 1: *Carrick-on-Shannon-Carrigart 322 km (200 miles)*. The popular centre of Carrick-on-Shannon well known for cruising and coarse fishing is the starting point for this tour. The first town on this route is Boyle - 3 km (2 miles) from Lough Key Forest Park, with its numerous facilities, from boating to nature trails. Your drive will continue to Collooney, entering the magical country of Yeats. Share his experiences as you drive through Ballisadare, Kilmacowen and Strandhill on your way to Sligo, a beautifully situated town, surrounded by mountains. Pay a visit to Sligo Abbey and the museum, situated in the county library. Follow the road through Drumcliff (Yeats' burial place) to Grange and Cliffoney into Bundoran - a resort where you'll find enjoyment for all the family.

Begin your tour of Donegal from Ballyshannon, heading north to Donegal town and on to Killybegs by way of Mountcharles, Inver and Dunkineely. Following the coast to Glencolumbkille, a popular holiday centre, you are now in a part of Ireland's 'Gaeltacht' or Irish speaking region. This area of Donegal is noted for its excellent crafts and the production of handmade Donegal tweed. From Glencolumbkille head east to Ardara, Maas and Dungloe - a remarkable tract of rocky lakeland. Drive north from Crolly to the lovely fishing village of Bunbeg, along the coast to Gortahork and Dunfanaghy, with its lovely beaches and superb cliff scenery. Turn off at Creeslough for Carrigart beautifully situated on Mulroy Bay. Spend the night here.

Day 2: *Carrigart-Carrick-on-Shannon 193 km (120 miles)*.
From Carrigart there is a charming twelve-mile trip around the little Rosguill Peninsula,

Rossnowlagh Beach, Donegal at evening

taking in Tranarossan Bay and Rosapenna. Continue south to Letterkenny via Milford. Before driving south for Donegal town again you could take a trip around the Inishowen Peninsula, an extra 192 km (129 miles) in all, giving unrivalled views, a top class resort at Buncrana and some very interesting antiquities, such as the cross of Carndonagh. Complete your tour from Donegal by Ballyshannon, Bundoran, Kinlough, Manorhamilton, Killarga, Drumkeeran and along the shores of Lough Allen by Drumshanbo into Carrick-on-Shannon.

North-East Tour

Two circular tours - one north, the other south of Belfast.

Day 1: North Coast Tour 288 km (180 miles).

Travel north out of Belfast through Carrickfergus to the car ferry port of Larne. Continue along the scenic route to Cushendall and Ballycastle, enjoying the gently scooped-out contours of the Antrim Glens to your left. (You can turn inland to visit Glenariff Forest Park, where wooded paths lead to superb viewpoints.) Continue to the popular town of Ballycastle famous for its Ould Lammas Fair - before following the road to Portrush via the Giant's Causeway. (Bushmills, home of the world's oldest distillery, is only 5 km (3 miles) away, and can be visited.) Pass through Portrush and Coleraine towards Downhill and Limavady, taking in the view from the Binevenagh plateau on the way. Then head for Derry, whose historic features deserve to be explored. When you are ready to leave, turn south-east towards Dungiven and cross the Glenshane Pass into Castledawson.

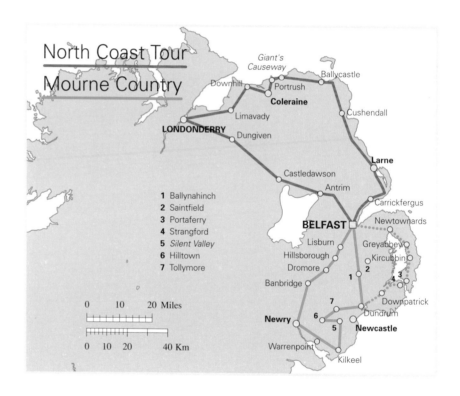

From here you can go on to Antrim town and back to Belfast.

Day 2: *Mourne Country 166 km (104 miles).* Leave Belfast on the south side and drive via Lisburn to Hillsborough, a remarkably pretty small town with adjacent fort, park and lake - ideal for a quiet stroll. Continue through Dromore and Banbridge to Newry, where you can turn eastwards along the shores of Carlingford Lough to the picturesque fishing port of Kilkeel. Take a walk down by the harbour to admire the fleet - and perhaps buy some freshly-landed fish - before heading north and inland towards the Silent Valley, in the

heart of the beautiful Mourne Mountains (follow Hilltown directions). It is worth stopping the car for a breath of the clear mountain air and the chance to enjoy the wonderful views. Then proceed via Tollymore (with its forest park) to Dundrum, whose long, unspoilt beach is always inviting. From here you can head straight back to Belfast through Ballynahinch, or travel to Downpatrick and Strangford, visiting Castleward before taking the ferry across Strangford Lough to Portaferry. Drive up the Ards Peninsula via Kircubbin and Greyabbey (interesting ruins) to Newtownards, overlooked by Scrabo Tower. From here it's only a short drive back to your Belfast base.

DUBLIN AND THE EAST

Dublin has all the attractions of any major European city. The Phoenix Park is Europe's largest, while the city gives on to the sea at the great beaches of Sandymount and Dollymount, and the fishing village of Howth. There are many cultural attractions, among them the National Gallery, National Library, National Museum and the Chester Beatty Library and Gallery of Oriental Art, together with many smaller galleries, museums, eighteenth-century houses and three cathedrals.

North of Dublin, seaside towns like Skerries lead on to the great historic sites: Drogheda, Trim and the Boyne Valley with prehistoric Newgrange. To the south, Killiney Bay is positively Italianate in its coastal vista, while Powerscourt Gardens are also Italian in style. The Wicklow mountains, with the medieval ecclesiastical centre of Glendalough, have some of Ireland's finest uplands.

Wall reliefs on the corner of Essex Quay / Parliment street, Dublin

Key to Guide Entry:
Each entry contains several types of information

NAME OF SITE —— **Avoca** *26 km (16 miles) S of Wicklow Town.* —— LOCATION
See Thomas Moore's tree, near the Meeting
of the Waters, where he spent many hours
DESCRIPTION —— lost in poetic contemplation.
The Ballykissangel TV series is filmed in —— LOCAL
the village. ***Avoca Handweavers,*** open daily, —— ATTRACTION
TELEPHONE —— all year, ☎ (0402) 35105 is in 1723 mill. —— OPENING HOURS
NUMBER —— Shop, restaurant.

Dublin Pop.1 million. TIOs Suffolk Street; Arrivals Hall, Dublin Airport, Baggot Street Bridge, ☎ 1 550 112233.

Few European capitals have a more natural setting, with the sea bordering the city, countryside within half an hour's drive and to the immediate south of the city, the Dublin and Wicklow mountains, a great range of hills that are unspoiled and unpolluted.

Dublin is nearly 2,000 years old and has been in turn a Viking, a Norman and an English city. Today, as the capital city of Ireland, it's a very European and cosmopolitan city. World renowned for its writers, artists and musicians, the city has always been proud of its culture, which has flourished in recent years. The city has numerous venues for traditional and classical music, especially since the advent of the National Concert Hall and many visual arts galleries.

Since 1922, Dublin has been the capital of an independent state, making up 26 out of the 32 counties of Ireland. The setting up of the new State was financially draining and the city experienced 40 years of financial hardship, including during the Emergency period of World War II, before it once again began to flourish as it had done in the 18th century. Unfortunately, in their eagerness to encourage new business, developers from the 1960s to the present day have destroyed many Georgian buildings in favour of modern commercial and residential blocks. Despite the developers' ravages, many parts of the city, such as the Liberties, retain their inherent interest and atmosphere.

People who enjoy the "buzz" of great cities and those who like open-air splendours and delights will find everything they wish in and around this lively and very human city, where strangers and visitors are made very welcome.

Major festivals and events include St Patrick's Week (starting 17 May); Festival of Classical Music in Great Irish Houses (June);

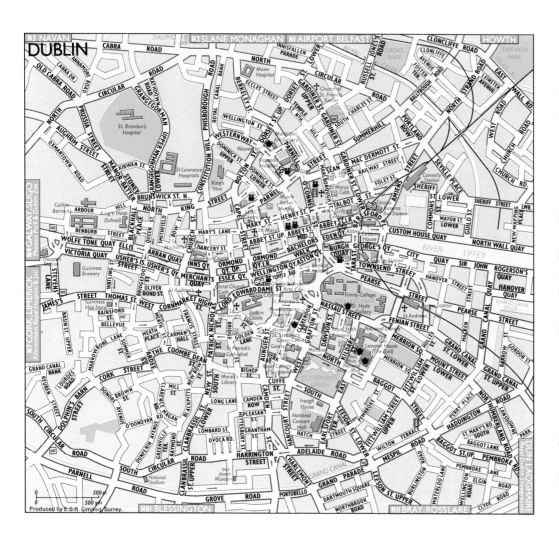

There's no bone in the tongue, but it
often broke a man's head.

There are two sides to every story
and a hundred versions of every song.

Thirst is the end of drinking and
sorrow is the end of drunkeness.

The work praises the man.

An extract from *A Little Book Irish of Sayings*
published by Appletree Press

Kerrygold Dublin Horse Show (July or Aug);
Irish Antique Dealers Fair (Aug); Dublin
Grand Opera Society winter season
(Nov/Dec).

CATHEDRALS AND CHURCHES

Christ Church Cathedral (CI)
Christchurch Place. Open daily, all year.

Founded 1038 and rebuilt by the Normans
in 1169. Magnificent stonework in aisles
and naves. Alleged tomb of Strongbow.
Visits to the Norman crypt.

St Patrick's Cathedral (CI) *St Patrick's
Close.* Open daily, all year. Founded 1190,
extensively restored with Guinness money
about 1860. Jonathan Swift, Dean from 1713
to 1745, is buried in the south aisle, 'where
savage indignation can no longer rend his
heart'. Monument to Turlough O'Carolan,
last of the Irish bards.

St Michan's Church (CI) *Church Street,
near the Four Courts.* Open 10am-4.45 pm,
Mon-Fri, Mar-Nov, 12.30pm-3.30pm, Mon-
Fri, Dec-Feb, 10am-1pm, Sat, all year.
☎ (01)872 4154. Dates from the 17th c.
and is famous for the bodies in its vaults-
the dry atmosphere has helped prevent their
decomposition. Handel is said to have played
the 18th c. organ.

Pro-Cathedral (C) *Marlborough Street,
near O'Connell Street.* Built in the early
19th c. as an imitation of St Philippe du Roule
church in Paris. Its famous Palestrina choir

sings Mass in Latin on Sundays. Visitors can
inspect the creepy crypt.

The Abbey Presbyterian Church
*Parnell Square, almost beside the Writers'
Museum.* Open daily during summer. Dates
from 1864, with a fine interior. It was funded
by Alex Findlater, a noted Dublin grocer.

St Audeon's Church (CI) *High Street,*
dates back in part to the 12th c., while the
nearby *St Werburgh's Church (CI), High
Street,* has foundations from the same period,
although the present building is 18th century.

GALLERIES

National Gallery *Merrion Square West.*
Open 10am-5.30pm Mon-Sat (8.30pm,
Thurs), 2pm-5pm, Sun, all year.
☎ (01)661 5133. Has some 2,000 paintings
from all major European schools, including
works by Gainsborough, Goya and Poussin. In
the Irish Rooms, outstanding works by Jack
B Yeats, together with Hone, Osborne, Lavery
and Orpen. Turner watercolours are only
shown in weak light in January. The building

has been extensively renovated and extended and further extensions are planned. Frequent exhibitions. Reference library by arr. Shop, restaurant.

Hugh Lane Municipal Gallery
Parnell Square. Open 9.30am-6pm Tues-Fri, 9.30am-5pm, Sat, 11am-5pm Sun. ☎ (01) 874 1903. Fine collection of Irish Impressionists, Lane Collection of paintings, sculptures, stained glass. Shop, restaurant.

RHA Gallagher Gallery *Ely Place.*
Open 11am-5pm Mon-Wed, Fri, Sat, 11am-5pm Thurs, 2pm-9pm Sun. ☎ (01) 661 2558. A vast new gallery built from unadorned concrete, with great spaces for hanging works. It's an ideal place to see contemporary art.

Irish Museum of Modern Art
Royal Hospital, Kilmainham. Open 10am-5.30pm Tues-Sat, 12 noon-5.30pm, Sun. ☎ (01)671 8666. Another fine collection of 20th c. Irish and international art, including the Gordon Lambert and Sidney Nolan collections. Frequent exhibitions. Shop, cafe.

Douglas Hyde Gallery *Trinity College.*
Open 11am-6pm Mon-Fri, 11am-7pm, Thurs, 11am-4.45pm Sat. ☎ (01) 608 1116. Contemporary art exhibitions.

Solomon Gallery *Powerscourt Townhouse*
Centre. Open 10am-5.30pm Mon-Sat, 12 noon-5.30pm Sun. ☎ (01) 679 4237.

Kerlin Gallery *Anne's Lane, off South*
Anne Street. Open 10am-5.45pm Mon- Fri. 11am-4.30pm Sat. ☎ (01) 670 9093. Contemporary paintings and sculpture.

Davis Gallery *11 Capel Street.*
Open 10am-5pm Mon-Fri, 11am-5pm, Sat. ☎ (01)872 6969.

Oriel Gallery *17 Clare Street.*
Open 10am-5.30pm Mon-Fri, 10am-1pm Sat. ☎ (01) 676 3410. Regular exhibitions of mainly 20th c. paintings.

Gallery of Photography *Meeting House*
Square, Temple Bar. Open 11am-6pm Mon-Sat. ☎ (01) 671 4654. Regular photographic exhibitions, Irish and international.

City Arts Centre *Moss Street, opposite*
Custom House. Open 11am-5.30pm Mon-Fri, 11.30am-5.30pm, Sat. ☎ (01)677 0643. Contemporary work.

Guinness Hop Store *Crane Street, off*
Thomas Street, Dublin 8. Open 9.30am-5pm Mon-Sat, 10.30am-4.30pm, Sun, BH. ☎ (01) 408 4800. Regular exhibitions of historical and contemporary material.

United Arts Club *3 Upper Fitzwilliam*
Street. ☎ (01) 661 1411. Exhibitions of members' works.

Alliance Francaise *1 Kildare Street.*
☎ (01) 676 1732. Exhibitions on French themes and artists.

LIBRARIES

National Library *Kildare Street.*
Open 10am-9pm Mon 2pm-9pm Tues and Wed 10am-5pm Thurs and Fri 10am-1pm Sat, all year. ☎ (01) 603 0200. Vast repository of printed information about Ireland in book, magazine, newspaper and MS formats. Copies of virtually everything ever published in Ireland can be found here. More recent newspapers are on microfilm. Frequent exhibitions.

Marsh's Library *St Patrick's Close,*
beside St Patrick's Cathedral. Open 10am-5pm Mon, Wed-Fri, 10.30am-12.45pm Sat. ☎ (01) 454 3511. Early 18th c. library with some 25,000 volumes. Interior has great atmosphere, complete with cages where readers are locked in with rare books. Library has own bindery and restoration section.

EXHIBITIONS

Royal Irish Academy *Dawson Street.*
Open 9.30am-5.30pm Mon-Fri, Sept-July. ☎ (01) 676 2570. One of Ireland's largest collections of ancient Irish MSS.

National Archives *Bishop Street.*
Open 10am-5pm Mon-Fri, all year. ☎ (01) 478 3711. Old State papers and other archival material can be read in elegant, comfortable surroundings.

Chester Beatty Library and Art
Gallery *20 Shrewsbury Road, Dublin 4.* Open 10am-5pm Tues-Fri, 2pm-5pm Sat, all year. Guided tours at 2.30pm on Wed and Sat. ☎ (01) 269 2386. Books, paintings, papryi, clay tablets and bindings from 2700 BC to present day. Also visual arts, including vast array of Japanese prints. It's one of the most important collections in the world of Islamic art. The whole foundation is being moved to new premises at Dublin Castle.

Trinity College Old Library
Open 9.30am-5pm Mon-Sat, 12 noon-5pm Sun, all year. ☎ (01) 677 2941. Many rare MSS and books in a venerable setting. Its main treasure, the Book of Kells, is on display in the new ground floor Colonnades Gallery.

Central Catholic Library *74 Merrion*
Square, Dublin. Reading room open 12 noon-7pm Mon-Fri, 12 noon-6pm Sat, all year. ☎ (01) 676 1264. About 80,000 volumes of general, religious and Irish interest.

Irish Architectural Archive *73 Merrion*
Square, Dublin 2. Open Mon-Fri, all year. ☎ (01) 676 3430. Reference material on historic Irish buildings. Reading room.

Irish Traditional Music Archive
63 Merrion Square, Dublin 2. Open Mon-Fri, all year, by arr. ☎ (01) 661 9699. Lovers of traditional Irish music will feel they've gone to heaven here.

Pearse Street Library ☎ (01) 677 2764.
Material on Dublin history.

ILAC Centre Library *Off Henry Street.*
☎ (01) 873 4333. High tech,with extensive reference, business and music sections.

Goethe Institut *37 Merrion Square.*
☎ (01) 661 1155. German reference material.

Dublin Diocesan Library *Clonliffe*
Road, Dublin 3. ☎ (01) 874 1680. Extensive reference facilities.

Genealogical Office *Kildare Street.*
☎ (01)661 8811.

NOTABLE BUILDINGS

Ashtown Castle *Phoenix Park.* Open
9.30am-4.30pm Sat, Sun, Nov-Feb, 9.30am-5.30pm daily Mar-May, Oct, 10am-6pm daily, June-Sept, ☎ (01) 677 0095. Tower house, probably 17th c., has adjoining visitor centre detailing park's history, its flora and fauna. Exhibitions, audio-visual presentations, restaurant.

Bank of Ireland Arts Centre
Foster Place, off College Green. 10am-4pm 2pm Mon-Fri, 2pm-5pm Sat, 10am-1pm Sun, all year. ☎ (01) 671 1488. Museum tells story of past 200 years of banking in Ireland. Also tours, during banking hours, of the historic bank itself, next door, which was once the Irish Parliament in late 18th c.

Brazen Head *Bridge Street, opposite Four*
Courts. Reputedly Dublin's oldest pub, dating back to 1198.

Casino *Off Malahide Road, Marino, Dublin*
3. Open 9.30am-6pm daily, Apr-Oct, 9.30am-5pm Mon-Fri, 10am-6pm Sun, Oct-Mar. ☎ (01) 833 1618. One of Ireland's finest classical buildings. Includes four State rooms.

City Hall *Dame Street, facing top*
of Parliament Street. Open 9am-5pm Mon-Fri, all year. ☎ (01)679 6111. Late 18th c., with impressive entrance hall and historical material.

Custom House *Custom House Quay,*
city centre. Open 10am-5pm Mon-Fri, 2pm-5pm Sat, Sun, mid-Mar-Oct, 10am-5pm, Wed-Fri, 2pm-5pm Sun, Nov-mid-Mar. ☎ (01)878 7660. Designed by James Gandon and completed in 1791, it is one of Dublin's most impressive buildings, restored in last few years. The new visitor centre (entrance

Goverment Buildings, Merrion square

Dublin Castle Clock Tower

from steps at quayside front) is on two levels and tells the story of the building in detail. Audio-visual presentation. Also many related themes, including Customs & Excise history. Exhibits include a great famine register, c. 1850, from the Cashel workhouse, Co Tipperary.

Drimnagh Castle *Long Mile Road, Dublin 12.* Open 12 noon-5pm Wed all year, Sat, Sun Apr-Oct, or by arr. ☎ (01) 450 2530. Dublin's only authentic medieval castle, incongruous amid a bleak industrial landscape. The Great Hall and the original gardens, complete with moat, have been restored.

Dublin Castle *Entrance opposite top of Parliament Street.* Open 10am-5pm Mon-Fri, 2pm-5pm, Sat and Sun, all year. ☎ (01) 677 7129. An elaborate restoration programme has been completed and the State apartments have been restored to their former glory. St Patrick's Hall was built in the mid-18th c. as a ballroom. Church of the Most Holy Trinity in lower yard was designed in early 19th c. by Francis Johnston of GPO fame and has elaborate interior decorations. Heritage Centre. The castle also has records of the Company of Goldsmiths, the Garda museum and will soon accommodate also the Chester Beatty Library and Gallery. Restaurant, shop.

Dublin Experience *Trinity College.* Presentations 10am-5pm daily, May-Sept. ☎ (01) 608 2320. Elaborate audio-visual presentation on Dublin's history.

Dublin Tourism Centre *Suffolk Street, off lower Grafton Street.* Open daily, all year. Plenty of tourist information, tour bookings, cafe, shops.

Dublinia *Next to Christchurch cathedral.* Open 10am-5pm daily Apr-Sept, 11 am-4pm Mon-Sat, 10am-4.30pm Sun, BH, Oct-Mar. ☎ (01) 679 4611. Impressive scale models and recreated streetscapes of medieval Dublin. From tower top, panoramic views of the city.

Four Courts ☎ (01) 872 5555. Beside the River Liffey, this 1785 building is at the heart of Ireland's legal system. It was restored with some incongruities after the civil war, during which the adjoining Public Records Office and its contents were disastrously destroyed. Central hall can be inspected, while the dome affords good views over the city.

GPO *O'Connell Street.* Open daily, all year. Early 19th c., much restored after 1916. Recently restored,with central hall and portico brought back to pristine condition. The Statue of Cuchulainn can still be seen.

Kilmainham Jail *Dublin 8, near Royal Hospital.* Open 9.30am-4.45pm daily, Apr-Sept, 9.30am-4pm Mon-Fri, 10am-4.45pm Sun Oct-Mar. ☎ (01) 453 5984. Many of Ireland's political leaders were held captive here and their stories are told in audio-visual presentations, artefacts and chilling tours of the cells and execution area.

Newman House *85-86 St Stephen's Green.* Open 12 noon-5pm Tues-Fri, 2pm-5pm Sat, 11am-2pm Sun, or by arr. ☎ (01) 706 7422. Two finely restored Georgian houses where the Catholic University of Ireland began in 1850. Exquisite plasterwork and other interior features. Exhibition on the restoration work.

Number 29 Lower Fitzwilliam Street Open 10am-5pm Tues-Sat, 2pm-5pm Sun, all year. ☎ (01) 702 6165. This corner house, owned by the Electricity Supply Board, has been totally and authentically restored to show lifestyle of a typical Dublin middle class household c. 1790-1820.

Powerscourt House *South William Street.* Open daily. Late 18th c. town house has been elaborately restored, now a fashionable shopping centre with Craft Council gallery, craft shops and interesting restaurants.

Rathfarnham Castle Open 10am-6pm daily, May-Oct. ☎ (01) 493 9462. Parts are now open to visitors, although restoration work still goes on.

Royal Hospital *Kilmainham.* Open 10am-5.30pm,Tues-Sat, 12 noon-5.30pm Sun, BH. ☎ (01) 671 8666. This late 17th c. structure, replicating Les Invalides in Paris, has been finely restored in recent years. Great hall, chapel and central courtyard. Also houses Irish Museum of Modern Art, qv.

Shaw House *33 Synge Street, off South Circular Road, Dublin 8.* Open 10am-6pm Mon-Sat, 11.30am-6pm Sun, BH, May-Oct. ☎ (01) 475 0854. The house where George Bernard Shaw was born and lived until he was 10 years old, has been totally restored to 19th c. ambience.

St Mary's Abbey *Off quays end of Capel Street.* Open 10am-5pm Wed, June-Sept. ☎ (01) 872 1490. 12th c. Benedictine abbey. Historical exhibition on its origins.

Tailor's Hall *Back Lane, near Christchurch cathedral.* ☎ (01) 454 4794. Early 18th c., last surviving Dublin Guild Hall, well restored and now headquarters of An Taisce (National Trust for Ireland).

Trinity College ☎ (01) 677 2941 Founded just over 400 years ago, although nothing remains of the original college. The buildings around the great central square, including the marvellous chapel, date from 18th c. Various historical collections and cultural events on campus.

MUSEUMS

National Museum *Kildare Street and Collins Barracks, Benburb Street.* Open 10am-5pm Tues-Sat, 2pm-5pm Sun, all year. ☎ (01) 677 7444. Now in two locations. The original museum in Kildare Street has much material on prehistoric, early Christian and medieval Ireland. Highlights include the Treasury Room, while antiquities include the Ardagh Chalice, the Cross of Cong and the Tara Brooch. Frequent exhibitions. Cafe, shop. The extension (entrance in Merrion Row) is used mainly for exhibitions.

The Collins Barracks extension, near Heuston Station, is brand new and includes much material on decorative arts, economic, social and military history. Exhibits include the gauntlets worn by King William at the Battle of Boyne in 1690 and the pocket book carried by Wolfe Tone when he was imprisoned here in 1798. The conversion of what was Europe's oldest military barracks is most impressive. Shop, cafe.

Natural History Museum *Upper Merrion Street, Dublin 2.* Open 10am-5pm Tues-sat, 2pm-5pm, all year. ☎ and opening hours as National Museum. Part of the National Museum, this section is devoted to zoological material and includes some impressive skeletons.

Dublin Civic Museum *South William Street.* Open 10am-6pm Tues-Sat, 11am-2pm Sun, all year. ☎ (01) 679 4260. Material on Dublin history, frequent exhibitions. Dublin Corporation city archive has much printed material on Dublin history.

Dublin Writers' Museum *Parnell Square.* Open 10am-5pm Mon-Sat, 1pm-5pm Sun, BH, all year. ☎ (01) 872 2077. Memorabilia on Ireland's most famous writers. Exhibitions. Cafe, restaurant.

The Grand Canal, Dublin

Education Museum *Church of Ireland College of Education, 94 Upper Rathmines Road, Dublin 6.* Open 2.30pm-5.30pm Wed, all year, by arr. ☎ (01) 497 0033. The story of Ireland's schools. Interactive displays. 19th c. classroom.

Findlater's Museum *Harcourt Street Vaults, 10 Upper Hatch Street.* Open 10am-6pm Mon-Sat, all year. ☎ (01) 475 1699. Fascinating wine cellars, beneath old Harcourt Street railway station and has much memorabilia on the Findlater family and the chain of grocery and wine shops it owned until the 1960s. Also material on theatrical history. It's a veritable social history of Dublin over the last 150 years.

Freemason's Hall *Molesworth Street.* ☎ (01) 679 9799/679 5465. This 18th c. building with fine portico is headquarters of the Masonic Order in Ireland. Interior and historical contents can be seen by arr.

Garda Siochana Museum *Dublin Castle.* Open 9am-5pm Mon-Fri, all year. ☎ (01) 671 9597. Fine collection of material on Irish police history, in new location at Dublin Castle, following its transfer from Garda headquarters in the Phoenix Park.

Guinness Museum *Hop Store, Crane Street.* Open 9.30am-5pm Mon-Fri, 10.30am-4.30pm, Apr-Sept, 9.30am-4pm Mon-Sat, 12 noon-4pm Sun, BH, Oct-Mar. ☎ (01) 453 6700, extn 5155. A 19th c. hop store has been converted into a fine museum and exhibition centre. An elaborate audio-visual presentation details the history of the brewery since 1759. You can sample the product in the ground floor bar. Shop. Adjacent secure car park.

Heraldic Museum *Kildare Street.* Open 10am-4.30pm Mon-Fri, all year. ☎ (01) 661 4877. Collection of family coats of arms, details on genealogical research.

Irish Jewish Museum *3-4 Walworth Road, off South Circular Road.* Open 11am-3pm Tues, Thurs, Sun, May-Sept, 10.30am-2.30pm Sun Oct-Apr. ☎ (01) 676 0737. Memorabilia and artefacts recording the Jewish community's history in Ireland over the past 150 years.

Irish Railway Records Society *Heuston Station.* Open 8pm-10pm Tues, all year. Much printed and photographic material on Irish railway history.

Jameson Distillery Museum *Smithfield, Dublin 7, near Four Courts.* Open 9.30am-5pm daily, all year. ☎ (01) 807 2335. This new 'old' museum has taken over where the former Irish Whiskey Corner left off, with much more space. It's an impressive natural-looking display on the history of whiskey making in Ireland, from barley to bottle, with many old artefacts and photographs. Audio-visual presentation, guided tour. Excellent restaurant, bars. The adjacent Smithfield area is being developed as Dublin's next Temple Bar, complete with a traditional music museum, galleries, hotel and restaurants.

James Joyce Museum *Sandycove.* Open 10am-5pm Mon-Sat, 2pm-6pm Sun, BH, Apr-Oct, or by arr. ☎ (01) 872 2077. This Martello tower, where Joyce once lived, very briefly, is now a fine museum devoted to one of the most oustanding writers of the 20th c.

National Maritime Museum *Haigh Terrace, Dun Laoghaire.* Open 2.30pm-5.30pm Tues-Sun, May-Oct, 2.30pm-5.30pm Sat, Sun, Nov-Apr. ☎ (01) 280 0969. Old church has been converted to house extensive collection, including models of ships and working optic formerly used in the Baily lighthouse at Howth. Exhibitions.

National Wax Museum, *Granby Row, off Parnell Square.* Open 10am-5.30pm Mon-Sat, 12 noon-5.30pm Sun, all year. ☎ (01) 872 6340. Chamber of Horrors. Children's world of fantasy and fairytales. Many Irish entertainment stars and other personalities in wax.

Pearse Museum *St Enda's, Grange Road, Rathfarnham, Dublin 16.* Open 10am-4pm daily, Nov-Jan, 10am-5pm daily, Feb, Mar, Apr, Sept, Oct, 10am-5.30pm daily, May-Aug. ☎ (01) 493 6120. School formerly run by Patrick Pearse, leader of 1916 Easter Rising. Exhibitions, audio-visual presentation, tea room. Adjoining gardens.

National Print Museum *Beggar's Bush, Dublin 4.* Open 10am-12.30, 2.30pm-5pm, Mon-Fri, 12 noon-5pm, Sat, Sun, BH, May-Sept, 2pm-5pm, Tues, Thurs, Sat, Sun, Oct-Apr. ☎ (01) 660 3770. Old military garrison chapel has been converted into museum that includes audio-visual show, detailing old ways of printing.

Steam Museum, *Straffan, Co Kildare.* Open 12 noon-5pm Sat, 2pm-5pm Sun, all year. ☎ (01) 627 3155. Exhibition of models and working stationary steam engines. Garden, Steaming Kettle tea house.

Waterways Visitor Centre *Pearse Street, beside Grand Canal Basin.* Open 9.30am-6.30pm daily, June-Sept, 12.30pm-5pm, Sun, Oct-May. ☎ (01) 677 7510. Photographs, models and artefacts detailing the history of Ireland's inland waterways, in modern centre also worth seeing for its design.

PARKS AND GARDENS

Beech Park *Clonsilla, Dublin 15.* Open 2pm-6pm first weekend every month, Mar-Oct, also Sun, BH, July, Aug. ☎ (01) 821 2216. Large walled garden with some 10,000 species.

Fernhill Gardens, *Sandyford, Co Dublin.* Open 11am-5pm Tues-Sat, 2pm-6pm Sun, Mar-Nov. ☎ (01) 295 6000. On slopes of

Three Rock Mountain, with specimen trees, rhododendrons, rock and water gardens. Nursery.

Garden of Remembrance *Parnell Square, facing Writers' Museum.* Open daily, all year. Tribute to Ireland's war dead, including those of 1916 and the subsequent War of Independence.

Arbour Hill cemetery *Dublin 7.* Open 9am-4.30pm Mon-Sat, 9.30am-12 noon, Sun, all year. Burial place of the executed leaders of 1916 Easter Rising.

Herbert Park *Ballsbridge, near US Embassy.* Delightful park, with tennis courts, bowling, pond, music in summer, flower displays, built partly on site of 1907 International Exhibition.

Iveagh Gardens *Rear St Stephen's Green South.* Entrance: Clonmel Street, off lower Harcourt Street. Daily, all year. Excellent but little known city centre park with fountains, water cascades and statue-lined walls.

Marlay Park *Rathfarnham,* daily all year. Extensive parkland, model steam railway, craft courtyard with interesting workshops. Start of Wicklow Way long distance walk.

Merrion Square *City centre.* Plans to build a Catholic cathedral here never came to fruition. Instead, what was once a closed garden in the centre of Dublin's most extensive Georgian square is now open to all.

National Botanic Gardens *Glasnevin, Dublin 9.* Open 9am-6pm Mon-Sat, 11am-6pm Sun, summer, 10am-4.30pm, Mon-Sat, 11am-4.30pm Sun, winter. ☎ (01) 837 7596. Dating back to 1795, the gardens contain about 20,000 species of plants and cultivars, a rose garden and a vegetable garden. Delightful stroll beside the River Tolka. New alpine house. The main attraction,the enormous mid-19th c. Turner built Palm House, has been restored most meticulously.

North Bull Island 5 km (3 miles) long island created by the action of the tides in the last century. Vast beach and dunes, nature conservancy area. There's a good walk along the Bull Wall itself, as far as the statue. The South Wall, another great walk, but on the opposite side of the River Liffey, seems tantalisingly close.

Phoenix Park Open 9.30am-sunset daily, all year. ☎ (01) 677 0095. Europe's largest public park, extending to 709 ha (1752 acres), with numerous tree-lined roads, several lakes, deer herds. Furry Glen nature trail in NW of park has many trees and plants. Dublin Zoo, with plans for extension, dates back to 1830s and has many exotic species. Children's corner, cafe, restaurant. The park also has an elaborate visitor centre at Ashtown Castle.

St Anne's Park rose garden *Mount Prospect Park, Clontarf.* Open daily all year. Magnificent rose displays in fine park setting.

St Catherine's Park *Off Thomas Street, near Guinness Hop Store.* Small, secluded inner city oasis created from old graveyard. There are plans to restore nearby historic church of St Catherine's.

St Enda's Park *Rathfarnham, Dublin 16.* Open daily, all year. Charming park near the Pearse Museum, with riverside walks, waterfall, walled garden.

St Stephen's Green *City centre, top of Grafton Street.* Open daily, all year. Probably Ireland's oldest public park, an oasis of lakes and walks, surrounded by flowers, shrubs. Lunchtime concerts in summer.

War Memorial Gardens *Islandbridge, Dublin 8.* Near Royal Hospital. Dedicated to the memory of the Irish soldiers who were killed in World War I, about 50,000 in all. The gardens were designed by Sir Edwin Lutyens and have been well restored in recent years.

PUBS

Ryans *Parkgate Street, near Heuston station.* Superb traditional bar, with snugs and old-fashioned lamps.

Stag's Head *Off Dame Street, behind Olympia Theatre.* Founded in 1770, remodelled last during 19th c.

Palace Bar *Fleet Street, just off Westmoreland Street.* Genuine, old-time Dublin bar, dark panelling and mirrors.

Bowes *Fleet Street, off D'Olier Street.* Another small, dark pub that's popular with journalists.

Mulligan's *Poolbeg Street.* Dark, ancient, noisy. It used to be the favourite watering hole for journalists from the now closed Irish Press, almost next door.

Long Hall *South Great George's Street.* It's all done with mirrors in this, the city's most ornate, traditional pub, decorated with carved interior woodwork, many mirrors and chandeliers.

McDaid's *Harry Street, off Grafton Street.* Literary and theatrical pub.

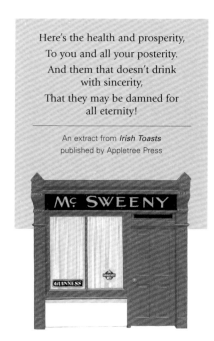

Here's the health and prosperity, To you and all your posterity. And them that doesn't drink with sincerity, That they may be damned for all eternity!

An extract from *Irish Toasts* published by Appletree Press

Waterloo House *Upper Baggot Street.* Once part of Paddy Kavanagh's territory, this pub, dating back nearly a century, is one of the few Dublin pubs that hasn't yet been swept by the tide of modernisation.

Davy Byrne's *Duke Street.* Famous meeting place, complete with murals.

Toner's *Lower Baggot Street.* Old-style pub with stone floor. The nearby Doheny & Nesbitt's pub also retains its traditional look and atmosphere. O'Donoghue's in Merrion Row is a music pub, made famous by the Dubliners.

ROUND AND ABOUT

Royal Dublin Society *Ballsbridge, Dublin 4.* ☎ (01) 668 0645. Many exhibitions and lectures, also concerts in its fine new concert hall, not to be confused with the National Concert Hall in Earlsfort Terrace.

National Concert Hall *Earlsfort Terrace.* ☎ (01) 671 1888. Frequent music events, at lunchtime and in the evenings. Restaurant.

Dunsink Observatory *Castleknock.* ☎ (01) 838 7911. Open to the public two nights a month; for free tickets, telephone first. Planning a visitor centre.

James Joyce Centre *35 North Great George's Street, near Parnell Square.* Open 9.30am-5pm, Mon-Sat, 12 noon-5pm Sun, Apr-Oct, 10am-4.30pm Tues-Sat, 12.30pm-4.30pm Sun, Nov-Mar. ☎ (01) 878 8574. Much material and many events relating to James Joyce, who shares the title with Samuel Beckett of being Ireland's greatest 20th c. writer. Reference library, audio-visual presentations, exhibitions.

Bewley's Cafes *Grafton Street, South Great George's Street, Westmoreland Street.* City centre cafes that have great atmosphere. Grafton Street has some fine Harry Clarke stained glass windows and a museum, qv.

Geological Survey of Ireland

Beggar's Bush, Dublin 4. ☎ (01) 666 0951. Exhibitions relating to geology. The Irish Labour History Museum on the same site has exhibitions on labour history, while the National Print Museum is also located here, qv.

Sandymount Strand
South Dublin's answer to North Bull Island, it's a great stretch of sand that is enlarged greatly at low tide. A promenade walk runs between it and the Strand Road. The South Wall provides another fine walk,this time with the sea on both sides, but the stones on the breakwater are very uneven. An elaborate science museum is planned for the old power station here.

Traditional markets
For traditional banter and bargains, Dublin has several markets. You could try the Iveagh Market, at the top of Francis Street, itself now home to most of the city's antique dealers, or the Liberty Market in Meath Street. Also in this area is Mother Redcap's Market in Back Lane. On the opposite side of the River Liffey, there's a market in St Michan's Street, behind the Four Courts, as well as the fruit and

vegetable markets. Moore Street, off Henry Street, is the best-known and has managed to survive the developers. In the suburbs, there are weekend markets in various locations, including Blackrock and Rathmines.

Temple Bar
The Temple Bar district stretches from Westmoreland Street to Parliament Street and from Dame Street down to the quays on the south side of the River Liffey. Thanks to tax incentives, the whole area has been transformed, not only with many apartments, but pubs, restaurants and lots of tourist attractions and sites. It has been described as Dublin's answer to the Left Bank. At this stage, building is almost completed, but the curved Poddle Bridge across the Liffey, connecting the area with the north quays, is due to be completed in time for the Millenium. In the meantime, there's much to see and do in Temple Bar.

The best place to start is the ***Temple Bar Information Centre,*** *18 Eustace Street,* ☎ (01) 671 5717, fax (01) 677 2525 and on the Web, http://www.temple-bar.ie. It has a large scale model of the entire district with all individual attractions clearly marked. The centre also has plenty of information on what's on. Places worth visiting include ***Africa Calls sculpture gallery and cultural centre,*** *2 Temple Lane South,* ☎ (01) 671 5107, ***The Ark,*** a cultural centre for children, *Eustace Street,* ☎ (01) 670 7788, the ***Arthouse Multimedia Centre for the Arts,*** *Curved Street,* ☎ (01) 605 6800, the ***Black Church print studio,*** *4 Temple Bar,* ☎ (01) 677 3629, the ***Bank of Ireland arts centre,*** *Foster Place,* ☎ (01) 671 1488, ***DESIGNyard*** jewellery, decorative, applied art, *12 East Essex Street,* ☎ (01) 677 8467, Graphic Art Studio, 8A Cope Street, ☎ (01) 679 8021, the ***Original Print Gallery,*** *4 Temple Bar.* ☎ (01) 677 3657, ***Seomra an Cheoil/ The Music Room,*** *43 East Essex Street,* ☎ (01)671 7009, the ***Temple Bar Music Centre,*** *Curved Street,* ☎ (01) 679 0202 and the ***Temple Bar Gallery and Studios,*** *5-9 Temple Bar,* ☎ (01) 671 0073.

It's billed as the largest studio and gallery complex in Ireland. As if all that wasn't enough to be going on with, there's the renowned ***Gallery of Photography*** at Meeting House Square, ☎ (01) 671 4654 and the ***National Photographic Archive,*** also at Meeting House Square, ☎ (01) 603 0238. ***Dublin's Viking Adventure,*** *Essex Quay,* ☎ (01) 679 6040, tells the story of Viking Dublin 1,000 years ago. You can also enjoy Viking feasts and entertainment. Open daily. The ***Olympia Theatre,*** *Dame Street,* ☎ (01) 677 7744, is included in Temple Bar. The ***Irish Film Centre*** is in *Eustace Street,* ☎ (01) 679 3477. The Project theatre and gallery is temporarily at Henry Place off Henry Street, ☎ (01) 671 2321. For details of ***Temple Bar walking tours,*** contact the

Temple Bar audio-visual centre, ☎ (01) 671 5717.

THEATRES AND CINEMAS

Gate Theatre
Cavendish Row. ☎ (01) 874 4045. Revivals and contemporary work in Dublin's most exciting theatre.

Abbey and Peacock Theatres
Lower Abbey Street. ☎ (01) 878 7222. Irish and international plays at the Abbey, more experimental work at the Peacock.

Andrew's Lane Theatre
Off Dame Street. ☎ (01) 679 5720. Contemporary work in small, intimate theatre.

Gaiety Theatre
South King Street. ☎ (01) 677 1717. Plays and variety shows in late 19th c. theatre, one of only three such theatres in Ireland. The others are the Theatre Royal in Waterford and the slightly later Grand Opera House in Belfast.

Lambert Puppet Theatre
Monkstown, Co Dublin. ☎ (01) 280 0974. Puppet theatre and museum.

Olympia Theatre
Dame Street. ☎ (01) 677 7744. Variety, drama.

Point Theatre
Beside East Link Bridge. ☎ (01) 836 3633. The place for spectacular large scale concerts and shows. Restaurant, car parking.

Project @ The Mint
Henry Place, off Henry Street, Dublin. ☎ (01) 671 2321. Temporary home for leading experimental theatre.

Dublin has several city centre cinemas showing commercial releases, principally the *Savoy,* the *Virgin* cinema complex and the *Screen at D'Olier Street.* The *Irish Film Centre,* Eustace Street, ☎ (01) 679 3477 specialises in art films. Out of town multiplexes offer good cinema choice, with plentyof car parking. The *UCI Multiplex, Tallaght,* ☎ (01) 452 2611, has 12 screens, while the *UCI Multiplex* Malahide Road, ☎ (01) 848 5133 and the *Omniplex* complex, *Santry,* ☎ (01) 842 8844, have 10 screens each.

SPORT

Croke Park
Dublin 3. ☎ (01) 836 3222. Dublin's major venue for Gaelic Athletic Association games. The GAA plan to open a museum and interpretative centre on Gaelic games. ☎ (01) 877 1336.

Lansdowne Road
☎ (01) 668 4601. The major stadium for international rugby and soccer matches.

Dún Laoghaire

DUBLIN AREA

Ardgillan Demesne *3km (2 miles)*
W of Skerries. Open from 10am daily, all year.
☎ (01) 849 2212. Extensive house dating from early 18th c. Demesne, rose and herb gardens.

Blackrock *South Dublin.* Walk along the sea front terrace, explore the two big shopping centres. *Dublin Crystal Glass, off Carysfort Avenue.* Open daily, all year.
☎ (01) 288 7932/288 8627. Traditional style glassmaking.

Carton House *E end of Maynooth.*
☎ (01) 628 6250. Classical house built about 1740, with Shell House in gardens.
It is being refurbished.

Castletown House *24 km (15 miles) W of Dublin.* Likely to be closed for most of 1998 as restoration continues. ☎ (01) 628 8252.

Set at the end of a long drive, at the end of Celbridge village, this Palladian style house is one of Ireland's most distinguished 18th c. great houses. Among the interior highlights are the plasterwork, the long gallery, the downstairs nursery room and kitchen. Formal gardens, while in the distance, you can see a well-known obelisk, Conolly's Folly.

Celbridge Abbey *24 km (15 miles) W of Dublin.* Open daily, all year. ☎ (01) 627 5508. The abbey itself was built around 1697, while the grounds, beside the River Liffey, have been developed by the religious order of St John of God. Vanessa's Bower is where Jonathan Swift and his beloved Stella viewed the weir. Oldest stone bridge over the Liffey.

Dalkey *Near Dun Laoghaire.*
Delightful seaside village with medieval castle and some fine restaurants and an art gallery. Two small harbours, trips to Dalkey Island during the summer from Coliemore Harbour.

Good views from Dalkey Hill and the adjoining Killiney Hill Park, complete with obelisk.

Dún Laoghaire *11 km (7 miles)*
S of Dublin TIO St Michael's Wharf,
☎ 15501 12233, all year. Major ferryport. Walk along the east and west piers.
National Maritime Museum.

Howth *16 km (10 miles) N of Dublin.*
Attractive seaside village, with ruins of old abbey, Abbey Tavern and art galleries. Walk around the two arms of the pier, trips to nearby Ireland's Eye island. Walks around Howth Head and Howth Castle rhododendron gardens. *Transport Museum.*

Kilcock *35 km (22 miles) W of Dublin.*
Village set beside Royal canal,which provides extensive towpath walks. *Bridestown Rare Breeds Farm.* Open 12 noon-5pm daily. Includes Kerry cows, four horned Manx sheep

and a horse museum. **Larchill Arcadian Garden,** open 11am-6pm daily, Apr-Sept, ☎ (01) 628 4580, includes walled garden, lakeside gazebo, rare breeds and many other features.

Malahide *14 km (9 miles) N of Dublin.* New marina. **Malahide Castle** dates from 12th c. Features include Great Hall, library, drawing room, National Portrait Gallery, botanic garden, parklands. **Fry Model Railway Museum** has detailed model railway, canal and river layouts. Open 10am-5pm Mon-Fri 11am-6pm Sat Sun, BH, Apr-Oct. ☎ (01) 846 2184/846 3779.

Maynooth *28 km (18 miles) W of Dublin.* University town. **Maynooth Castle,** open 3pm-6pm daily, June-Sept. At campus entrance, castle dates in part from 13th c. **Maynooth Museum,** open 2pm-4pm Tues, Thurs, 2pm-5pm Sun, summer or by arr. ☎ (01) 628 5222. Ecclesiastical relics and 19th c. electrical equipment.

Monkstown *South Dublin suburb.* **Comhaltas Ceoltoiri Eireann,** 32 Belgrave Square, ☎ (01) 280 0295. An Irish cultural institute, with summer entertainment.

Newbridge House *18 km (11 miles) N of Dublin.* Open 10am-5pm Tues-Fri, 2pm-6pm Sat, Sun, BH, Apr-Sept, 2pm-5pm Sat, Sun, BH, Oct-Mar. ☎ (01) 843 6534. 18th c. mansion includes old kitchen,craft workshops, walled garden, farm animals, parklands. Nearby **Lusk Heritage Centre,** open 10am-5pm daily mid-June-mid-Sept, ☎ (01) 843 7683. In old church, centre has many local historical items. Round tower.

Skerries *30 km (19 miles) N of Dublin.* Seaside town with busy fishing pier and seafront walks. Some cottages still have thatched roofs.

Straffan *13 km (8 miles) S of Maynooth* **Steam Museum,** ☎ (01) 627 3155 qv and **Butterfly Farm,** ☎ (01) 627 1109, qv.

Swords *5 km (3 miles) W of Malahide* Church of Ireland church, on west side of town, has round tower dating from 6th c. monastery. Castle. **Town Museum,** Carnegie Library Building, open 2.30pm-5.30pm, Sun, all year: fascinating local items.

BOYNE VALLEY AND CO LOUTH

Annagassan *5 km (3 miles) SE of Castlebellingham.* Walk along the shores of Dundalk Bay to Salterstown, a secluded bathing place. Heritage centre.

Ardee *20 km (13 miles) SW of Dundalk.* **St Mary's church (CI)** has part of 13th c.

Carmelite church. Also 13th c. Castle keep, in Main Street.

Ballymascanlon *7 miles (4 km) NE of Dundalk.* **Proleek Dolmen,** one of the largest in Ireland, with huge capstone, is near the Ballymascanlon Hotel.

Baltray *8 km (5 miles) E of Drogheda.* Small village has one of Ireland's finest links golf courses and along the seashore, one of longest beaches on the east coast. An Grianan, home of Irish Countrywomen's Association, has a museum. ☎ (041) 22119.

Bective Abbey *8 km (5 miles) S of Navan.* Founded as a Cistercian House in 12th c. There are ruins of the original chapter house and church, as well remnants of the fortified house into which the abbey was converted after the Dissolution.

Bettystown *8 km (5 miles) E of Drogheda.* Sandy strand runs for 9 km (6 miles), ideal for walking at low tide. Horse races here for one day in August. Amusement park during summer.

Carlingford *20 km (13 miles) NE of Dundalk.* Much of this medieval town has been restored, including the town walls. Ruins of **King John's Castle,** 13th c. Also 16th c. **Taaffes Castle,** 15th c. Mint and 14th c. Dominican Abbey. **Holy Trinity Heritage Centre,** open 9am-5pm daily, all year. ☎ (042) 73454. Details of the town's history from its Anglo-Norman foundation to Thomas D'Arcy McGee, 19th c. poet

and Canadian statesman, who was born in the town. **Oyster Festival** held in August.

Clogherhead *14 km (9 miles) NE of Drogheda.* Short walk from village to Port Oriel fishing harbour and the headland, which gives fine views of Dundalk Bay, north to Mountains of Mourne.

Cooley Peninsula *Begins 8 km (5 miles) NE of Dundalk.* A drive round the peninsula from Dundalk is approximately a 40 km (25 miles) round trip. It offers many fine scenic views and small, secluded bathing places, such as **Gyles Quay** and pleasant resorts like **Omeath. Riverstown Old Corn Mill Crafts Centre,** open daily, ☎ (042) 76157 is a restored 18th c. mill.

Drogheda *48 km (30 miles) N of Dublin.* Pop.24,000. TIO ☎ (041) 37070 June-Sept. Hilly, medieval town set on slopes rising from the River Boyne. The river is spanned by a spectacular mid-19th c. railway viaduct. Not far from the quays, the old laneways and warehouses retain some of the atmosphere of a 19th c. port town.

St Peter's Church (C), *West Street,* houses the shrine of St Oliver Plunkett, which contains the martyr's head. **St Peter's Church (CI),** *top of Peter Street,* affords fine town views from the surrounding graveyard. The **Siena Convent,** *Chord Road,* decorated with 19th c. mosaics, is a haven of calm after the town's bustle. **St Lawrence's Gate** is only one of ten to survive from medieval times.

Laytown, near Drogheda, Co. Meath

Millmount Museum open 10am-5pm daily, summer, 3pm-5pm Wed, Sat, Sun, winter. ☎ (041) 36391. Fine collection of material on the town's history and crafts, as well as rocks from every county in Ireland, every country in Europe and every continent in the world. Also, restored *Governor's House.* Other houses in the former cluster of military barracks have been turned into craft workshops. The top of the adjoining tower gives the best views of Drogheda. Buttergate restaurant. In the town itself, Fridays and Saturdays are the liveliest days, with town markets. Sellers ply their wares along West Street, including fish merchants. Walks along the quays.

Dundalk *84 km (52 miles) N of Dublin. Pop. 26,000. TIO,* ☎ (042) 35484, open all year. The town fell in 1177 to the Anglo-Normans and for the next 300 years, it was repeatedly attacked as a frontier town of the English Pale. Most of its fortifications were removed during the 18th c. and little of Dundalk's historic past is to be seen today. Nevertheless, parts of the town are interesting, particularly the area around the Courthouse.

Industrial Heritage Centre, Jocelyn Street. Open Tues-Sun, all year. ☎ (042) 27056. Details of the town's manufacturing traditions, including brewing, shoe making, cigarette manufacture and railway engineering, besides many other aspects of the town's history, are featured. One highlight among many is the 1960 Bubble Car made in the town. Attractively situated in a converted 18th c. distillery warehouse, with adjacent local library. *Graveyard of St Nicholas (CI), Clanbrassil Street* has tomb of Agnes Galt, sister of Robert Burns, the 18th c. Scottish poet.

The nearby *St Patrick's Cathedral (C)* built in the mid-19th c., was modelled on King's College, Cambridge. *Seatown Castle, on eastern outskirts of the town,* has the ruins

of a 13th c. Franciscan monastery. *Carroll's* cigarette factory, ☎ (042) 36501, visits by arr. *Harp Lager brewery,* ☎ (042) 34793, visits by arr. Also horse and greyhound racing.

Dunleer *8 km (5 miles) N of Drogheda.* *White River Mills,* open Mon-Fri, all year. ☎ (041) 51141. A restored water-powered flour mill; the waterwheel is over three centuries old. Stoneground flour continues to be produced. *Monasterboice High Cross,* 5.4 metres (17' 8") tall, is one of Ireland's best preserved crosses.

Faughart *6 km (4 miles) N of Dundalk.* Robert the Bruce's brother is buried here. Outstanding scenic views from the graveyard.

Hill of Tara *9 km (6 miles) SE of Navan.* Once the seat of the High Kings of Ireland, the site has considerable historical and religious significance. On a clear day, you can see right across the Midlands to the mountains of the West. The former CI church nearby has been converted into a centre for audio-visual presentations. Open daily, May-Oct. ☎ (046) 25903.

Inniskeen *14 km (9 miles) W of Dundalk.* The poet Patrick Kavanagh was born here in 1906 and is commemorated in the *folk museum,* open daily, all year, by arr, ☎ (042) 78109 which also has local railway artefacts. The poet is specifically remembered in the *Patrick Kavanagh Literary Resource Centre* in the former parish church. Archives, exhibitions, audio-visual shows. Kavanagh is buried in the adjoining graveyard. Open daily, all year, ☎ (042) 78560.

Kells *16 km (10 miles) NW of Navan.* Ancient town in the Blackwater Valley, on site of a 6th c. monastic settlement founded by St Colmcille, where the Book of Kells (now in Trinity College, Dublin) was written. The medieval market cross that

stands in the centre of Kells is likely to be moved to a planned heritage centre.

Mellifont Abbey *9 km (6 miles) W of Drogheda.* Open 10am-5pm daily, May-mid-June, 9.30am-6.30pm daily, mid-June-mid-Sept, 10am-5pm daily mid-Sept-end Oct. ☎ (041) 26459. Ireland's first Cistercian monastery, founded in 1142. The octagonal lavabo, built around 1200, is its most unusual feature. Visitor centre details the work of medieval masons.

Mornington *5 km (3 miles) E of Drogheda.* Pleasant village beside the Boyne estuary. Moran's pub with its wooden interior and shelves has changed little since the 19th c.

Mosney Holiday Centre *8 km (5 miles) S of Drogheda.* This holiday centre has many attractions, including a water-based leisure centre, pets' corner, nature walks and *Brú na Bóinne,* an audio-visual presentation on Boyne Valley history. ☎ (041) 29200.

Navan *27 km (17 miles) W of Drogheda.* This hilly town set at the confluence of the Boyne and Blackwater rivers was once a walled and fortified outpost of the Pale. *Athlumney House, 3km (2 miles) from the town centre,* by the River Boyne, contains impressive remains of the original four-storey, 15th c. castle. *Mountainstown House* is a finely restored 18th c. mansion. By arr, ☎ (046) 54154. 5km (3 miles) S of Navan, the *Columban Mission Awareness Centre* has lots of artefacts and an audio-visual presentations on the Order's mission work. Open 10am-5pm, Mon-Fri, 2pm-5pm Sun, all year.

Newgrange *11 km (7 miles) W of Drogheda. TIO,* ☎ (041) 24274, Apr-Sept. Open 10am-4.30pm daily, Nov-Feb, 10am-5pm daily, Mar, Apr, 9.30am-6pm daily, May, 9.30am-7pm daily, June-Sept, 10am-5pm daily, Oct. ☎ (041) 24488. Dating from about 2,500 BC, Newgrange is one of the finest prehistoric passage graves in Europe, built with 250,000 tonnes of stones. The site also has considerable astronomical significance; on the day of the winter solstice, the sun shines straight down the passageway, if the weather is clear. The effect is recreated for visitors with electric light. *Knowth,* open 10am-5pm daily, May-mid-June, 9.30am-6.30pm daily, mid-June-mid-Sept, 10am-5pm daily, mid-Sept-end Oct. ☎ (041) 24824. It has the greatest collection of prehistoric tomb art ever found in western Europe. Beneath its great mound, there are two passage tombs and around it, 17 satellite tombs. Frequent guided tours. The third tomb, at Dowth, is still closed.

The *Brú na Bóinne* visitor centre is a new, high tech visitor centre detailing the whole Newgrange site - it's very impressive. All tours to Newgrange and Knowth start here. Open daily, all year, ☎ (041) 24488.

In nearby **King William's Glen,** the site of the Battle of the Boyne (1690) is marked. Development plans for this glen. Also nearby is **Newgrange Farm,** open 10am-5.30pm daily, Apr-Sept, ☎ (041) 24119. Animals, birds, old farm machinery, farm tours, gift shop, coffee shop. **Óengus Lodge,** open 10am-6pm Mon-Sat, Apr-Oct, ☎ (041) 24150. Next to Newgrange Farm, the lodge has farm machinery, a cooper's workshop and a blacksmith's forge. High quality fabrics are woven on hand looms. **Ledwidge Museum** in nearby Slane, open 10am-6pm Mon-Wed, Mar-Oct, or by arr, ☎ (041) 25201. Once the humble cottage home of Francis Ledwidge, a noted poet killed in the First World War. **Slane Hill,** where St Patrick proclaimed Christianity in 433, gives spectacular views in fine weather of the Boyne Valley, from Drogheda to Trim.

Sonairte National Ecology Centre
Laytown, 12 km (7 miles) SE of Drogheda. Organic garden, nature trails, lectures, exhibitions for anyone who's interested in an unpolluted environment. Daily, Easter-Oct, ☎ (041) 27572.

Trim *16 km (10 miles) S of Navan.* Trim Castle, in the centre of the town, is the largest Anglo-Norman castle in Ireland, and well worth a visit, especially for its massive keep. Across the river is Talbot's Castle, an impressive fortified manor house. Trim heritage centre has frequent exhibitions and entertainment. ☎ (046)37227.

THE MIDLANDS

An Dún Transport Museum
8 km (5 miles) SE of Athlone. Extensive display of old cars, lorries, bicycles and farm equipment. Open daily, Apr-Oct, ☎ (0902) 30106.

Ardagh *11 km (7 miles) SE of Longford.* Small, very neat and tidy village has splendid new **Heritage Centre** in the old national school. Displays and audio-visual presentations on local history. Coffee shop. Open 9am-5pm daily, all year. ☎ (043) 75277. The outbuilding of nearby Ardagh House have been converted into a **museum of rural life;** there's also a large herb garden and stables with old-fashioned equipment on display. Same opening hours as heritage centre.

Athy *19 km(12 miles) N of Carlow.* TIO, ☎ (0507) 31859,June-Aug. Modern Dominican church has stained-glass windows and Stations of the Cross by George Campbell, a noted 20th c. northern Irish artist. The new **Heritage Centre,** town centre, open daily, summer, ☎ (0507) 31444 has interesting material on the locality. Riverside walks beside the River Barrow begin at Emily Square.

Ballaghmore Castle *Near Borris-in-Ossory, just off main Dublin-Limerick N7.* Open daily, all year. ☎ (0505) 21453. Built in late 15th c. and rising five storeys high, the castle has been superbly restored in recent times.

Ballyjamesduff *16 km (10 miles) SE of Cavan town.* The Cavan County Museum has all kinds of material on the history and culture of the county. Audio-visual and interactive displays. Open 10am-5pm Mon-Fri, 2pm-5pm, Sat, Sun, all year. ☎ (049) 31799.

Birr *37 km (23 miles) SW of Tullamore.* TIO, ☎ (0509) 20110, May-Oct. A fine heritage town, full of Georgian features, well worth a day spent in exploration. **Birr Vintage Festival** has a lot to offer in August. **Birr Castle,** home of the Earl and Countess of Rosse, has demesne and gardens open to the public. Features include an ornamental lake, trees, shrubs, flowers and 200 year old box hedges, claimed to be the oldest in the world. Theme exhibitions in the castle.

Historic Science Centre is being developed here. Already, the huge telescope that was the largest in the world for the 75 years after it was built here in 1845 has been restored and put back in place. A whole range of stables and galleries are being converted to science galleries, demonstrating many aspects of the history of Irish science and the strong scientific interest by the owning family over the past two centuries. Open daily, all year, ☎ (0509) 20336.

Birr's new **Heritage Centre,** John's Hall, open 2.30pm-5pm daily, Apr-Sept, ☎ (0509) 20187 in a hall built in the style of a miniature Greek temple, details town history. **Slieve Bloom display centre,** Railway Road, open 10am-6pm Mon-Fri, 2.30pm-6pm Sat, Sun, July-Sept, ☎ (0509) 20029 details the wildlife of the Slieve Bloom mountains.

Carrickmacross *24 km (15 miles) W of Dundalk.* **Carrickmacross Lace Gallery,** Market Square, open 9.30am-5pm Wed-Sat, May-Oct, ☎ (042) 62506. Displays of locally made lace, which is offered for sale.

Carrigglas Manor *5 km (3 miles) NE of Longford.* Open 1pm-5.30pm Mon, Thurs-Sat, 2pm-6pm Sun. ☎ (043) 45165. Gothic house built in 1837 retains much of its original furnishings. The stable block dates from 1790 and was built on the site of an earlier house. Small museum. Woodlands, garden, tearooms.

Castleblayney *19 km (12 miles) SE of Monaghan.* Small town beside the shores of Lough Muckno. The **regional park** lake is ideal for water sports, boating, coarse fishing, while the surrounding wooded area offers nature trails, orienteering and golf. Bar, restaurant. Open daily, all year, ☎ (042) 46356.

In Whatever place, it is a tribesman's right to spear a salmon seen near the top of the water, (But one thrust of the spear is all that is allowed.)

An extract from *Traditional Irish Laws* published by Appletree Press

Cavan *30 km (19 miles) SW of Clones.* TIO, ☎ (049) 31942, all year. Small town set amid low hills, with excellent coarse fishing in nearby lakes. **Cavan Crystal factory,** Dublin Road, open 9.30am-3 pm Mon-Fri, all year. ☎ (049) 31800. Factory tours. Shop and video presentation suite are open the same hours, while the shop is also open 2pm-5pm, Sat, Sun. **Lifeforce Mill,** open daily, all year, ☎ (049) 62722 is a restoration of an 1840s water-powered flour mill which has been thoroughly restored as a visitor centre. It also produces its own bread.

Clones *21 km (13 miles) SW of Monaghan.* **Ancient Celtic cross** in Diamond, also 22m (75ft) high round tower in graveyard near the Cavan road and early Bronze age court cairn. Sarcophagus dates back to early Christian times. Exact origins unknown, but worth a close look. **Clones Lace Guild,** open daily, all year, ☎ (047) 51051/ 51729 has displays of locally made lace. Some items are for sale. Coffee shop.

Corlea Centre *13 km (8 miles)*
S of Longford. Open 10am-5pm daily, Apr,
May, 9.30 am-6.30pm daily, June-Sept,
☎ (043) 22386. A timber trackway found
here was dated to 147 BC, well preserved
by the bog. This unique example of Irish
prehistory is documented in the new
Corlea Trackway Exhibition Centre, which
also has an audio-visual show. Tearoom.

Dún A'Rí Forest Park, *34 km (21 miles)*
W of Dundalk. Open daily all year,
☎ (042) 67320. Set by the Cabra River, some
of the main highlights include walks, nature
trails, red deer enclosure, wishing well, ruins
of old flax mill and an old ice house.

Emo *9 km (6 miles) S of Portlaoise.*
Gardens open daylight hours, daily, all year.
House open 10am-6pm, Mon, June-Sept.
☎ (0502) 26573. Wonderful gardens with
ornamental lake, fine trees and statuary
complementing the 1790 house designed by
James Gandon (qv Custom House, Dublin).
House approached by 1.6 km (1 mile) long
avenue of Wellingtonias.

Fore *5 km (3 miles) E of Castlepollard.*
The ***Seven Wonders of Fore*** include water
that never boils and a mill without a race.
Ask for details at Abbey pub in Fore.
Also ***Fore Abbey*** dates from 13th c.

Heywood Gardens *6 km (4 miles)*
SE of Abbeyleix. Open daily, all year.
☎ (0502) 33563 or (056) 21450. The formal
gardens, completed in 1912,were designed
by Sir Edwin Lutyens, who designed the War
Memorial park in Dublin, qv. The Heywood
gardens were landscaped by Gertrude Jekyll
and include formal Italianate gardens, lakes
and woodlands.

Kilbeggan *11 km (7 miles) N of Tullamore.*
Locke's Distillery, open 9am-6pm daily, Apr-
Oct, 10am-4pm Nov-Mar. ☎ (0506) 32134.
Founded in 1757 and closed down in 1947,
it has been restored as a fascinating industrial
museum, complete with beam engine,
waterwheel and old stills. Folk museum.
Shop, restaurant.

Kildare *13 km (8 miles) SE of Naas. TIO,*
☎ (045) 522696, June-mid-Sept. ***St Brigid's
cathedral (CI)*** is 19th c. restoration of a
13th c. building. Visitors can climb to the top
of the adjacent round tower. ***National Stud,***
open 10am-6pm, where breeding stallions
are stabled, now includes visitor centre.
Irish Horse Museum, open 10am-6pm,
☎ (045) 21617 tells the story of the horse
in Ireland and includes the skeleton of Arkle,
the Irish racehorse that won numerous races
in Ireland and England in the late 1960s.
The Japanese Gardens, open 10am-6pm
daily, Easter-Oct, are considered the finest
of their kind in Europe. They were laid out
in the first decade of this century and
symbolise man's passage through life.
Bridges, trees and flowers make the gardens

Locke's Distillery, Kilbeggan, Co. Westmeath

an earthly paradise. Garden centre with bonsai
trees, restaurant.

Longford *44 km (27 miles) NW of
Mullingar.* TIO, Main Street, ☎ (043) 46566,
all year. ***St Mel's Cathedral (C)*** was designed
in 1840 in the Italianate style. ***Diocesan
Museum,*** in the right transept of the
cathedral, open 11am-1pm Mon-Wed, 1pm-
3pm Sat, 4pm-6pm Sun, June-Sept. Has many
interesting items, including the 10th c.
St Mel's crozier. The ***Town Museum*** in the
old post office, open 2pm-6pm daily, summer,
☎ (043) 45052 has many interesting items
of local folk and social history.

Monaghan *22 km (14 miles) NE of
Castleblayney. TIO,* Market House,
☎ (047) 81122, all year. ***St Macartan's
Cathedral (C) on the Dublin Road*** was built
between 1859 and 1892 in the French Gothic
style and is one of a number of interesting
public buildings in the town. The ***County
Museum,*** Hill Street, open 11am-5pm Tues-
Sat, all year, ☎ (047) 82928 has a remarkable
and well-presented collection of local
artefacts. These range from prehistory to the
middle ages and include the 14th c. ***Cross of
Clogher.*** Local canals, railways, lacemaking
and historical figures are well represented.
Also art gallery. ***St Louis Convent,*** open
10am-12 noon, 2.30pm-4.30pm, Mon, Tues,
Thurs, Fri, 2.30pm-4.30pm Sat Sun, all year.
☎ (047) 83529. Formerly a brewery, the
convent has a heritage centre tracing the
history of the Order in Monaghan and Ireland.

Rossmore Forest Park, 3.5 km (2 miles) has
lakeside and forest walks, nature trails,
rhododendron arbours and fishing. Panoramic
views from the site of Rossmore Castle.

Castle Leslie, *Glaslough, 11 km (7 miles)*
NE of Monaghan. Open 12 noon-7pm daily
June-Aug,12 noon-7pm Sat, Sun, Easter-Oct.
☎ (047) 88109. Late 17th c. edifice, the
castle was once a favourite haunt of WB Yeats.

Mountmellick *9 km (6 miles)*
N of Portlaoise. ***Visitor centre, Irishtown.***
Open 9.30am-5pm Mon-Fri, 2pm-6pm Sat,
Sun, all year. ☎ (0502) 24525. Has details
of Quaker history in the town, local industrial
heritage and Mountmellick lace.

Mullagh *9 km (6 miles) E of Virginia.*
Small, attractive village has ***heritage centre***
for one of Ireland's first Christians, St Kilian,
who was born in the immediate area.
St Kilian's connections with Wurzburg in
Germany are highlighted. Open 10am-6pm
Mon-Sat, 12 noon-6pm, Sun, Apr-Oct.
☎ (046) 42433.

Mullingar *51 km (32 miles) SE of Longford.*
TIO, Dublin Road, ☎ (044) 48650, all year.
Cathedral of Christ the King (C) is a striking
structure, built in 1936. The mosaics in
the chapels near the high altar were done
by a Russian artist, Boris Anrep. ***Cathedral
Museum*** open by arr, ☎ (044) 48333
includes a letter written by St Oliver Plunkett,
together with his vestments. ***Town Museum***
open 2pm-5.30pm Mon-Fri, June-Sept.
Located in 18th c. Market House, the museum
has many local history relics. The Military
Museum, Columb Barracks, open by arr,
☎ (044) 48391 has mementoes of the Army
in Mullingar and on UN service.

***Midlands Arts Resource Centre, Austin Friar
Street,*** open daily, ☎ (044) 43308.
Contemporary Irish art exhibitions.

Mullingar Pewter, renowned pewter maker, open 9am-5.30pm Mon-Fri, all year. ☎ (044) 48791. Canton Casey's pub, town centre, dates back 200 years and has a suitably historic interior.

Belvedere House Gardens, 5 km (3 miles) S of Mullingar. Open 12 noon-6pm daily, May-Sept. ☎ (044) 40861. Terraced gardens descend in three levels to shores of Lough Ennell. Also walled gardens, landscaped parkland. Plans to restore mansion to its former glory.

Newbridge *11 km (7 miles) W of Naas. Newbridge Cutlery* makes attractive tableware. Visitor centre open daily, all year. ☎ (045) 431301.

Newtowncashel *Near Corlea Centre, Co Longford. Heritage Centre* has a farmhouse parlour with decor in early 1930s style, with utensils and farm implements to match. Open 2pm- 6pm daily, or by arr, ☎ (043) 25306. *Peatland World, Lullymore 24 km (15 km) N of Kildare.* Open 9.30am-5pm Mon-Fri all year, 2pm- 6pm Sat, Sun, Apr-Oct. ☎ (045) 860133. The interpretive centre highlights the history and development of the bogs that cover much of the flat central plain of Ireland, as well as their flora and fauna. Nearby Lullymore Heritage Centre recreates times past.

Portarlington *27 km (17 miles) SW of Tullamore.* Once home to a strong French-speaking Huguenot community, who built the French church in 1696 (it was rebuilt in 1853). Many of the French settlers are buried in the graveyard. *Town Museum, Main Street,* open 2pm-5pm Sun, all year. Details some French history relating to the town, besides Bronze Age artefacts and an 1866 pillar box, one of the oldest in Ireland.

Rathdowney *14 km (9 miles) W of Durrow. Donaghmore Workhouse Museum,* open 2pm-5pm daily, summer. ☎ (0505) 46212. Once a workhouse, the museum now has a fine collection of old farm implements, kitchen utensils. Matron's room has been reconstructed, as has the dairy house. *Rock of Dunamase*, 6 km (4 miles) E of Portlaoise. This rock, rising from the plain, is capped by a ruined fortress. Excellent views of the surrounding countryside from the 60 m (200 ft) high summit.

Slieve Bloom Environment Park, Kinnity *18 km (11 miles) E of Birr.* Forest walks on slopes of Slieve Bloom mountains. Waterfalls and wildlife.

Stradbally *11 km (7 miles) E of Portlaoise.* Most attractive main street, steeply sloping and flower lined. The Steam Museum, open 10am-4pm Tues-Sat, Easter-Oct, ☎ (0502) 25444, has a collection of old steam powered machinery, including

threshing machines. Narrow gauge railway runs for 1.6 km (1 mile) through adjacent woods. Vintage steam rally held on August bank holidays. Steam train trips, ☎ (0502) 60609/46535.

Timahoe *8 km (5 miles) S of Stradbally.* Attractive village set around an extensive green, with 12th c. round tower in good condition. A memorial on the green marks the visit here by a former President of Ireland, Erskine Childers, in 1974. The late Richard Nixon, US President 1969-1974, came here in 1970 in search of his family's ancestral links.

Tullamore *40 km (25 miles) SE of Athlone. TIO* ☎ (0506) 52617, mid-June-mid-Sept. Attractive heritage town that owed much of its earlier development to the opening of the Grand Canal in 1798. *Charleville Castle,* open 2pm-5pm Sat, Sun, BH, Apr, May, 11am-5pm Wed-Sun, June-Sept. ☎ (0506) 21279. Just outside the town, on the Birr road, this magnificent Gothic revival building dates from 1812 and was designed by Francis Johnston, who was also the architect of Dublin's GPO and Emo Court in Co Laois. With 56 rooms, this castle has been extensively renovated in recent years. Set in fine woodland grounds. Tullamore Dew heritage centre being planned, named after the town's famous liqueur.

Tullynally Castle *2 km (1 mile) W of Castlepollard.* Open 2pm-6pm daily, July, Aug and by arr. Gardens open 10am-5pm daily, May-Oct. ☎ (044) 61159. This castle, built in the 18th c. and extended the following century, is the largest castellated house in Ireland, the seat of the Earls of Longford and the Irish base of the Pakenham literary family. Portraits, furnishings, library, large kitchen worth seeing, also landscaped park, flower and kitchen gardens.

Tyrellspass *24 km (15 miles) SW of Kinnegad.* Village set around an impressive half-moon shaped green. *Tyrellspass Castle,* open 10am-6pm Mon-Sat, 12.30pm-6pm Sun, all year. ☎ (044) 23105. This 15th c. castle has a museum, antiques and books.

Virginia *83 km (52 miles) NW of Dublin.* Charming village in south Cavan. Main street leads to yew-lined grounds of Church of Ireland church. Walks to shores of Lough Ramor.

CARLOW AND KILKENNY

Abbeyleix *35 km (22 miles) N of Kilkenny.* Attractive town with a broad main street and interesting parish church (CI). The new *heritage centre,* open 9am-5pm Mon-Fri, 1pm-5pm Sat, Sun, Mar-Oct, ☎ (0502) 31653, details the story of this planned town, including the de Vesci estate. Its defunct manufacturing traditions are also portrayed, including the carpet factory that made carpets for the ill-fated Titanic. The de Vesci demesne, open daily in summer, is also worth seeing. *Morrissey's pub on the main street* is a perfect heritage place, preserving its 1900 style, complete with photographs, old bottles and other old time packaging. You can enjoy a drink here - including coffee - and buy groceries and newspapers, in the old style of country shopping.

Altamont Gardens *9 km (5 miles) SE of Tullow.* Open 2pm-6pm Sun, BH, Apr-Oct, or by arr, ☎ (0503) 59128. Fine gardens on the banks of the River Slaney, with views of the Wicklow Mountains. Ornamental lakes, walks and nature paths. *Ballykeenan House* is a pet farm and aviary. Open 11am-6pm Mon-Fri, 2pm-6pm Sat, ☎ (0503) 57665.

Ballitore *4 km (3 miles) N of Moone.* The *Quaker Museum,* open 11am-6pm Tues-Sat, 2pm-5pm Sun, during the summer, ☎ (01) 668 3684. The museum is housed in an 18th c. schoolhouse and has a great deal of materials on the Quakers who lived in the area. *Crookstown Mill,* open daily, all year, ☎ (0507) 23222, has many fascinating artefacts from the old milling industry and it records the changing social order.

Callan *16 km (10 miles) SW of Kilkenny. Edmund Ignatius Rice,* founder of the Christian Brothers, was born in an old farmhouse here, which can be seen daily, by arr with the adjoining monastery. ☎ (056) 25141. *Kilkenny Crystal* can be visited by arr, ☎ (056) 25132.

Carlow *38 km (24 miles) NE of Kilkenny. TIO* ☎ (0503) 31554, all year. This modest town was formerly an Anglo-Norman stronghold and is the capital of one of Ireland's smallest counties. Interesting walks through the narrow laneways and along the banks of the River Barrow. Carlow Castle: much of this 13th c. edifice was destroyed in the early 19th c. when a local doctor used explosives when he was trying to turn the place into a lunatic asylum. *County Museum* 11am-5pm Tues-Fri, 2pm-5pm Sat, Sun, all year. ☎ (0503) 40730. Many local history exhibits, including a blacksmith's forge, a dairy and a country kitchen. Also an old printing press once used by the local Nationalist & Leinster Times newspaper. *Cathedral of the*

River Barrow at Boris, Co. Carlow

Assumption (C), Tullow Street. Consecrated in 1833, this edifice has windows by Harry Clarke and a distinctive spire, the recent reorganisation of the interior has been the subject of much local controversy. Oak Park Agricultural Research Station, 3 km (2 miles) N of Carlow, open 9am-5pm Mon-Fri, all year, ☎ (0503) 31425. Run by Teagasc, it has extensive woodland lakes and a wildfowl sanctuary. **Browne's Hill Demesne,** *3 km (2 miles) E of Carlow* has a magnificent dolmen; its capstone is the largest in Ireland. **Castletown Tower House,** medieval tower house, by arr. ☎ (0503) 40283.

Castlecomer *20 km (12 miles) N of Kilkenny.* Built to a classical design in the 17th c., it still has a gracious air, despite its coalmining past. Reddy's pub has some relics of the old coal mines in the vicinity.

Castledermot *14 km (9 miles) SE of Athy.* Two well-preserved medieval high crosses and a 10th c. round tower in equally good condition. Only the chancel walls remain of the 14th c. Franciscan friary.

Dunmore Cave *11 km (7 miles) N of Kilkenny.* Open 10am-7pm daily, summer, 10am-5pm Sat, Sun, BH, winter. However, ongoing work in the caves may restrict opening times, so check first, ☎ (056) 67726. Arguably the finest limestone caves in Ireland, made up of a series of caverns. There was a Viking massacre here in 928. The visitor centre has exhibitions and displays.

Graiguenamanagh *32 km (20 miles) SE of Kilkenny.* Attractive village set on banks of the River Barrow. Duiske Inn, near the bridge, has many photographs of the old village. **Duiske Abbey,** the largest Cistercian foundation in Ireland, built in the 13th c., has been restored to its original glory. Open daily, all year, ☎ (0503) 24238.

Inistioge *8 km (5 miles) SW of Thomastown.* Thoroughly unspoiled and good looking village by the banks of the River Nore. Tree-lined square and walks by the river. Two interesting churches, one C, the other CI. In the graveyard of the latter,

Mary Tighe, the celebrated late 18th/ early 19th c. poet, is buried. Ruins of 13th c. castle. Armillary sphere in square is ancient Greek device to depict the progress of the earth and moon.

Woodstock Park, *1.5 km (1 mile) S of the village* was once the estate of the local landowner. The ruins of the mansion, burned down during the civil war, stare out over what had been the formal gardens and arboretum. Visitors can walk through the grounds. Open daily, all year.

Jerpoint Abbey *3 km (2 miles) SW of Thomastown.* Open 10am-5pm Wed-Mon, Mar-May, mid-Sept-Oct, 9.30am-6.30pm daily, June-mid-Sept. ☎ (056) 24623. Cistercian foundation dating from late 12th c. is one of Ireland's finest monastic ruins. Unique cloister carvings. Small visitor centre.

Kells Priory *13 km (8 miles) S of Kilkenny.* Founded in 12th c., the extensive ruins run down to the King's River.

Kilkenny *117 km (73 miles) SW of Dublin.* Pop. 8,500. TIO Rose Inn Street, ☎ (056) 51500, all year. This medieval city, set on the banks of the River Nore, is one of Ireland's main designated heritage towns, with a wealth of sites and facilities for visitors. During the 17th c., Kilkenny came close to upstaging Dublin as the administrative capital of Ireland, but is now renowned as a cultural and historical centre, well worth the time spent in exploration. Kilkenny has a very varied and comprehensive arts festival in August.

The **Kilkenny CityScope Exhibition,** *Rose Inn Street,* daily, all year, ☎ (056) 51500. The best place to start a tour of the city. The audio-visual presentation in the former Shee Alms House is centred around a model of Kilkenny as it was in 1640. **Kilkenny Castle,** open 10.30am-5pm daily, Apr, May, 10am-7pm daily, June-Sept, 10.30am-5pm Tues-Sat, 11am-5pm Sun, Oct-Mar. ☎ (056) 21450. Built in the 12th c. and extensively remodelled in the 19th c., with extensive refurbishment in the last few years. The rooms have been restored and are open to view, including the Long Gallery. A suite of servants' rooms has been turned into the **Butler Art Gallery,** a fine venue for contemporary art exhibitions. The castle houses the National Furniture Collection. Audio-visual room. The grounds, with woodland walks, lake and formal terraced gardens, have also been restored.

St Canice's Cathedral (CI). Open 9am-6pm Mon-Sat, 2pm-6pm Sun, Easter-Oct, 10am-4pm Mon-Sat, 2pm-4pm Sun, Oct-Apr. Built in the 13th c., St Canice's is one of the most striking medieval churches in Ireland. The view from the top of the round tower, next to cathedral, is equally impressive, provided you have a head for heights.

Jerpoint Abbey, Kilkenny

Rothe House, Parliament Street, open
10.30am-5pm Mon-Sat, 3pm-5pm Sun,
Mar-Oct, 1pm-5pm, Mon-Sat, Nov-Mar.
☎ (056) 22893. Three houses make up
this Tudor masterpiece, meticulously restored
to form an elaborate museum of Kilkenny
history. Items on show are many and
varied, from old picture postcards to an
1850 Kilkenny-made double bass.
Includes interpretative and genealogy centre.
Gardens.

Kyteler's Inn, St Kieran's Street, has been
an inn since 1324. Dame Alice Kyteler, a
noted Kilkenny witch, was born here in 1280.
Black Abbey (C), Abbey Street. Built in 1225,
the nave and transept have been restored as
a Dominican church. *Smithwick's Brewery,*
open Mon-Fri, all year. ☎ (056) 21021.
Video of brewery and tour of the 14th c.
abbey in its grounds. *Kilkenny Design
Workshops,* opposite the castle entrance,
open daily, all year. Many excellent craft
lines for sale, while the courtyard behind
the shop and restaurant has many
craft workshops.

Tynan's Bridge Bar, near the castle, has an
authentic Edwardian interior, with marble
counter and gas lights, while the *Club House
Hotel, Patrick Street,* has intriguing collection
of 19th c. political cartoons.

Leighlinbridge *11 km (7 miles) S of
Carlow.* Pleasant village set on banks of
River Barrow, with ruins of 16th c. tower.
Walks along the river bank.

Moone *19 km (12 miles) NE of Carlow.
Moone High Cross* has 51 elaborate carved
panels. The walls of the nearby *Moone High
Cross Inn* are lined with fascinating historical
newspaper cuttings and photographs.
The *Irish Pewter Mill and High Cross
centre,* open daily, all year, ☎ (0507) 24164.

Thomastown *18 km (11 miles) S of
Kilkenny.* Delightful but badly congested
town on the banks of the River Nore.
Walks in the town and in surrounding
demesnes. *Water Garden,* open 10am-6pm
daily, May-Sept, ☎ (056) 24478 is small
and very peaceful, with lots of aquatic plants.

Tullaroan *15 km (9 miles) W of Kilkenny.
Lory Meagher Heritage Centre,* open 2pm-
5pm Sat, Sun, Mar-May, Sept-Nov, 10am-
5.30pm Mon-Sat, 2pm-6pm Sun, June-Aug.
☎ (056) 69107/ 69202. Fascinating
restoration of two storey thatched house,
GAA museum.

Tullow *12 km (7 miles) SE of Carlow.*
Tullow Museum, beside bridge over River
Slaney, open 10am-1pm, 2pm-5pm, Mon-Fri,
2pm-5pm, Sun, BH, Mar-Oct. ☎ (0503)
51286. *The Cottage Collection, Ardattin,
near Tullow:* domestic appliances from early
20th c. Open daily, all year, ☎ (0503) 55639.

WICKLOW MOUNTAINS

Arklow *14 km (9 miles) S of Wicklow
Town. Maritime Museum,* St Mary's Road,
near railway station, open 10am-5pm Mon-
Fri, all year, or by arr, ☎ (0402) 32868.
Display of many items relating to Arklow's
long maritime history. *Wicklow Vale Pottery,*
open daily, all year, ☎ (0402) 39442.
Factory shop, tearoom.

Aughrim *14 km (9 miles) NW of Arklow.*
Pleasant riverside village, surrounded by
forests, excellent for walking.

Avoca *26 km (16 miles) S of Wicklow
Town.* See Thomas Moore's tree, near the
Meeting of the Waters, where he spent
many hours lost in poetic contemplation.
The Ballykissangel TV series is filmed in
the village. *Avoca Handweavers,* open daily,
all year, ☎ (0402) 35105 is in a 1723 mill.
Shop, restaurant.

Avondale Estate *2.5 km (1.5 miles) S of
Rathdrum.* Open 10am-6pm daily, May-Sept,
11am-5pm daily, Oct-Mar. ☎ (0404) 46111.
Charles Stewart Parnell, the great late 19th c.
political leader who fell from grace, lived in
this charming house which was built in 1799
and has been well restored. An audio-visual
presentation details his life and the main
rooms have fascinating mementoes. The estate
has an arboretum, river walks, car parks and
a tea-shop.

Baltinglass *30 km (19 miles) SW of
Blessington.* Impressive ruins of a 12th c.
abbey on the banks of the River Slaney.
Baltinglass Hill, 2 km (1 mile)
E of Baltinglass is worth the arduous climb
to see the Bronze Age cairn and enjoy the
excellent views. *Humewood Castle* at nearby
Kiltegan, open by arr, ☎ (0508) 73215 is
an exotic castellated 19th c. mansion that
has been sumptuously restored. It has an
extensive walled estate and two lakes.

Blessington *27 km (18 miles) SW of
Dublin.* Broad, tree-lined Main Street is
very French in appearance. *Ardenode Deer
Farm, Ballymore Eustace,* open Wed and Sat.
Tel.(045) 64428. Cruises on Blessington
Lake, daily in season, ☎ (045) 65850.

Bray *12 km (8 miles) S of Dublin.*
Seaside town with long promenade and
shingle beach. *Bray Heritage Centre,
Lower Main Street, beside Royal Hotel,*
open 10am-4pm daily, summer.
☎ (01) 286 7128. Many mementoes and
artefacts of local historical interest.
The derelict aquarium on the seafront has
been taken over by a UK firm, which plans
to reopen it in 1998 as the National Sea
Life Centre.

Brittas Bay *13 km (8 miles) S of Wicklow
Town.* Popular sandy beach stretching for
5 km (3 miles), backed by dunes.

Derrynamuck *9 km (4 miles) SE of
Donard. Dwyer McAllister Cottage.* Michael
Dwyer, a late 18th c. rebel leader, was based
here in 1799. The cottage has been restored
to its original state. Open 2pm-6pm daily,
June-Sept.

Enniskerry *19 km (12 miles) S of Dublin.*
Attractive village with craft shops and
restaurants, beside Wicklow Mountains.

Glendalough *24 km (15 miles) W of
Wicklow Town.* TIO, ☎ (0404) 45581, June-
Sept. One of Ireland's most attractively set
and extensive *monastic sites.* The principal
ruins, just E of the lower lake, are the
cathedral, an 11th c. nave, chancel and
St Kevin's Church, usually called St Kevin's
Kitchen, which is a fine example of early
Irish barrel-vaulted oratory. Beside the church
is an almost perfectly preserved round tower.
The site is open 9.30am-5pm daily, mid-Oct-
mid-Mar, 9.30am-6pm daily, mid-Mar-May,
9am-6.30pm daily, June-Aug, 9.30am-6pm
daily, Sept-mid-Oct. ☎ (0404) 45325/45352.
The Visitor Centre nearby, open daily, has
exhibitions and an audio-visual presentation.
Craft Centre, open daily, ☎ (0404) 45156,
features jewellery making, weaving.
Gallery, tearoom.

Less accessible than the main monastic site,
on the S shore of the upper lake, are
Teampaill na Skellig (Church of the Rock)
and *St Kevin's Bed,* cut into the rock face.
*Glendalough Woods, 1.5 km (1 mile) W of
Laragh,* have nature trails and forest walks.
There are guided walks from the information
point at the upper lake, through the new
Wicklow National Park.

Greystones *8 km (5 miles) S of Bray.*
Seaside village with harbour and walk along

Ní gnách cosaint ar díth tiarna
Rarely is a fight continued when
the chief has fallen.

An extract from *Classic Irish Proverbs*
published by Appletree Press

Glendalough Lake, Co. Wicklow

seafront, best seen before proposed development of marina gets under way.

Kilcoole *5 km (3 miles) S of Greystones.* A popular TV soap opera, Glenroe, is filmed on location here. ***Glenroe Open Farm*** has animals, shop, cafe. Open daily, Apr-Sept, but closed during filming. ☎ (01) 287 2288.

Kilruddery Gardens *2 km (1 mile) S of Bray, just off Greystones road.* Open 1pm-5pm daily, May-June, Sept. ☎ (01) 268 3405. Ireland's only 17th c. gardens, set near splendid mountain landscapes.

Mount Usher Gardens *Ashford, 8 km (5 miles) NW of Wicklow Town.* Open 10.30am-6pm, daily, Mar 17-end Oct. ☎ (0404) 40116/ 40205. These attractive gardens beside the River Dargle have more than 5,000 species of plants, from azaleas to rhododendrons. Tea room, craft shops.

National Garden Centre *Kilquade, 8 km (5 miles) SE of Greystones.* Open 10am-6pm Mon-Sat, 1pm-6pm Sun, all year. ☎ (01) 281 9890. Extensive garden layouts, mountain ponds and streams.

Newtown Mount Kennedy *11 km (7 miles) S of Bray.* **Model World** depicts Ireland's history since 5th c. BC in model format. Open daily, all year.

Powerscourt Estate, *1.5 km (1 mile) S of Enniskerry.* Gardens open 9.30am-5.30pm daily, Mar-Oct, Waterfall open 9.30am-7pm daily, summer, 10.30am-dusk, winter. ☎ (01) 286 7676. Vast estate in the shadow of the Wicklow Mountains has Italian and Japanese gardens, complete with sweeping terraces, antique sculpture and fountains. The ruined great house has been turned into an upmarket shopping and dining experience.

Agricultural Heritage Display Centre *Coolakay House, just SW of Enniskerry.* Open daily, all year. ☎ (01) 286 2423. Working farm with good displays of old implements and machinery, dating from early 18th c. Restaurant.

Rathdrum *16 km (10 miles) SW of Wicklow Town.* Small, attractive town surrounded by forests. ***Parnell Memorial Park*** commemorates the great leader. ***Kilmacurragh Arboretum*** was created in the 19th c. Open daily, all year. ***Clara Lara Fun Park,*** *Vale of Clara, near Rathdrum.* Open daily, all year, ☎ (0404) 46161. Water-based sports, picnic area, restaurant.

Roundwood *19 km (12 miles) SW of Bray.* Highest village in Ireland, 238 m (780 ft) above sea level. Walk along the main street for distant glimpses of the reservoir. Market in parish hall on Sunday afternoons. ***Ballinastoe Studio Pottery,*** *Enniskerry Road, 5 km (3 miles) from Roundwood.* Open 10am-6pm daily, all year. ☎ (01) 281 8151. Close by are ***Loughs Tay and Dan,*** *3 km (2 miles) W of Roundwood.* The countryside

which surrounds them is among the most desolate and remote in eastern Ireland and is very Scandinavian looking.

Russborough House *3 km (2 miles) SE of Blessington.* Open 10.30am-5.30pm Sun, BH, Apr-May, Sept, Oct,10.30am-5.30pm daily June-Aug. ☎ (045) 865239. Great Palladian house, built 1740-1750,has Beit art collection, with works by Goya, Rubens, Velasquez, Vermeer. Irish silverware, magnificent Francini plasterwork. Furniture, carpets, tapestries. Shop, restaurant, children's playground.

Shillelagh *8 km (5 miles) S of Tinahely.* Good walks in the hills surrounding this attractively set village. A portion of the nearby ancient oak forest at Coolattin Woods has been preserved for posterity.

Wicklow Gap The R756 runs for some 32 km (20 miles) across some of the most spectacular mountain landscapes in Ireland, including the Wicklow Gap, between Hollywood in west Wicklow and Glendalough.

Wicklow Town *48 km (30 miles) S of Dublin.* Pop.6,000. TIO, Fitzwilliam Square, ☎ (0404) 69117, all year. The administrative centre of Ireland's Garden County, Wicklow has a strong maritime feel, enhanced by its busy harbour and two piers. Its best-known son is Captain Robert Halpin, born in the Bridge Inn in 1836,who became captain of the Great Eastern cable-laying ship. The *Fitzwilliam Square Memorial* commemorates Capt. Halpin. Many historic items relating to him can be seen at *Tinakilly Country House Hotel and Restaurant, 2 km (1 mile) N of the town,* which he built as his retirement home.

The town's busy and straggling main Street, which is divided into two levels, has many small craft and gift shops. *St Lavinius Church (CI)* has an informative memorial to the aforesaid Halpin and a Russian-style copper dome. On the headland beyond the harbour are the remains of the castle, built in the late 12th c. In the town, directly opposite the *Grand Hotel,* the ruins of the 13th c. Franciscan friary can be seen by arr. with the parish priest in the adjoining presbytery.

Wicklow's *Old Jail heritage* centre has finally opened, after years of delays. It was worth the wait: a fine renovation job has been carried out on the building, which details such questions of local history as the 1798 rising, the 19th c. famine and transportation of Wicklow convicts to Australia. Audio-visual presentation and interactive displays. Open 10am-6pm daily, Apr- Oct, ☎ (0404) 20100.

Enjoyable walks beside the River Leitrim, along the quays. At Rathnew, 3km (2 miles) N of Wicklow Town, *Hunter's Hotel* has fine riverside gardens and some interesting historical photographs. S of Wicklow Head is *Silver Strand,* an attractive and popular sandy beach.

Woodenbridge *8 km (5 miles) NW of Arklow.* One of the best looking villages in Ireland, set where three valleys meet.

WEXFORD SHORES

Ballyhack *1.5 km (1 mile) E of Passage East, across Waterford Harbour by car ferry.* Attractive seaside village. *Ballyhack Castle,* open 12 noon-6pm Wed-Sun, Apr-June, Sept, 10am-6pm daily, July, Aug. To view, Pierce McAuliffe ☎ (051) 389468/ 388348. This large tower house is believed to

have been built about 1450 by the Knights Hospitallers of St John at the time of the Crusades. The structure is still substantially intact. Nearly adjacent Neptune restaurant.

Bunclody *21 km (14 miles) NW of Enniscorthy.* Spaciously laid-out town with broad main square divided by a fast-flowing stream. Set in the shadow of the Blackstairs Mountains.

Courtown *6 km (3.5 miles) SE of Gorey.* Popular seaside resort, with small but interesting harbour and entertainments.

Craanford *8km (5 miles) W of Gorey* 17th c. restored cornmill. Open 11am-6pm daily, June-Oct, 11am-6pm Sat, Sun, Apr, May. ☎ (055) 28124.

Dunbrody Abbey *20 km (12 miles) S of New Ross. Near Campile.* Great roofless church dating from 12th c., built by Cistercian monks from St Mary's Abbey, Dublin. Visitor centre, museum, maze. Open 10am-6pm daily, Apr-Sept, ☎ (051) 388603. Nearby Tintern Abbey, 13th c., is being developed for visitors, including visitor centre, maze and woodland walks.

Duncannon Fort *E side of Waterford Harbour.* Old military structures, mostly 16th c., rather like Charles Fort near Kinsale, is being restored. Open 10am-5pm daily, May-Sept, ☎ (051) 389454.

Enniscorthy *24 km (15 miles) N of Wexford.* TIO, in Castle, ☎ (054) 34699, mid-June-end Aug. Delightful and historic town set beside the River Slaney. The main part of the town rises up steeply from the river. Lots of historical atmosphere; it's worth exploring the quaysides and many narrow laneways.

The imposing *Enniscorthy Castle,* rebuilt in late 16th c., houses the *Town Museum,* open 10am-8pm Mon-Sat, 2pm-6pm Sun, July, Aug, Mon-Sat, 11am-6pm, 2pm-6pm Sun, Apr-June, Sept, 2pm-6pm daily, Oct, Nov, 2pm-5pm daily, Dec-Mar. ☎ (054) 35926. Folk section, relics of 1798 and mementoes of Enniscorthy's industrial history. *Vinegar Hill* on *E outskirts of the town* is where the decisive battle of 1798 was fought. The site offers fine views over the town. A brand new multi-million IR£ multimedia *1798 visitor centre* opened in 1998 to commemorate those stirring events. Open 9.30am-6.30pm daily, all year. ☎ (054) 33540.

St Aidan's Cathedral (C) was designed by Pugin in the 1840s and has been substantially restored in recent years.

There are three fascinating potteries near Enniscorthy. The oldest, going back over 300 years, is *Carley's Bridge Pottery,* open 9am-5pm Mon-Fri, all year, ☎ (054) 33512.

Paddy Murphy's Hillview Pottery, open daily all year, ☎ (054) 35443, makes pots the traditional way. *Kiltrea Bridge Pottery,* open daily, all year, ☎ (054) 35107, does very modern, stylish pottery, mostly glazed. Also a weaving workshop.

Ferns *34 km (21 miles) N of Wexford.* Once the capital of Leinster, this small village has some impressive ruins, including a 13th c. castle, a 12th c. Augustinian abbey and a cathedral.

Hook Peninsula *E side of Waterford Harbour.* This narrow finger of land concludes with the *Hook Head lighthouse,* one of the oldest lights for shipping in the world. Now that it has been automated, it's being turned into a maritime heritage centre. The main village on the peninsula is *Fethard-on-Sea,* with its "shell" garage, the facade of which is covered in seashells. Nearby lifeboat memorial. *Tintern Abbey,* the impressive ruins of a 13th c. Cistercian foundation, is 6km (4 miles) N of Fethard-on-Sea. On the E side of the peninsula is Slade, with its tiny harbour,18th c. fish salting house and 14th c. castle. *Baginbun Bay* is the site of the first Norman landing in Ireland, in 1169. On the W side of the peninsula is *Dollar Bay,* one of several sandy bays that are reputed to hide Danish treasure.

The large crack in the ceiling of the 18th c. Loftus Hall is supposedly the spot where the Devil exited in a hurry and as a result, cannot be repaired. The entire Hook Peninsula drive is well signposted.

Irish National Heritage Park *5 km (3 miles) N of Wexford.* Open 9.30am-6.30pm daily, Apr-Oct. ☎ (053) 20733. Full size replicas of the homesteads, burial locations and places of worship in prehistoric times. This living lesson in history continues up to Viking and Norman times. The park has been substantially refurbished. Audio-visual presentations, lectures, guided tours, restaurants.

John F. Kennedy Park *8 km (5 miles) S of New Ross.* Open 10am-8pm daily, May-Aug, 10am-6.30pm daily, Apr, Sept, 10am-5pm daily, Oct-Mar. ☎ (051) 388171. This 165 ha (410 acre) park commemorates the late John F. Kennedy, President of the US from 1961-1963, some of whose ancestors came from this immediate area. *Arboretum* with large selection of trees and shrubs from around the world, forest garden. Tremendous views from summit of nearby Slieve Coillte hill. Visitor centre, pony and trap rides, miniature railway, cafe. At nearby *Dunganstown,* there's a one room homestead shrine to JFK's 1963 visit to Ireland.

Johnstown Castle *6 km (4 miles) S of Wexford.* The castle itself, which contains an agricultural research centre, is not open to

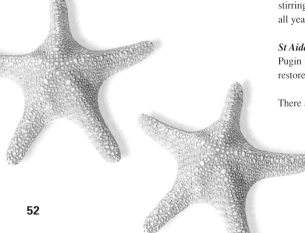

Late evening, Wexford

the public, but the ornamental grounds, with over 200 species of trees and shrubs, together with a large lake, can be seen. On working days, visitors can also see the walled gardens and hothouses.

The *Irish Agricultural Museum,* open 9am-5pm Mon-Fri, 2pm-5pm Sun, June-Aug, 9am-12.30pm, 1.30pm-5pm, Mon-Fri, Sept-May. ☎ (053) 42888. This is an excellent presentation of the old rural way of life, with sections on transport, dairying and farming, besides farmhouse interiors and country furniture. Replica workshops on rural crafts, including a blacksmith's forge, basket and harness makers.

Kilmore Quay *16 km (10 miles) S of Wexford.* A long, straggling main street with a dozen thatched cottages, runs down to the harbour, now much refurbished. The old Guillemot lightship has been turned into a full-scale *maritime museum,* with sections on lightships, the Irish Navy, the old Irish Shipping fleet and modern fishing. Also ships' models. Open 12 noon-6pm daily, June-Sept. ☎ (053) 29655/ 29832. Pubs in the village have maritime artefacts. Marina.

In calm summer weather, boats take visitors to the two offshore *Saltee Islands,* renowned bird sanctuaries. If the weather permits, landings are possible.

Lady's Island *10 km (6 miles) SW of Rosslare, just W of Carnsore Point.* A place of pilgrimage on 15 August. A causeway joins the island to the mainland. Ruins include a Norman tower that leans at a greater angle than the Leaning Tower of Pisa.

New Ross *37 km (23 miles) E of Wexford. TIO, The Quay,* ☎ (051) 421857, mid-June-end August. The streets of this town set on the River Barrow are positively medieval. The town rises steeply from the quaysides, with its Dutch-style buildings, to the hilltop area of New Ross, which is full of medieval fortifications. There are substantial ruins of the 13th c. parish church at St Mary's, Church Lane. *The Tholsel* (Town Hall) has civic insignia and documents, including charter of King James II. *New town theatre. Berkeley Doll and Costume Museum,* just outside the town, on Enniscorthy side, open 11.30am-6.30pm Sat, May-Sept, or by arr, ☎ (051) 421361. Includes collections of dolls and rocking horses. At New Ross harbour, a reconstruction of a three-masted famine barque, the *Dunbrody,* is under construction. It's due to set sail for Boston in 1999. Open daily, all year. ☎ (051) 425239. *River cruises* along River Barrow and River Nore, with dinner served on board, summer only. ☎ (051) 421723.

Rosslare Harbour *25 km (16 miles) S of Wexford. TIO,* ☎ (053) 33662, May-Sept.The port may be the busy terminal for ferries from Wales and northern France, but the town itself will repay closer inspection. The area has many fine sandy beaches, as well as clifftop walks. The bar of the Hotel Rosslare has a well-presented maritime museum, with many relics and artefacts, even an old-style diving suit.

Tacumshane Windmill *3 km (2 miles) W of Lady's Island lake.* The windmill is not easy to find, amid the labyrinth of lanes in south Wexford, but it's in good condition and can be viewed. Built in the 19th c., it was restored about 45 years ago. Both sails and interior are in near perfect condition. Keys at nearby Myler's pub.

Wexford *144 km (90 miles) S of Dublin. Pop.10,000. TIO, The Crescent,* ☎ (053) 23111, all year. An ancient town whose name is derived from its Viking title, set on the broad expanses of the River Slaney estuary. The narrow main street with many slate-fronted buildings winds its way through the town. Many laneways run off the main street, some of the wooden quaysides, others to the heights of the town. In summer, Wexford is understandably popular, packed with cars and people, while the autumn *Wexford Opera Festival,* ☎ (053) 22240, attracts the cosmompolitan black-tie crowd to the small, but gloriously refurbished and now extended *Theatre Royal.* Many fringe events and exhibitions are staged during the festival.

Westgate Heritage Centre, open 10am-5pm Mon-Fri, 10am-2pm Sat, May-Oct, ☎ (053) 42611, uses audio-visual techniques to tell the long and tortuous story of this sea-faring, culture-loving town. See the adjoining town walls, dating back to Norman times, which are now restored. Substantial ruins of 12th c. *Selskar Abbey, Westgate.* Henry II spent Lent here in 1172 as penance for the murder of Thomas a Becket.

Wexford has some fine churches, including the so-called "Twin Sisters", the *Church of the Immaculate Conception (C), Rowe Street* and the *Church of the Assumption (C), Bride Street,* both 19th c. and almost identical in external appearance. *St Francis (C), School Street* is a Franciscan friary church founded in 1230, plundered in Cromwell's time in the mid-17th c. and remodelled in 1748. *St Iberius' Church (CI), North Main Street,* was built in the 17th c. and has been substantially restored. There has been a church on this site for the past 1,500 years.

White's Hotel, where the opera festival was founded, has many interesting photographs, while the town library, next door, has much material on Wexford. *Wexford Arts Festival, Cornmarket,* open daily, all year, ☎ (053) 23764, hosts concerts, exhibitions and other events.

Wexford Wildfowl Reserve *North Slob, Wexford.* Open 9am-6pm daily, mid-Apr-Sept, 10am-5pm daily, Oct-mid-Apr. ☎ (053) 23129. Over a third of the world's population of white-fronted Greenland geese winter here. The visitor centre has an audio-visual show, exhibitions and guided tours.

Yola Farmstead *5 km (3 miles) E of Rosslare Harbour, on main N25.* Open daily all year. ☎ (053) 31177. This tourist-related development commemorates the Yola dialect created and used in Wexford by the Normans from the 12th c. onwards. By the early 19th c., it had largely died out. The farmstead has several thatched buildings and outbuildings, including a privy made for two! Crystal glass making, craft shop, genealogy centre, cafe, nightly entertainment in summer.

THE SOUTH

Travelling south, into Tipperary and on to Cork, one of Ireland's great sights suddenly comes into view: Cashel's massive ruins perched, Acropolis-like, on a rock outcrop that dominates the surrounding plain. Cashel has smaller delights too, like Bru Boru, its folk village and the Bothan Scoir, a venerable one-roomed thatched cottage. The south is like that, set pieces that startle and surprise besides innumerable smaller places. Cork, both city and county, has an immense variety of sights. East Cork contains Midleton's whiskey heritage centre and the Queenstown Experience in Cobh, while Youghal, with its unsurpassed town walls, has rediscovered its rich past. The bays, inlets and peninsulas of West Cork have their own natural magic, culminating in the unspoiled, desolate splendour of the Beara peninsula. The most spectacular vistas of all in the south are to be found from one end to the other of the Ring of Kerry, a spectacular coastal route, while all through the Dingle peninsula more mountains and deserted beaches entice the traveller.

Beara Peninsula, Co. Cork

TIPPERARY CASTLES

Athassel Abbey *8 km (5 miles) W of Golden.* Extensive ruins of 12th c. Augustinian foundation in delightfully rural location.

Cahir *17 km (11 miles) S of Cashel. TIO,* ☎ (052) 41453, May-Sept. Small, quiet town beside the River Suir, with Georgian buildings and unusual churches. *Cahir Castle,* open 9.30am-5.30pm daily, Mar- mid- June, mid-Sept-mid-Oct ,9am-7.30pm daily, mid-June-mid-Sept, 9.30am-4.30pm daily, mid-

Oct-Feb. ☎ (052) 41011. This magnificent 12th c. structure has been elaborately restored and features include a courtyard and hall, a massive keep and high enclosing walls. Good views of the town from the parapets. Audio- visual show on all main sites in the area.

The Swiss Cottage open 10am-4.30pm Tues-Sun, Mar, Apr, Oct, Nov, 10am-6pm daily, May-Sept. ☎ (052) 41144. A cottage ornee built in early 19th c. to a design by John Nash, the noted Regency architect. It has been lovingly restored in recent years, both the interior and exterior. Cahir Park, immediately S of the town, offers walks and scenic views by the River Suir.

Carrick-on-Suir *27 km (17 miles) NW of Waterford.* Scenically set, rising up from the banks of the River Suir, with the Comeragh Mountains to the immediate south. *Ormonde Castle,* open 9.30am-6.30pm daily, mid-June-Sept. ☎ (051) 640787. Splendidly restored, this 15th c. castle is fronted by a 16th c. Elizabethan manor house with some of the finest Tudor plasterwork in Ireland. The buildings are surrounded by parkland. *Heritage Centre,* open daily, all year, ☎ (051) 640200, is in a converted church and is packed with mementoes of local customs and crafts. Frequent exhibitions. *Tipperary Crystal,* 5 km (3 miles) E of Carrick-on-Suir on the main N24 to Clonmel. Open 9am-5.30pm Mon-Fri, 9am-5pm Sat, 11am-5pm, Sun, BH, all year. ☎ (051) 641188. Former Waterford Crystal craftsmen set up this crystal glassmaking operation, which has gained a fine reputation for itself. Factory tours and showrooms.

Cashel *160 km (100 miles) SW of Dublin. Pop.2,500. TIO, Main Street,* ☎ (062) 61333, Apr-Sept. This small town set at the foot of the Rock of Cashel has an abundance of places to visit. A good first introduction to the town could come from a trip on the Heritage Tram - see TIO for details.

Cashel Heritage Centre, Main Street, open 9.30am-5.30pm Mon-Fri, Jan-Mar, 9.30am-5.30pm daily, Apr-June, 9.30am-8pm daily, July, Aug, 9.30am-5.30pm daily Sept, Oct,9.30am-5.30pm Mon-Fri, Nov-Feb. ☎ (062) 62511. Multimedia presentation on Cashel; it's the best place to start your tour of the town.

The Rock of Cashel. Open 9.30am-4.30pm daily, mid-Sept-mid-Mar, 9.30am-5.30pm daily, mid-Mar-early June, 9am-7.30pm daily, early June-mid-Sept. ☎ (062) 61437. The Rock dominates the town and the surrounding plain and is one of Ireland's great historic sites, the country's equivalent of the Acropolis. Main features are the 12th c. round tower, *Cormac's Chapel,* styled as a miniature cathedral, *St Patrick's Cross* and the **Cathedral of St Patrick**. In the **Hall of the Vicars Choral,** which you go through on entering the site, there are many fascinating relics and replicas, which will give you a feel for the site and prepare you for scrambling round these extraordinary ruins. Audio-visual presentation, full guide service.

Brú Ború, open 9am-12 midnight daily, mid-June-mid-Sept (entertainment at 9pm), 9am 5pm daily, mid-Sept-mid-June (no shows). ☎ (062) 61122. In the shadow of the Rock, has folk theatre, genealogy centre, restaurant, shop. **Cashel Folk Village,** *Chapel Lane,* open 9.30am-6pm daily, Mar, Apr, 9.30am-7.30pm daily, May-Oct, ☎ (062) 62525. Many historical artefacts, a 19th c. house and shop fronts.

Bothain Scoir, *on the Clonmel Road,* open by arr., ☎ (062) 61360 is a totally authentic single room 17th c. thatched cottage, well worth a visit. **Cashel Palace Hotel,** built in Queen Anne Style about 1730, was formerly the residence of the local Church of Ireland archbishops. It was restored recently, but retains its magnificent interiors, with original panellings and carvings. **Bolton Library,** *beside the CI cathedral,* open 11am-4.30pm daily, May-Sept, or by arr, ☎ (062) 61232 has one of the finest collections in Ireland of 16th and 17th c.books, together with ancient maps. In Cashel main street, **Padraig Ó Mathuna** creates exquisite jewellery with Celtic themes, together with paintings and sculptures, all on display in his shop.

In Chapel Lane,opposite the folk village, you can see the extensive ruins of a **Dominican friary,** while just W of the Rock of Cashel is **Hore Abbey,** a Cistercian abbey ruin.

Clonmel *48 km (30 miles) NW of Waterford.* TIO, ☎ (052) 22960, all year. Tipperary's main town, set most attractively beside the River Suir, is an excellent base for exploring the Comeragh and Knockmealdown mountains. **The Museum and Art Gallery,** *Parnell Street,* open 10am-5pm Tues-Sat, all year, ☎ (052) 25399 has a large collection of local historical material and paintings. **St Mary's Church (CI)** is mainly a 19th c. structure but includes part of an earlier 14th c. church and is surrounded by extensive sections of the old town walls. Other interesting churches in the town include the **Franciscan (C)** in Abbey Street, a 19th c. church which has been restored. Celebrated Tipperary Trials, Courthouse, daily, June-Sept, ☎ (052) 22960. 19th c. trials recreated in story, song and music.

Hearn's Hotel, *Parnell Street,* has been refurbished at the expense of much of its old character. It was here that Bianconi started his horse-drawn car service in 1815. The **Main Guard** is a very old building at one end of O'Connell Street - it's about 350 years old- and faces West Gate at the other end of Clonmel's main thoroughfare. This gate is a

Lough Derg looking towards Clare, from Garrykennedy

19th c. reconstruction of the 14th c. original. Enjoyable walks along the quaysides (prone to flooding) and through the riverside park.

Dromineer *10 km (6 miles) W of Nenagh.* Fine but small resort on the E shores of Lough Derg, a sailing mecca in summer.

Dundrum *13 km (8 miles) W of Cashel.* **Celtic Plantarum** has over 60,000 plants, trees and shrubs, representing some 2,500 species. Also Celtic theme reconstructions, like a dolmen and a crannog. Open 9am-dusk, daily, all year, ☎ (062) 71303.

Fethard *14 km (9 miles) NW of Clonmel.* It's a marvellously atmospheric small town. Large sections of the medieval town walls

have been restored. The **Farm, Folk and Transport Museum** started off next to the old railway station and since been much expanded. There's a great collection of items, some 3,000 in all, everything from old prams, a Victorian hearse and craft tools to a sizeable section devoted to old farm implements. Open 10am-6pm Mon-Sat, all year, or by arr., ☎ (052) 29727.

Holy Cross *6 km (4 miles) S of Thurles.* Open 10am-6pm daily, all year, ☎ (0504) 43241. The restored abbey was founded in 1168 by the Benedictines but was soon afterwards transferred to the Cistercians. It's a most impressive place in an equally fine location, beside the River Suir. Audio-visual centre.

Nenagh *39 km (24 miles) NE of Thurles.* TIO, Connolly Street, ☎ (067) 31610, May-Sept.

Nenagh Heritage Centre, open 10 am-5pm Mon-Fri, 2.30pm-5pm Sun, Apr-Oct, ☎ (067) 33850. The former governor's house in the old county jail has been turned into a fascinating reconstruction of aspects of the old country way of life, including a shop and a schoolroom. Also hosts temporary exhibitions. *Nenagh Castle, nearby,* has a circular keep that was part of a larger early 13th c. castle. The *Castle Brand* factory has a visitor centre, cookware museum and factory shop. Open daily, all year, ☎ (067) 31711. Ballyartella Woollen Mills, factory shop and visitor centre. Open 9.30am-5.30pm daily, all year, ☎ (067) 33250.

Roscrea, *34 km (21 miles) N of Thurles.* Interesting market town with strong heritage that's been well preserved. *Damer House,* early 18th c. was saved from demolition and fully restored, with its richly carved main staircase a notable feature. The formal garden at the side and rear has been restored.

The most recent restoration project here has been *Roscrea Castle,* open daily, Apr-Sept. ☎ (0505) 21850. Dating from the late 13th c., it comprises a gate tower, curtain wall and two corner towers.

The round tower on the road into Roscrea from the Dublin direction is seen to full advantage in its landscaped surroundings. *Mount St Joseph's, 3 km (2 miles) W of Roscrea,* ☎ (0505) 21711 is Ireland's only silk farm, in a Cistercian abbey that's the sister foundation of Mount Mellerary, Co Waterford.

Terryglass *24 km (15 miles) N of Nenagh.* This lakeside village at the NE corner of Lough Derg is full of character and has a 13th c. castle. It was the overall winner in the 1997 National Tidy Towns competition.

Thurles *21 km (13 miles) N of Cashel.* Market town on banks of the River Suir. Remnants of two Norman castles by the bridge, while in the spacious Liberty Square, *Hayes Hotel* was where the Gaelic Athletic Association was founded in 1884. The *GAA Museum, just off Liberty Square,* open daily, Mar-Oct, ☎ (0504) 23579 is strong on the history of the Association, with models, memorabilia and audio-visual reruns of historic matches. It's so interesting that even someone with no knowledge of Gaelic sports will find it fascinating. The *Cathedral (C),* built in late 19th c. has a richly decorated interior, while its campanile is a landmark for miles around. Nearby *famine museum is in St Mary's Church (CI)* and has much detail on the 19th c. famine in the area. Open 2pm-5pm Mon-Sat, June-Aug, 2pm-6pm, Sun, BH, all year, or by arr, ☎ (0504) 21133.

Tipperary Town *40 km (25 miles) SW of Thurles.* TIO, James Street, ☎ (062) 51457, May-Oct. Tipperary was immortalised in the First World War marching song, "It's a long way to Tipperary", which has been sung around the world ever since. That song and many other aspects of Tipperary's heritage are commemorated in the new heritage centre. The old jail is restored and open to visitors. Open daily, all year, ☎ (062) 52725. *Tipperary Excel Centre:* multimedia, arts, crafts. ☎ (062) 33466. The town also has interesting riverside walks and some streets in the centre have fine old shopfronts. *Immediately S of Tipperary Town,* the *Glen of Aherlow* is a noted beauty spot with outstanding mountain views.

WATERFORD CITY AND COAST

Annestown *20 km (12 miles) W of Tramore.* Small resort with good sandy beach, on the coast road from Tramore to Dungarvan. Beware of disused mine workings in the area.

Bunmahon *18 km (11 miles) W of Tramore.* Tiny fishing village with sandy beach, surrounded by cliffs.

Cappoquin *30 km (19 miles) N of Youghal.* *Cappoquin House and Gardens,* open 9am-1pm Mon-Sat, Apr-July, ☎ (058) 54275. Noted coarse fishing location at head of tidal section of River Blackwater. Excellent views of the nearby Knockmealdown mountains and an impressive drive over the mountains to Clogheen. On the slopes N of Cappoquin is *Mount Mellerary Abbey* where the monks follow various crafts. Visitors can attend services in the chapel. From the front of the abbey, impressive views over the Blackwater valley. Details of visitations are recorded in the nearby grotto. Open daily, all year, ☎ (058) 54404.

Cheekpoint *13 km (8 miles) E of Waterford.* Small riverside village has peaceful atmosphere. Nearby Cheekpoint Hill gives fine views of Waterford city and harbour. Meade's pub is an historic, peaceful place with riverside setting.

Clonea *5 km (3 miles) E of Dungarvan.* Fine sandy beach.

Curraghmore House *Portlaw 16 km (10 miles) W of Waterford.* Open 2pm-5pm, Thurs, BH, Easter-mid-Oct. ☎ (051) 387101. 18th c. gardens in beautiful setting, overlooked by the great house.

Dungarvan *30 km (19 miles) NE of Youghal.* TIO, The Square, ☎ (058) 41751, all year. 'Capital' of west Waterford, this attractive town is set on the coast where the River Colligan broadens into Dungarvan harbour. Fine walks along the harbour and promenade. *Dungarvan Castle* is late 12th c., while Abbeyside, on the E bank of the river, has a tower from a 13th c. Augustinian priory which is used as a belfry by the next door church. The W wall is all that's left of 12th c. *Abbeyside Castle. Shell Cottage* has exterior walls covered in thousands of sea shells.

Dungarvan Museum, Lower Main Street, open 2.30pm-5pm, Mon-Fri, all year, ☎ (058) 41231, is housed in the 17th c. Market House and contains many relics and mementoes of Dungarvan's maritime history. The *Seanachie Inn, off the main Cork road,* just W of Dungarvan, has historical relics, including old furniture and kitchen utensils.

Touraneena Heritage Centre, Ballinamult, 16 km (10 miles) NW of Dungarvan. Open daily, all year. The now vanished rural way of life is depicted here, including buttermaking, dairy and forge.

Dunmore East *14 km (9 miles) SE of Waterford.* Agreeable fishing village with busy harbour. Neat, Breton-style thatched cottages along the main street. Walks around the harbour area, including breakwater, and down to the coves. Small, sandy beach.

Lismore *6 km (4 miles) W of Cappoquin.* The *Lismore Experience,* open daily, Apr-Oct, ☎ (058)54975. This impressive heritage centre in the old courthouse uses multimedia techniques to tell the story of the town since the arrival of St Carthage in 636. Historical display room.

St Carthach's Cathedral (CI) is a striking medieval church, with Gothic vaulting and impressive memorials, a complete contrast to the very Italianate Catholic cathedral nearby. See also streets with English-style Tudor houses and *Lismore Castle Gardens,* open 2pm-5pm daily, except Sat, May-Sept, ☎ (058) 54424. Magnificent verdant setting overlooking the River Blackwater.

Passage East *11 km (7 miles) E of Waterford.* Old world riverside village with fine views of Waterford harbour from the quays and from the hill close to the village. Frequent daily *car ferry* to Ballyhack on the Wexford side of the estuary, ☎ (051) 382488. *Geneva Barracks, 5 km (3 miles) S of Passage East,* is a settlement founded in 1785 by gold and silversmiths from Geneva but was never completed. It was later used to hold prisoners after the 1798 Rising and the extensive walls can still be seen.

Woodtown Strand, 5 km (3 miles) S of Passage East, is a pleasant, secluded beach.

Stradbally *10 km (6 miles) NE of Dungarvan.* Small, attractive village that is a mass of flowers in summer. Interesting coves and fine cliff walks in the vicinity.

Reginald's Tower

Tramore *13 km (8 miles) S of Waterford.*
TIO, Railway Square, ☎ (051) 381572,
open mid-June-end Aug. Busy seaside town
with new amenities for visitors. *Splashworld*
is a futuristic, water-based leisure centre.
Open daily, all year, ☎ (051) 390176.
Laserworld, next door, has electronic games
with Celtic themes. Open daily, Apr-Oct,
☎ (051) 386565. Other Tramore attractions
include the amusement park covering more
than 20 ha (50 acres) and a well modernised
racetrack which provides horse racing all
year, with the main event in August. Walks
along the excellent promenade and to the
nearby coves. *The Majestic Hotel, opposite
the TIO,* has interesting old photographs of
the town. There are also walks along both
sides of Tramore Bay to see the old style
navigation marks, including the most famous,
the early 19th c. Metal Man, on the W side
of the bay. *Knockeen Dolmen, 5 km (3 miles)
N of Tramore,* is a well preserved dolmen.

Waterford *166 km (103 miles) SW of
Dublin.* Pop.40,000. TIO, 41 The Quay,
☎ (051) 875788, all year. This busy port,
mainly on the S bank of the broad River Suir
has many interesting buildings and some
fascinating laneways. In recent years,
the city centre has been radically upgraded.

The *Waterford Heritage Centre,* open 10am-
5pm daily, Apr-Oct, 10am-5pm Mon-Fri,
Nov-Mar, ☎ (051) 871227. *Just off the
quays, near Reginald's Tower,* the centre has
many relics of Viking and Norman Waterford
which were discovered during excavations
in recent years.

Reginald's Tower, on the quays, open 10am-
5pm daily, Apr-June, Sept, Oct,10am-8pm
Mon-Fri,10am-5pm Sun, July, Aug, 10am-
5pm, Mon-Fri, Nov-Mar, ☎ (051) 873501.
The symbol of Waterford, this tower, built
in 1003 by the Vikings, has been much
refurbished. It houses the civic museum,
with collections of archive material and
regalia. There are plans to develop a major
heritage centre on the quays, near the offices
of The Munster Express newspaper. It is due
to be located in a disused warehouse and no
firm date for opening has yet been set.

The *French Church, Greyfriars Street,*
was built in 1240 as a Franciscan foundation.
Later, it housed Huguenot refugees from
France. *Holy Trinity Church (C),
Barronstrand Street,* just off the quays, has a
remarkable late 18th c. interior. *Christ Church
Cathedral (CI), off the Mall,* is equally
impressive, this time for both its exterior and
interior. It dates from 1773. Audio-visual
presentation, daily, ☎ (051) 396270.

*Blackfriars Dominican Friary in Arundel
Square:* the square tower is the only major
part of the building left from the 13th c. The
Chamber of Commerce building *in George's
Street,* just off the quays, has a fine late 18th
c. interior. Also see the council chamber in
the *City Hall.* The Waterford *Municipal Art
Collection* can be seen here, 10am-5pm Mon-
Fri all year, ☎ (051) 873510. Nearby, there
are sections of the old city walls

The Waterford Room in the nearby City
Library, Lady Lane, has a wealth of material

on the city's ancient and modern history.
☎ (051) 873501.

The *Theatre Royal, The Mall,* has a lovely
and finely refurbished Victorian interior,
one of only three in Ireland (the others are
the Gaiety Theatre, Dublin and the slightly
later Grand Opera House, Belfast).
The *Waterford International Light Opera
Festival* is staged here every autumn.
The *Garter Lane Arts Centre, 22A O'Connell
Street,* ☎ (051) 855038 has established a fine
reputation as a cultural powerhouse,
with regular events and exhibitions, cinema
and theatre performances. The Red Kettle
Theatre Company is applauded far beyond
its native city.

Waterford Crystal has a magnificent new
visitor centre that includes an audio-visual
presentation and factory tours to see glass
blowers and cutters at work. Restaurant.
*Main Cork road, 5 km (3 miles) W of city
centre.* Open 8.30am-4.30pm daily, Apr-Oct,
9am-3.15pm Mon-Fri Nov-Mar.
☎ (051) 373311.

The *People's Park, off the Dunmore East
road,* has fine open spaces, while *Mount
Congreve Demesne, 8km (5 miles) W of
Waterford,* ☎ (051) 384115 offers attractive
gardens in a woodland setting. *Tory Hill,
13 km (8 miles) N of Waterford,* affords superb
views of the surrounding plain, Waterford
city and harbour.

EAST CORK

Ardmore *13 km (8 miles) E of Youghal.*
TIO, ☎ (024) 94444, May-Sept. Pleasant
seaside resort with some thatched cottages
and long, sandy beach. Cliff walks above the
village. St Declan's 7th c. monastic settlement
includes a round tower. *Ardmore Pottery, on
coastal road to Cliff House Hotel,* has lots of
locally made craft items. See the grave of
Molly Keane, the noted Anglo-Irish writer,
who died in 1996; she's buried in the tiny
CI graveyard, just off the main street.
Amusement park open during summer.
The new tourist information office is on
the seafront promenade; its design is most
unusual, like a sandcastle.

Ballycotton *32 km (20 miles) W of Youghal.*
Fishing village overlooking bay and lighthouse.
Sandy beaches, cliff walks, good views.

Carrigtwohill *12 km (8 miles) E of Cork
city.* **Barryscourt Castle,** b*etween Fota Island
and Cobh,* open 10.30am-6.30pm daily,
Apr-Oct, ☎ (021) 883864, is a 13th c. castle
with courtyard and towers which have been
restored. Craft and coffee shop.

Cloyne *29 km (18 miles) E of Cork.*
Cloyne Cathedral (CI) is a restored, spacious
14th c. building, with a monument to the one-

Middleton Whiskey Distillery, Middleton, Co. Cork

time bishop of Cloyne, George Berkeley (1685-1753),the noted philosopher. **Cloyne Round Tower,** *opposite the cathedral,* was built in 900,but is still in good condition and can be climbed. Key from house in corner of the cathedral grounds.

Cóbh *24 km (15 miles) E of Cork city.* This fine 19th c. seaside town, with a Brighton-style "Crescent" or terrace of Georgian houses, is enjoying a revival. The main reason for Cóbh's resurgence is the **Queenstown Story,** open 10am-6pm, daily, all year, ☎ (021) 8213591. *Located in part of the railway station,* it tells how innumerable people emigrated through Cóbh (formerly Queenstown) to North America during the past two centuries. It also records the details of the great trans-Atlantic liners that once called to Cork Harbour (these days, liners like the QE2 still call from time to time) and the sinking of the Lusitania, off Kinsale Head in 1915. The **Lusitania Memorial,** *on the quayside.* Many victims of the tragedy are buried at Cóbh's Old Church cemetery.

Cóbh Museum, open 3pm-6pm Wed, May-Sept, 30m-6pm Sun, all year, ☎ (021) 811562, in the former Presbyterian church, has many items relating to the town's history. **St Colman's Cathedral (C)** *on the hill above the town* is a magnificent 19th c. Gothic edifice with carillon to match. Recitals are often given in summer. **Regular harbour trips** *are run from Kennedy Pier,* Cóbh. Tel. Marine Transport, ☎ (021) 811485. A new car ferry connects Cóbh to Ringaskiddy, across Cork Harbour, which means that you can avoid driving through Cork city. The new River Lee tunnel, due to open late summer 1998, will also be useful for avoiding city centre traffic jams, especially if you are coming from

Dublin and going towards Cork airport, Ringaskiddy or West Cork.

Fota Island *16 km (10 miles) E of Cork.* **Wildlife Park,** has many exotic species of animals, including antelopes, giraffes, emus and ostriches. The arboretum is one of the finest in Ireland. Walled gardens. Open 10am-6pm Mon-Sat, 2pm-6pm Sun, all year. ☎ (021) 812678.

Glanmire *6 km (4 miles) E of Cork.* **Dunkathel House,** open 2pm-6pm Wed-Sun, May-Oct, ☎ (021) 821014, is an attractive 18th c. building, full of antiques and paintings. **Riverstown House,** open 2pm-6pm Thurs-Sat, May-Sept, ☎ (021) 821205. Built in 1602 and rebuilt in 1745, the house features fine plasterwork and an art gallery.

Midleton *22 km (14 miles) E of Cork.* **Jameson Heritage Centre,** open 10am-6pm daily, Mar-Oct. Last tour at 4.30pm. Mon-Fri, tours at 12 noon and 3pm, Sat, Sun, 2 pm and 3.30pm, Nov-Feb. ☎ (021) 613594. The old whiskey distillery, in use between 1825 and 1975, is now an impressive centre detailing the history and methods of whiskey distillation.

Shanagarry *3 km (2 miles) NW of Ballycotton.* This castle, which belonged to William Penn, 17th c. Quaker who founded the US State of Pennsylvania, has been restored by Stephen Pearce, owner of the nearby pottery.

Youghal *48 km (30 miles) E of Cork.* Pop.5,500. TIO, ☎ (024) 92390, June-mid-Sept. This historic walled town and seaport is starting to realise its tourist potential, with the opening of its new heritage centre.

Go and see the place before it's over-developed. Youghal is most attractively set, between steep hillsides and the broad expanse of the Blackwater estuary. Founded by the Anglo-Normans in the 13th c., many of the town's medieval buildings can still be see along the 1.5 km (1 mile) long Main Street.

The Heritage Centre, *in the Old Market House,* open 9.30am-5.30pm Mon-Fri, all year, ☎ (024) 92390, tells the story of Youghal and its seaborne trade. The four storey clock tower, nearby, was built in 1777 to straddle the main street and during a period of insurrection in the late 1790s, rebels were often hanged from the windows to discourage others. The **Devonshire Arms Hotel** *in Pearse Square, at the S end of Main Street,* has many old photographs of the old Youghal sailing schooners. The **Moby Dick pub,** *just off the quays,* has film stills and other photographs of the making of the film Moby Dick in Youghal in 1954.

St Mary's Collegiate Church (CI) was built in the 11th c. and is one of Ireland's finest medieval churches. Standing in the shadow of the towns walls, **Myrtle Grove House,** ☎ (024) 92274, is where Sir Walter Raleigh lived. He brought the potato and tobacco to this part of the world and lived in this house when he was Mayor of Youghal in the 16th c. Regular guided tours.

Perk's Amusement Park *is on the S side of the town, near the former railway station* for the old Youghal-Cork line. There are also some 8 km (5 miles) in the vicinity of Youghal.

NORTH CORK AND THE BLACKWATER VALLEY

Annes Grove Gardens *1.5 km (1 mile) SE of Castletownroche.* Open 10am-5pm Mon-Fri, 1pm-6pm Sat, Sun, Easter-Sept, ☎ (022) 26145. The gardens sweep down to the River Awbeg, a tributary of the Blackwater. Several of them, including the cliff garden and the walled garden, contain many rare trees and shrubs, which are displayed in a naturalistic manner, a 'must' for every true gardener.

Ballyporeen *13 km (8 miles) E of Mitchelstown.* The great grandfather of Ronald Reagan, US President, 1981-1989, lived here over 150 years ago. Ronald and Nancy Reagan visited the area in 1984. The heritage centre at the cross roads has material commemorating that visit.

Buttevant *11 km (7 miles) N of Mallow.* **Buttevant Friary,** beside the River Awbeg,

Evening From Mount Gabriel, Co. Cork

was an Augustinian foundation built in the 13th c. Its chancel walls are still largely intact, as is the dovecote. The world's first steeplechase was staged in this area in 1752, from the steeple at Doneraile to the steeple at Buttevant.

Churchtown, *5 km (3 miles) NW of Buttevant.* Delightful small village; many of its houses were estate houses. A detailed heritage centre is being planned.

Doneraile
10 km (6 miles) NE of Mallow. Canon Sheehan, the author, was parish priest here 1895-1913 and is commemorated by a memorial. *Doneraile Wildlife Park* has herds of deer in mature parkland setting. Open 8am-8.30pm Mon-Fri, 10am-8.30pm Sat, 11am-7pm Sun, BH, Apr-Oct, 8am-4.30pm, Mon-Fri, 10am-4.30pm Sat, Sun, BH, Nov-Mar. ☎ (022) 24244. The ruins of Doneraile Court are being restored.

Fermoy *30 km (19 miles) E of Mallow.* Delightfully situated on the banks of the River Blackwater, the town has some fine riverside walks. The promenade is lined with stately trees, while on the opposite side of the river are the wooded grounds of *Castlehyde House.*

Kanturk *16 km (10 miles) NW of Mallow.* This fine looking market town is set on the Rivers Allua and Dallua which are spanned by three bridges. The main bridge has interesting 18th c. poetic descriptions carved on its parapet. Work on *Kanturk Castle* stopped about 1609, because the English Privy Council decided it was too grand for an Irish subject (the local chieftain was MacDonagh MacCarthy). Consequently, the building was never finished, although the substantial ruins can still be seen. *Assolas House,* a 17th c. manor house, is now a hotel and has many fine furnishings and a well-tended garden.

Kilcoman *5 km (3 miles) N of Doneraile.* The 16th c. English poet, Edmund Spenser, lived in *Kilcoman Castle* for eight years and is said to have written much of the Fairie Queen here. Access to the ruins is difficult and in any case, they are best seen from afar. *Kilcoman Bog* ☎ (022) 24200 is a bird observatory, with many rare species, including Greenland white-fronted geese.

Kildorrery *13 km (8 miles) W of Mitchelstown.* Site of *Bowen's Court,* where

the distinguished novelist Elizabeth Bowen once lived. The location is marked, although the house was sold in 1959 and later demolished.

Killavullen *10 km (6 miles) E of Mallow.* This 250 year old house, once the ancestral home of the Hennessy brandy family, stands on a cliff overlooking the River Blackwater. There are caves nearby, although they have not been developed as a tourist attraction and should only be explored by experts.

Longueville House *5 km (3 miles) W of Mallow.* This fine early 18th c. house has been converted into an hotel. It has its own vineyard, one of several in the N Cork/ Waterford area. The restaurant has portraits of all the Presidents of Ireland.

Macroom *37 km (24 miles) NW of Cork.* Lively mid-Cork market town was once the property of Admiral Sir William Penn, whose son founded Pennsylvania. Penn Castle, now mostly demolished, stands in the town square. Browne's drapery store in the square is a rare survivor from the old days of Irish retailing. The riverside *Bealick flour mill* is being restored to its former glory.

Mallow *35 km (22 miles) N of Cork. Pop.6,000.* Tourist information point, Bridge Street. Now a prosperous market town and agricultural processing centre, Mallow had a much livelier reputation in the 18th and 19th c., when visitors would come to take the waters and indulge in riotous living. Their antics are reflected in the song, The Rakes of Mallow. The present day town is altogether more sedate. *Mallow Castle* is not open, but visitors can wander the grounds, which extend to the River Blackwater, and see the herds of deer on the estate. Thomas Davis, the 19th c. patriot writer, was baptised in 1814 in *St Anne's Church,* which dates from the 13th c. The ruins of a 17th c. church can be seen at the entrance to the demesne. *Mallow Racecourse* has been imaginatively redeveloped. ☎ (022) 21592. *Nano Nagle Heritage Centre, 12 km (7 miles) W of Mallow.* The centre commemorates the 18th c. educational pioneer, who founded the Presentation Sisters in Cork was a formative influence on Irish education.

Millstreet *40 km (25 miles) SW of Mallow.* Small, enterprising town, a horse racing centre. Museum. *Country Park* has open landscapes, deer farm, audio-visual theatre. Open 10am-7pm daily, Apr-Oct.

Mitchelstown *34 km (21 miles) NE of Mallow.* This undistinguished-looking town with its busy Main Street is a thriving agricultural processing centre. The monument in the main square commemorates men shot at a Land League meeting in 1887. See also *St Fanahan's Holy Well;* the saint died over 1,500 years ago. The water in the well is said to have curative powers. *Burncourt House,*

13 km (8 miles) NE of Mitchelstown. See the shell of the 17th c. house which the owner burned before he would allow Cromwell to occupy it.

Mitchelstown Caves, *16 km (10 miles) NE of Mitchelstown.* Open 10am-6pm daily, all year. ☎ (052) 67246. Access to the new cave is easy and a guide will take you on a 3 km (2 miles) tour of the passages and chambers. The old cave can only be reached by rope or ladder.

CORK CITY AND LEESIDE

Ballincollig *8 km (5 miles)W of city centre.* The late 18th c. gunpowder mills have been restored as a Heritage Centre. Open 10am-6pm daily, Apr-Sept. ☎ (021) 874430.

Blackrock *3 km (2 miles) SE of Cork city centre.* **Cork Heritage Park** has a centre detailing many aspects of local history, including the fire service, transport and the Pike family, Quakers who gave sustenance during the 19th c. famine. Also details of boatbuilding, other local crafts and Cork Harbour. Open 10am-5.30pm daily, Apr-Sept, ☎ (021) 358854.

Blarney *8 km (5 miles) NW of Cork city.* Blarney Castle and Stone, open from 9am daily all year. Closing time varies. ☎ (021) 385282. Climb more than 100 steps to the battlements of the central keep, which is all that's left of this 15th c. castle. Hang upside down, with an attendant holding your feet, and kiss the stone, whereupon you'll be blessed with the gab. If you want to stay the strong silent type, simply admire the lush pastoral views. The castle gardens have pleasant walks and include a grove of ancient yew trees.

Three days is the stay of your cattle in the pound for a quarrel in the ale house, injury of thy chief, over-working a valuable horse, maiming thy chained dog, disturbing a fair or a great assembly, or striking or violating thy wife.

Five days for satirizing a man after his death

An extract from *Irish Laws* published by Appletree Press

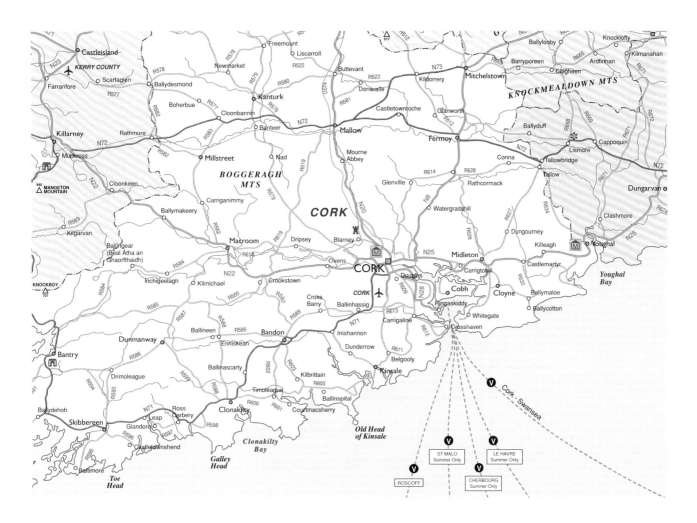

Blarney Castle House, open 12 noon-6pm
Mon-Sat, June-Sept. Built in the Scottish
baronial style, complete with turrets and
gables. The interior has been fully refurbished
and has many family portraits. Many craft
shops are clustered around the green, near
the castle entrance. The biggest store is the
Blarney Woollen Mills, in a converted 19th c.
factory. **Blarney Woodland Farm,** *Waterloo
Road,* open 10am-6pm daily, ☎ (021) 385733.
Has many farmyard pets, tearoom.

Cork *259 km (161 miles) SW of Dublin.*
Pop. 130,000. TIO, Grand Parade,
☎ (021) 273251,all year. The second city
of the Republic retains a strong hold on its
originality and separateness. In the 19th c., it
emerged as a centre of the Fenian movement,
earning Cork the title of "Rebel City". A large
portion of the city centre was burned down
during the War of Independence, only to be
rebuilt in a flat, dull style. Today, Cork is
keenly aware of its cultural, social and literary
heritage and this is reflected in various new
developments. The **Cork Choral Festival**
in May, its **Film Festival** in October and the
Jazz Festival, also in October, are just three
of the year's cultural highlights.

St Finbarre's Cathedral (CI) *near the South
Mall,* was built in the early French Gothic
style over a century ago and has fine carvings
and mosaics. See the cannonball fired during
the 1690 siege of Cork, which was found

embedded in the tower of the previous
church on this site. **Christ Church** is now
an archives centre at South Main Street,
☎ (021) 277809. Built in 1702, some
foundations date from the Norman church
built on this site about 1270 and badly
damaged in the 1690 siege. **Church of Christ
the King (C),** *Turner's Cross, NW Cork,*
is one of Ireland's most stunning modern
churches, with equally impressive views over
the city. **Red Abbey, between George's Quay
and Douglas Street.** The square tower is all
that's left of this medieval abbey, the oldest
structure in Cork. **St Anne's (CI):** would-be
Quasimodos can ring tunes on the Shandon
bells. The church has a small, interesting
historical exhibition, including books.
Honan Chapel, University College, was built
in 1915/16 and has superb stained-glass
windows by Harry Clarke and Sarah Purser.

Public Museum, open 11am-5pm Mon-Fri,
3pm-5pm Sun, all year. Closed on BH.
☎ (021) 276871. Located in Fitzgerald Park,
the museum has a natural history section,
an ogham stone collection, old photographs,
notably of the 1916-1922 period, old
documents and a reference library. The former
Women's Gaol, *Sunday's Well,* has been
turned into a fine heritage centre, with very
realistic cell reconstructions and an audio-
visual presentation. The building was the
improbable setting for Cork's first radio
station, 6CK, in the late 1920s. The new

Wireless Story broadcasting museum
includes a recreation of that first studio,
old radio equipment and other memorabilia.
Open daily, all year, ☎ (021) 305022.
Collins Barracks has a Michael Collins
museum, with memorabilia of the great man
and a second museum, devoted to Irish troops
who have served with the UN since 1960.
By arr, ☎ (021) 514000. Cork's mainline
railway station has an 1848 **steam locomotive**
that clocked up nearly half a million miles
for the old Great Southern Railway.

Triskel Arts Centre, *Tobin Street, off South
Main Street,* ☎ (021) 272022 has regular
performances, exhibitions, restaurant, wine
bar. It's expanding its facilities in 1998.
Crawford Municipal School of Art, open
10am-5pm Mon-Fri,10am-1pm Sat, all year.
Displays of many local scenes depicted in
watercolour and oils, together with sculptures
and a collection of classical statues from the
Vatican. Restaurant. There are also frequent
exhibitions at the **Cork Arts Society Gallery,**
16 Lavitt's Quay, open 11am-6pm Tues-Sat,
☎ (021) 277749. The **Opera House,**
Emmet Place, ☎ (021) 270022 has regular
performances of drama, opera and variety.

The **Everyman Palace Theatre,**
MacCurtain Street, is a revival of a 19th c.
theatre originally built as a music hall.
University College, *Cork,* has a new theatre
at the Mardyke and the **Cork School of**

St. Finbarr's Cathedral, Cork City

Cork has a good selection of pubs, including Le Chateau, Patrick Street, frequented by Examiner journalists and opera singers; An Bodhran, Oliver Plunkett Street, for traditional Irish music; Dan Lowery's, MacCurtain Street, for period atmosphere and the Long Valley, Winthrop Street, a traditional pub.

The *Lee Walk Fields* offer good riverside walks opposite the County Hall on the western approaches to the city and there are excellent strolls along the riverside quays upstream from the city centre. *Fitzgerald Park* has sculptures as a diversion from walking. The *Marina Park, 3 km (2 miles) downstream from the city centre* and *The Lough, S of the city centre,* is a wildlife habitat full of bird species.

Crosshaven *27 km (17 miles) SE of Cork.* The narrow main street of this delightful seaside town has interesting pubs and shops. Walk up the hill to *St Brigid's Church (C)* for fine views of the surrounding area. The *Royal Cork Yacht Club* here was founded in 1720, making it the oldest in the world. Climb the headland road from Crosshaven to *Fort Camden,* a great military fortification built in the late 18th c., for fine views over Cork Harbour, the largest natural harbour in Europe. *Carrigdhoun Pottery,* open daily, all year, ☎ (021) 372305.

Kilcrea Abbey *8 km (5 miles) W of Ballincollig.* The grave of Noble Art O'Leary is here; he was killed in 1773 because he wouldn't sell his horse for £5. At that time, Catholics were forbidden to own a horse worth more. *Opposite the abbey* are the ruins of *Kilcrea Castle.*

Tracton *5 km (3 miles) S of Carrigaline.* See the aptly named 'Overdraft' pub and enjoy extensive forest walks. Continue S for about 16 km (10 miles) to Nohaval; a maze of side roads here bring you to the very quiet coastline.

WEST CORK

Adrigole, Beara Peninsula
20 km (12 miles) SW of Glengarriff. The road over the *Healy Pass* was started during the great mid-19th c. famine and only completed in 1931. It's an arduous drive, but if the weather is clear, you will be rewarded with tremendous views.

Ahakista *18 km (12 miles) SW of Bantry.* Just before the tiny windswept village is the impressive memorial to the 329 victims of the Air India jumbo jet that crashed into the Atlantic in 1985. The narrow, winding road continues for a further 16 km (10 miles) to the tip of the *Sheep's Head peninsula.*

Music, Union Quay, has regular evening recitals.

Elizabeth Fort, near the Beamish & Crawford brewery, was built in the early 17th c. and has had many changes of use since then. There are excellent views over the city from its parapets. Daly's Suspension Bridge, Sunday's Well, also offers fine vistas of the River Lee, while the Tanto Footbridge at Blackrock also gives good river views. Carey's Lane, off Patrick Street, was once home to Cork's Huguenots; now, it's an interesting quarter for craft shops and restaurants.

Shandon Craft Centre, opposite St Anne's Church, has interesting workshops, while the adjoining *Cork Butter Museum* tells the story of how butter used to be brought from other parts of Co Cork and from Co Kerry into Cork city for export. The *English Market* dates from Victorian times and is a fine, covered food emporium. Food specialities sold here include two that are unique to Cork, crubeens (pigs' trotters) and drisheen (a type of black pudding). For those unaccustomed to such delicacies, a strong stomach is recommended! There's also an open air market at Coal Quay.

Allihies *9 km (6 miles) W of Castletownbere.* The remains of the 19th c. copper mine should be explored with care. Near the village is a fine strand.

Ballinascarthy *8 km (5 miles) N of Clonakilty.* Site of the homestead (private property),where William Ford, father of Henry Ford, the US motor pioneer, was born. Plans to develop a museum.

Ballinspittle *8 km (5 miles) SW of Kinsale.* Kilmore flour mill dates back to mid-17th c. and has been excellently restored. Open daily.

Ballydehob *16 km (10 miles) S of Bantry.* Quaint harbour. The winding and decorative village streets have craft workshops, but the main highlight is the former railway viaduct that has been converted into a walkway, giving panoramic views of *Roaring Water Bay.*

Baltimore *13 km (8 miles) SW of Skibbereen.* Centuries old fishing village, full of atmosphere. From the White Beacon atop the cliffs above Baltimore, you get fine views of the harbour and Sherkin Island, as far as Cape Clear Island. From the *Baltimore Diving and Water Sports Centre,* ☎ (028) 20300 visitors can go down to explore the many wrecks in the area.

Bandon *21 km (13 miles) NW of Kinsale.* Busy, if straggling, market town. The *Heritage Centre* in former Christ Church (CI), built in 1610 and one of the very first Protestant churches in Ireland. Now detailed displays of local history, with old shops and pubs recreated. Open daily, summer. *Bandon Weir,* open by arr., ☎ (023) 41533 has a salmon leap viewing area and a wildlife sanctuary. See pottery being made at *R & J Forrester's Craft Shop and Gallery, 83 North Main Street,* ☎ (023) 41360.

Bantry *92 km (57 miles) W of Cork. TIO, The Square,* ☎ (027) 50229, June-Sept. Delightfully placed town at head of Bantry Bay. *Bantry House* was built in the mid 18th c. and is exquisitely furnished with tapestries and furniture. The hall, dining and drawing rooms are especially interesting. Some upstairs rooms are open to visitors. The gardens, with their Italianate terraces, more than repay exploration, particularly with the stunning views across the bay. It's one of the locations for the West Cork classical music festival, Aug. Craft shop, tea room. The new *French Armada Centre,* open 10am-6pm daily, Mar-Oct, ☎ (027) 51796, details the abortive French landing in Bantry Bay in 1796. The *Kilnaurane Inscribed Stone, near the Westlodge Hotel,* has an early 7th c. carving and is unique to West Cork, an area full of such ancient artefacts.

Béal-na-mBláth *3 km (2 miles) SW of Crookstown.* Memorial to General Michael Collins, killed here in 1922. The house where he was born, at *Woodfield, 8km (5 miles) SW of Clonakilty,* has been turned into a Collins memorial centre.

Bere Island *3 km (2 miles) E of Castletownbere.* Frequent ferries, daily, all year. The ferry trip across from Castletownbere takes about 30 minutes in calm weather. Tourist accommodation on this island with a permanent population of about 230 is limited. Explore the ruins of the former Royal Navy base, abandoned in 1938. Sailing tuition at the *Glenans Sailing Centre,* ☎ (027) 75012. Sea angling.

Castletownbere *51 km (32 miles) SW of Bantry.* This small fishing town is a good centre for exploring the rugged beauties of the Beara Peninsula. The large town square is surrounded

The health of the salmon to you,
A long life,
A full heart
And a wet mouth.

An extract from *Irish Toasts*
published by Appletree Press

by some interesting shops and pubs. Just S of the town is the great ruined shell of *Dunboy Castle,* built in the 19th c. by the Puxley family, who owned the copper mines at Allihies on the other side of the peninsula (qv). The castle was burned down in 1921, during the War of Independence.

Castletownshend *8 km (5 miles) SE of Skibbereen.* Very attractive single street village. The road descends steeply to the tiny harbour and used to be divided halfway down by two great trees. Edith Somerville and Violet Martin, co-authors of The Irish RM and his Experiences, and other humorous stories of the old Anglo-Irish way of life in West Cork, lived in the village and are buried in the graveyard of *St Barrahane's Church (CI), up steps off the end of the main street.*

Charles Fort *5 km (3 miles) S of Kinsale on E shores of the estuary.* Open 10am-6pm daily, Apr-Oct, ☎ (021) 772263. This star-shaped fort, built in late 17th c., is in a good state of preservation. Fine views out to see. Enjoyable walk back to Kinsale, taking in the Church of Ireland graveyard in nearby Summercove, enjoying refreshments in the 200 year old Bulman pub here and concluding in the Spaniard in Kinsale, dating back to the 17th c.

Clear Island *10 km (6 miles) SW of Baltimore.* Ferry from Baltimore all year and from Schull in summer. ☎ (028) 20125. The new pier on the island helps improve access. A tiny museum with relics of the island's history and a bird observatory are virtually the only man-made attractions on the island, which is one of the last places in West Cork where Irish survives as a living language.

Clonakilty *35 km (22 miles) SW of Kinsale.* TIO, Rossa Street, ☎ (023) 33226, July, Aug. An attractive angling centre at the head of Clonakilty Bay. Many of the shopfronts in its winding streets have their names in traditional Irish lettering. The Wheel of Fortune, a cast iron contraption, dates from about 1840 when the town got its first proper water supply. *Emmet Square* has well-preserved Georgian-style houses near Kennedy Gardens. *West Cork Regional Museum,* Western Road, open 10.30am-5pm Mon-Sat, 2.30pm-5.30pm, Sun, May-Sept, has archaeological relics, mementoes of the town's industrial past, including brewing, the post office, social life and much on Michael Collins. The new highlight of the town is the *Model Village,* open daily, all year, ☎ (023) 33224. It's virtually completed now and has models of the main buildings in the towns of West Cork and a miniature of the much-missed West Cork Railway. The station building, which houses a restaurant, is a full-sized replica of Clonakilty's original station on the line.

Lisselan Castle, 3 km (2x miles) from Clonakilty on the Bandon road, has

West Cork landscape

homestead farm and gardens. Open 10am-5pm Thurs, Apr-Sept, ☎ (023) 33249.

Coppinger's Court *3 km (2 miles) SW of Rosscarbery.* Ruins of the 1610 mansion which burned down 30 years after it was built. It was said to have had a chimney for every month, a door for every week and a window for every day of the year.

Courtmacsherry *5 km (3 miles) E of Timoleague.* Attractive seaside village looking out on the estuary and backed by woods. Sea angling centre.

Creagh Gardens, *6 km (4 miles) SW of Skibbereen.* Open 10am-6pm daily, Easter-Sept. ☎ (028) 22121. These privately owned gardens covering about 12 ha (5 acres) run to the banks of the River Ilen. They have a variety of trees and shrubs.

Crookhaven *20 km (12 miles) SW of Schull.* This tiny harbour is near the end of the Mizen Head peninsula. Just W of the harbour is the site of the Pilchard Palace, once used for storing fish. Nearby Barley Cove, with its magnificent sandy beach, is a popular resort.

Derreen Woodland Garden

Near Lauragh, on N shores of Beara peninsula. Open 2pm-6pm Sun, Tues, Thurs, Apr-Sept, ☎ (064) 83103. First planted over a century ago, a splendid location for many specimen trees and shrubs.

Dursey Island *25 km (15 miles) W of Castletownbere.* This small, sparsely populated island has few facilities for visitors, but the trip across on the cable car is an experience in itself. There are regular daily services, ☎ (027) 73018. There is only one tiny village on the island, Kilmichael. The island has only one road, but it leads to the old and new lighthouses at the W end. Otherwise, the main delight is plenty of fresh sea air!

Garinish Island *off Glengarriff*
Open 10am-4.30pm Mon-Sat, 1pm-5pm Sun, Mar, Oct, 10am-6.30pm Mon-Sat, 1pm-7pm Sun, Apr-June, Sept, 9.30am-6.30pm Mon-Sat, 11am-7pm Sun, July, Aug.
☎ (027) 63040. Regular boats from the mainland, last landing 30 minutes before closing. Marvellous Italianate gardens designed early this century, with Grecian-style temple, old Martello tower, shrubberies, miniature Japanese and rock gardens.

Garretstown Courtmacsherry Bay, *10 km (6 miles) SW of Kinsale.* Good beaches on the shores of the bay and woodland walks. See what is left of the Manor House that once stood here and the orange groves.

Glandore *6 km (4 miles) W of Rosscarbery.* Extravagantly set village overlooking Glandore harbour. The higher part of the village, with its broad main street, gives fine views of the harbour.

Glengarriff *18 km (11 miles) W of Bantry.* Small coastal village set in a glen. The Eccles Hotel, built in early 19th c., and refurbished, has mementoes of George Bernard Shaw, the author and dramatist. Glengarriff Woods offers excellent walks. Boats to Garinish Island, qv.

Goleen , *15 km (9 miles) SW of Schull.* This tiny village on the Mizen Head peninsula has a new **Heritage Centre** *in the former CI church,* open daily, summer, ☎ (028) 21766. Has old agricultural implements and quirky local historical items.

Gougane Barra *24 km (15 miles) NE of Bantry.* This lake, surrounded on three sides by mountains, seems almost Norwegian in its severity; it's the source of the River Lee that flows through Cork city. Oratory on the island is reached by a short causeway from the mainland.

Inchadoney Island, *3 km (2 miles) S of Clonakilty.* Despite its name, it's actually part of the mainland. The long, golden sands are ideal for bathing and surfing.

Inishannon, *13 km (8 miles) NW of Kinsale.* This small village with broad main street is home to Alice Taylor, well-known Irish author. The ruins of the 15th c. *Dundaniel Castle stands on the banks of the River Bandon.*

James's Fort *4 km (2.5 miles) SW of Kinsale.* On the W side of the estuary at Kinsale, James's Fort was built in the early 17th c. and is approached by the bridge over the Bandon River. An older structure, Charles' Fort, is on the opposite side of the river, qv. Free access at all times.

Kinsale *29 km (18 miles) SW of Cork.* Pop.1,800. TIO, Pier Road, ☎ (021) 772234, Mar-Nov. Kinsale is an extravagantly set town overlooking the Bandon River estuary. It is a consistent winner in the Tidy Towns competition and is popular with holidaymakers, the yachting and sea angling fraternity and gourmets. Many experts consider Kinsale to be the gourmet capital of Ireland. The town was captured by the Spanish in 1601-2; they held it against English armies. Somehow, that Spanish flavour seems to have lingered. The narrow, winding street of Kinsale have been compared with those of Toledo. However, Kinsale has become a victim of its own success; it's so packed with visitors at peak times that it's best to visit at quieter times of the year. Many local people also consider that the town has been over-prettified in the interests of tourism.

BAKED SALMON

An expensive but fine dish…

1 whole fresh salmon (about 5 lb/2kg), parsley, salt & pepper, ¹/₂ cup butter, ¹/₂ cup dry cider, ¹/₂ pt/250 ml/ 1 cup double cream (serves eight to ten)

Clean and descale salmon, cut of the head and tail and trim the fins. Stuff the parsley into the gullet. Butter some aluminium foil and form an envelope around the fish, sealing both ends, leaving the top open for a moment. Dot the rest of the butter over the salmon, season and pour over the cider and the cream. Seal the top leaving a small vent. Bake in the oven for 1¹/₄ hours at gas mark 4, 350°F, 180°C. When ready take from the oven, remove the skin and reduce the sauce by boiling, stirring all the time. Serve with boiled potatoes and fresh garden peas.

An extract from *A Little Irish Cook Book* published by Appletree Press

St Multose Church (CI) has a fine interior, with old town stocks and flags from the Battle of Waterloo. Some victims of the Lusitania sinking off the Old Head of Kinsale in 1915 are buried in the graveyard here. *St John the Baptist Church (C), Friar's Street,* has an ornate, T-shaped, 19th c. interior. There are excellent views over the town from front of Carmelite Friary.

Desmond Castle, open 10am-6pm,Tues-Sun, Apr-Oct, ☎ (021) 774026. Also known as the "French prison", the castle is a three storey town house built around 1500. It now houses the *Wine Museum,* telling the story of the Wine Geese, Irish people who set sail for foreign lands and contributed much to wine production in such regions as Bordeaux in France and the sherry district of S Spain.

Kinsale Museum, in the 17th c. courthouse, open 11am-5pm Mon-Sat, 3pm-5pm Sun, all year, ☎ (021) 772044, has many relics and memorabilia on the town's history, besides much material relating to the Lusitania. Kinsale is also planning a heritage centre, nearby. See also the *Bowling Green,* a delightful small park *halfway up the hill on the W side of the harbour.*

Lough Hyne *6 km (4 miles) S of Skibbereen.* This enclosed lake, with a narrow outlet to the sea, is a marine nature reserve, with many rare species. It's not suitable for bathing. The vantage point in the forest on the N side of the lake offers fine views.

Mizen Head *25 km (15 miles) SW of Schull.* The old lighthouse on the head has been turned into a *Heritage Centre,* open daily, Mar-Oct, ☎ (028) 35591. It details local history and nature and the building of the Fastnet lighthouse. Wrecks in the area are also detailed.

Old Head of Kinsale *15 km (9 miles) SW of Kinsale.* Although much of the Head is now covered by a golf course, it still has some good walks and you can also see some fine seascapes, plus the ruins of a 15th c. de Courcey castle.

Ross Carbery *21 km (13 miles) E of Skibbereen.* Set around a square of enormous proportions, Rosscarbery has a striking 17th c. cathedral (CI) and some ruins of a 6th c. monastery. Safe, sandy beaches in the vicinity.

Schull *6 km (4 miles) SW of Ballydehob.* Delightful village set around an almost totally enclosed harbour, replete with craft shops, restaurants and bookshops. The *Planetarium,* ☎ (028) 28552 has frequent shows. However, Schull is so popular that it's over-crowded in the peak summer months, when it is known as Dublin 4 on sea, because so many of the inhabitants of Dublin 4 come to their holiday homes in this area.

Sherkin Island *Just off Baltimore, the crossing takes about 10 minutes.* Attractions include an outdoor pursuits centre, marine station, natural history museum and the ruins of 15th c. Franciscan friary. Some safe, sandy beaches.

Skibbereen *34 km (21 miles) SW of Bantry.* TIO, North Street, ☎ (028) 21766, all year.

Busy market town on the River Ilen. The *West Cork Arts Centre, North Street,* ☎ (028) 22090 has frequent events and exhibitions all year. The *Southern Star* newspaper offices, Ilen Street, has files of the old Skibbereen Eagle newspaper, which kept an eye on the Czar of Russia. The *Pro-Cathedral* dates from 1826.

At *Abbeystrewery, on W outskirts of Skibbereen,* many local victims of the mid-19th c. famine are buried and commemorated. *Sky Gardens, 3 km (2 miles) W of Skibbereen.* Open 2pm-6pm Tues-Thurs, all year, ☎ (028) 22368. A natural wildlife garden, complete with waterfall and wildflower meadow. Also contemporary sculpture.

Timoleague *16 km (10 miles) W of Kinsale.* Small village on the estuary of the Argideen River. *Timoleague Castle Gardens,* open 12 noon-6pm daily, Easter weekend and mid-May-mid-Sept, ☎ (028) 46116. The gardens have been developed over the past 150 years and include palm trees, besides two old-style walled gardens, one for flowers, the other for fruit and vegetables.

Unionhall *15 km (9 miles) E of Skibbereen.* On the opposite side of the harbour to Glandore. *Céim Folk Museum,* open daily, ☎ (028) 36280 is a unique collection of historical artefacts, including Stone Age, collected by one person, Therese O'Mahony.

RING OF KERRY AND KILLARNEY'S LAKES

Aghadoe Hill *5 km (3 miles) N of Killarney.* Ruins of a 7th c. church and castle and magnificent views of lakes and mountains surrounding Killarney.

Ballinskelligs *13 km (8 miles) NE of Waterville.* Miles of golden beaches on the shores of Waterville Bay. See also the Cill Rialaig village crafts centre.

Cahirsiveen *40 km (25 miles) E of Killarney. O'Connell Memorial Church (C), Main Street,* was built in 1888 to commemorate Daniel O'Connell, who was born just outside the village in 1775. The ruins of his birthplace, *Carhan House,* can still be seen. The new *heritage centre* looks rather like something out of Disneyland, with all its turrets and towers. Improbably, it used to be an RIC barracks, burned during the War of Independence. Today, the centre has much material on local history, including the Valentia Weather Observatory. Open 10am-6pm, Mon-Sat, all year, also 10am-6pm Sun, summer. ☎ (066) 72589.

Boats at anchor on the Kenmare River (Ring of Kerry)

Killarney *305 km (190 miles) SW of Dublin.*
Pop. 7,500. TIO, Town Hall, ☎ (064) 31633, all year. At first, it's a rather undistinguished looking town, packed with jaunting cars and tourists and owing its central location to Co Kerry's lake district. However, Killarney does have a good range of facilities for visitors, including restaurants and craft shops, and interesting historical buildings.

The *Cathedral of St Mary of the Assumption (C)* was designed by Pugin, that great 19th c. architect, while *St Mary's Church (CI) in the town centre,* has a richly decorated Victorian interior. The modern *Prince of Peace Church (C), Fossa, near Killarney,* was made by craftspeople from all over Ireland and its main door features dove and ark motifs by Helen Moloney. The *Franciscan Friary (C), College Street,* dates from 1860 and has a fine Harry Clarke stained glass window. Frequent arts and cultural events at the *Killarney Art Gallery, 47 High Street,* ☎ (064) 34628 and the *Frank Lewis Gallery, 6 Bridewell Lane,* ☎ (064) 31108.

The Museum of Irish Transport, town centre, open 10am-6pm daily, all year, ☎ (064) 34677, has many veteran and vintage cars. *Killarney Model Railway, Beech Road,* ☎ (064)34000, open daily, all year. *Coolwood Wildlife Sanctuary,* open 10am-6pm daily, all year, ☎ (064) 36288 has scenic walks, children's playground, coffee shop. *Reidy's shop in the Main Street* is worth seeing. It's one of the last traditional style grocery shops in Ireland. With its old-fashioned weighing scales, cash registers ringing up pounds, shillings and pence, and hooks in the ceiling for hanging Christmas hams and turkeys, it preserves the pre-supermarket era perfectly. It's an ideal nostalgia trip for visitors to the town, who can also relax in the bar at the back of the shop - in the old style. Open 9am-6pm Mon-Sat, all year. ☎ (064) 31011.

Derrynane House *Caherdaniel, 21 km (13 miles) W of Sneem.* Open 1pm-5pm Tues-Sun, Apr, Oct, 9am-6pm Mon-Sat, 11am-7pm Sun, May-Sept, 1pm-5pm Sat, Sun, Nov-Mar. ☎ (066) 75113. This invigorating house has many mementoes of Daniel O'Connell, the great 19th c. constitutional politician, including furniture, paintings and correspondence. Audio-visual show, tearooms. Surrounding coastal parklands, with nature trails.

Gap of Dunloe Tour *10 km (6 miles) W of Killarney.* Firmly on the tourist trail, this makes a memorable trip by jaunting car from either Killarney or by pony and trap from *Kate Kearney's Cottage.* It's also suitable for walkers who don't mind the busy equine traffic.

Glenbeigh *8 km (5 miles) SE of Killorglin.* Small village surrounded by mountains, with magnificent strand nearby. The bar of the Tower Hotel has many photographs of the locality. The *Kerry Bog Village Museum,* open 9am-6pm daily, Mar-Nov, has traditional 19th c. thatched cottages and blacksmith's forge.

Kells *13 miles (8 miles) W of Glenbeigh.* Midway between Glenbeigh and Cahirsiveen with panoramic views of Dingle Bay and the Blasket Islands. The old tunnels in the hillside were part of the railway that used to run from Cahirsiveen to Farranfore Junction, the latter now adjacent to Kerry County Airport.

Kenmare *34 km (21 miles) S of Killarney.* TIO, Market Square, ☎ (064) 41233, Apr-Oct. This delightful town was founded in 1670 and laid out with the three main streets forming a triangle. The *Heritage Centre,* in the same building as the TIO, open 10am-6pm Mon-Sat, Apr-Oct, ☎ (064) 41233, details Kenmare's history, including the nearby Bronze Age stone circle, local industries and personalities. Baroness Thatcher, a former British prime minister, claims descent from a Kenmare washerwoman who emigrated to England in 1811.

Killorglin *21 km (13 miles) W of Killarney.* Though this hilly town, set above the River Launce, may look desolate, it's full of warm, quixotic Kerry character. During the three days and nights of the *Puck Fair* in August, when a goat is hauled aloft to be crowned "King of the Fair", crowds make merry and enjoy the continuously intoxicated craic. The 17th c. *Kerry Woollen Mills, halfway between Killorglin and Killarney.* Open 9am-6pm Mon-Sat, Apr-Oct, 9am-5pm Mon-Fri, Nov-Mar.

Ladies' View *19 km (12 miles) SW of Killarney on N71.* Well over a century ago, Queen Victoria and her ladies-in-waiting were amused by this lovely view. Today, that view is enhanced by a tearoom and craft shops.

Leacanbuile Fort *5 km (3 miles) NW of Cahirsiveen.* Massive prehistoric fort. Excellent views of the nearby coast from its ramparts.

MacGillicuddy's Reeks *W of Killarney and Lough Leane.* Excellent mountain climbing range which includes *Carrantuohill,* Ireland's highest mountain, just over 1,040 metres (3,414 ft) high.

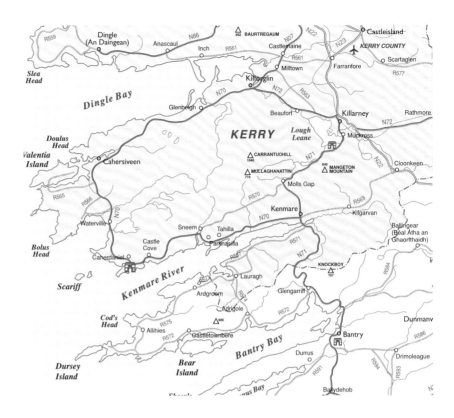

House ruins in Black Valley, MacGillicuddy's Reeks.

Mangerton *8 km (5 miles) S of Killarney, off N71.* Panoramic views of Killarney's lakes.

Meeting of the Waters *10 km (6 miles) S of Killarney, on N71 to Kenmare.* Another beauty spot, where rhododendrons and other sub-tropical species flourish in the mild Kerry climate.

Muckross House *7 km (4 miles) S of Killarney.* Built in the Elizabethan style in 1843, this baronial mansion has many rooms that still retain their original look. Craft workshops in the basement feature such skills as weaving, pottery, book-binding and printing, complemented by a 19th c. style pub. *Muckross Traditional Farm,* a recent addition, shows the old style way of farming and country living. The surrounding *National Park,* with its lake and mountain vistas, is noted for its oak woods and red deer herd. *Visitor Centre* open 9am-5.30pm daily, Nov-mid-Mar, 9am-6pm daily, mid-Mar-June, 9am-7pm daily, July, Aug, 9am-6pm daily, Sept, Oct, ☎ (064) 31440. The old Kenmare Road, from here to Kenmare, gives good walks across the mountains.

Parknasilla *3 km (2 miles) E of Sneem.* It's not a village, but a Great Southern hotel, with mementoes of George Bernard Shaw, the playwright and controversialist, who often stayed here. He and his wife just ignored everyone else in Sneem! Many walks in the grounds, golf.

Pass of Coomakista *8 km (5 miles) S of Waterville.* On the road between Sneem and Waterville, it offers fine views of Ballinskelligs Bay and the Skellig Islands.

Ring of Kerry The road which skirts the Iveragh Peninsula from Kenmare to Killorglin is called the "Ring of Kerry". It stretches for 203 km (126 miles) and a day's drive will take in many places of interest, besides innumerable scenic views.

Bagleo Nest, Long Range, Killarney (Ring of Kerry)

A window with wild flowers near Sneem

Ross Castle *3 km (2 miles) SW of Killarney.* Open 11am-6pm daily, Apr, 10am-6pm daily, May, Sept, 9am-6.30pm daily, June-Aug, 10am-5pm daily, Oct. ☎ (064) 35851. Probably built in the early 15th c. for one of the O'Donoghue Ross chieftains. The castle has been thoroughly restored and can be inspected by guided tour.

Rossdohan Island *Kenmare Bay, 5 km (3 miles) SE of Sneem.* ☎ (064) 45114. This delightful island has many botanical delights.

Skellig Islands *16 km (10 miles) S of Valentia Island.* These two dramatic rocks rise from the sea. Little Skellig is a bird sanctuary, while Skellig Michael contains an ancient monastic settlement on its summit, a fearsome climb. Boats in season from Valentia, also boat trip combining visit to the visitor centre on Valentia, qv.

Sneem *27 km (17 miles) W of Kenmare.* This charming village is situated where the

Ardsheelaun River runs into Kenmare Bay. The short pier is ideal for a stroll. Its two big squares are connected by a narrow bridge. Two presidents are commemorated here, Chaim Herzog, the Irish-born President of Israel and Cearbhaill Ó Dalaigh, a former President of Ireland, who lived nearby after his retirement and who died in 1976.

Sneem Museum, *in the W square,* is open daily in summer. It has a fascinating collection of bric-a-brac and is ideal for browsing. The Church of Ireland, with its tower and its white-painted exterior, may look Elizabethan but in fact it dates from around 1810. Its interior has many photographs from the local manor houses and the pew plates of the one-time owners. Fr Michael Walsh, a 19th c. priest better known as the "Father O'Flynn" of the famous song, is buried in the graveyard of St Michael's (C).

Staigue Fort *20 km (12 miles) W of Sneem. Turn right off the main road at Castlecove.* Probably the finest dry stone fort in Ireland, built about 2,000 years ago and still in almost perfect condition. It's worth climbing to the top of walls on this spectacular circular structure for some fine views.

Torc Waterfall *8 km (5 miles) S of Killarney, just off the road to Kenmare.* One of Ireland's finest waterfalls, which can be seen from an adjacent footpath which ascends alongside. Magnificent lake views.

Valentia Island *SW of Cahirsiveen, road bridge from Portmagee.* The modern **Visitor Centre,** open 10am-7pm daily, May, June, 9.30am-7pm July, Aug, 10am-7pm daily, Oct. ☎ (066) 76306. It tells the story of the Skelligs Islands in audio-visual form. The centre also has a craft shop and coffee shop. After they have seen the show, visitors are taken on a 90 minute cruise around the

Skelligs. Also on the island, see the disused slate quarry, with its grotto, and the site of the long-abandoned Western Union cable station, at the point where the first trans-Atlantic cable came ashore in 1866.

Bray Head *on the SW tip of the island* and **Geokaun Mountain** *on the N of the island,* form first class vantage points for scenic views. **Knightstown Harbour,** the main village on the island, has an atmospheric harbour.

Waterville *65 km (39 miles) W of Kenmare.* A popular resort town, although the main street is unimpressive. The **Butler Arms Hotel** has some fine photographs of Charlie Chaplin, the Hollywood comedian, and his family, when they stayed here for fishing holidays in the area. Fine sandy beaches and an inland drive beside Lough Currane.

DINGLE PENINSULA AND NORTH KERRY

Anascaul *16 km (10 miles) E of Dingle.* A road leads up for 5 km (3 miles) from this small, attractive village to the car park beside Anascaul Lake, one of the most isolated places on the peninsula.

Ardfert *10 km (6 miles) NW of Tralee.* Open 9.30am-6.30pm daily, May-Sept. A monastery was founded here by St Brendan the Navigator in the 6th c. The earliest building on the site is the cathedral, built between the 11th and 17th c. Much restoration work has been done in recent years. **Casement's Fort,** *2 km (1 mile) W of Ardfert.* Sir Roger Casement was arrested

Conor Pass (Owenmore Valley), Brandon Mountains

near this roadside earthen fort after landing on the nearby **Banna Strand** with German arms for the 1916 Rising. He is commemorated by a monument 2 km (1 mile) further on.

Ballybunion *34 km (21 miles) N of Tralee.* Seaside resort with wide sweep of beach, renowned for its summer **Bachelor Festival,** usually held in June, and its seaweed baths, which have restorative properties. The caves on the N side of the beach can be explored at low tide, but care is recommended. The ruins of the late 16th c. **Ballybunion Castle** can be seen on the promontory. Ballybunion **Heritage Museum,** open Tues-Sun, all year, ☎ (088) 2654127 has details of the many early Christian settlements in the area.

Ballyduff *13 km (8 miles) S of Ballybunion.* **Rattoo Heritage Centre,** open daily, all year, ☎ (066) 31000, has details of the archaeology, folklore and history of the area.

Ballyferriter *W Dingle Peninsula.* **Heritage Centre,** *Main Street,* open daily, summer, ☎ (066) 56100, has many items on the 19th c. way of life in the locality. **St Vincent's Church (C),** *on the opposite side of the street,* has all its signs in Irish. **Potadoireacht na CaolóigePottery,** open 9.30am-7pm daily, May-Sept, ☎ (066) 56229 has fine workshops and showrooms.

Ballyheige *16 km (10 miles) NW of Tralee.* The sandy beach is one of the finest in the country, stretching for 13 km (8 miles). Also ruins of 19th c. church. The **Ballyheigue Maritime Centre,** open daily, June-Sept, ☎ (066) 33666 has natural history exhibits and items on local history, including the boat that Casement used to come ashore at Banna Strand in 1916.

Blasket Islands *W of Slea Head.* The only one of the seven islands that was ever inhabited permanently is **Great Blasket,**

The Blasket Islands from Clogher Strand & Inishooskert, Dingle Peninsula

but that was abandoned in 1953. One of the smaller islands is owned by a former Taoiseach, Charles Haughey and is closed, but the other islands can be visited by boat from Dunquin. Some of the ruined buildings on Great Blasket Island may be restored.

In the meantime, the **Great Blasket Island Visitor Centre** *at Dunquin,* open 10am-6pm daily, Easter and June-Oct (7pm daily, July, Aug) ☎ (066) 56444, has lots of details on the heritage of the islands, including their strong literary tradition. The **Fuaim (Sound) Room** enables visitors to experience the sounds of the islands, from 'keening' (mourning the dead) to the crashing of the Atlantic waves. **Kruger Kavanagh** was a well-known personality in the area; you may see mementoes at the guest house he used to run at Dunquin.

Blennerville *3 km (2 miles) S of Tralee.* A steam railway runs from Tralee on a restored section of the old **Tralee-Dingle railway,** using a well refurbished locomotive from that line. Open daily, May-Oct, ☎ (066) 21064. The **windmill,** open 10am-6pm daily, Mar-Oct, ☎ (066) 27777 stands five stories high, a shining white beacon, fully restored to its original late 18th c. state. Also audio-visual show, emigration exhibition, craft workshops, pottery, restaurant. **Blennerville Art Gallery and Studio,** *Main Street, Blennerville,* is open 9.30am-6pm daily, all year. Also in Blennerville, you can see work under way on the reconstruction of the **Jeanie Johnston.** The original was a 19th c. famine ship that took emigrants to America. It's fascinating to watch the shipbuilding under way of her replica.

Brandon Bay *N Dingle Peninsula.* Cloghane, on an inlet of Brandon Bay, has an excellent strand and is a good base for climbing nearby Brandon

Mountain and exploring the coastline between Brandon Point and Brandon Head.

Brandon Mountain *N Dingle Peninsula.* A rough track leads up to the 900 m (3,000 ft) summit, which gives magnificent views of the whole peninsula and N Kerry in clear weather. St Brendan's Oratory is just below the summit.

Castleisland *18 km (11 miles) E of Tralee.* **Crag Caves,** open 10am-6pm daily, Mar-Oct (7pm, July, Aug), ☎ (066) 41244. The caves form part of one of Ireland's most impressive cave systems and have magnificent stalactites. Craft shop, restaurant.

Connor Pass *10 km (6 miles) NE of Dingle* Rising to a height of 450 m (1,500 ft), in some places, only a low stone wall protects drivers and walkers from a great fall to the valley below. In clear weather, the views are magnificent, although in cloudy weather, it's rather like being in an aircraft.

Dingle *50 km (35 miles) W of Tralee.* TIO, Main Street, ☎ (066) 51188, Apr-Oct. The main town on the Dingle Peninsula has a busy fishing harbour and marina, two festivals in August, some fine craft shops and a good spread of gourmet restaurants. In recent years, "Fungie" the dolphin has enlivened the harbour. **St Mary's Church (C),** was built in the 1860s and renovated in the 1970s. The next door library has much local historical material, some relating to the prominent local patriot, Thomas Ashe. **Craft village** on the Dunquin Road has some fine craft workshops and shops. Dingle Oceanworld/ Mara Beo, open 9am-8.30pm daily, July, Aug, 9.30am-6pm daily, May, June, Sept, 9.30am-5pm daily, Apr, Oct. ☎ (066) 52111. New aquarium is most impressive; it includes a walk-through tunnel tank. Many species from ocean depths.

69

Fenit Strand boats at evening, Tralee Bay

Multimedia interactive displays. Also Spanish Armada artefacts.

Dingle-Dunquin Road Some spectacular sea views skirting Ventry Harbour and then Slea Head. Archaeological remains on the mountainside, easily seen from the road, include over 400 prehistoric stone huts shaped like beehives.

Fenit *13 km (8 miles) W of Tralee.* Fine 1 km (0.5 mile) long L-shaped pier gives an excellent walk and equally excellent views of *Tralee Bay* and the *Dingle Peninsula* mountains. *Fenit Sea World,* open 10am-8pm daily, all year, ☎ (066) 36544, is a water-based theme exhibition featuring many aspects of marine life, even an old shipwreck. Visitors can also see dangerous species, such as conger eel, from a safe distance.

Gallarus Oratory *3 km (2 miles) NE of Ballyferriter.* The best preserved early Christian church in Ireland, believed to date from 8th c. Resembles an upturned boat. Open daily, mid-June- mid-Sept.

Glin Castle *48 km (30 miles) NE of Tralee on S shore of Shannon estuary.* Open daily, May, June or by arr, ☎ (068) 36230. Late 18th c. seat of the Knight of Glin, with fine neo-classical plasterwork and Adam-style ceilings. Good collection of 18th c. furniture, shop at gate. Fine gardens, including a walled garden. *Glin Heritage Centre.*

Inch *6 km (4 miles) E of Anascual. S Dingle Peninsula.* 6 km (4 miles) of long golden sandy strand at the entrance to *Castlemaine Bay* is one of the best bathing places in the region.

Listowel *27 km (17 miles) NE of Tralee.* TIO, St John's Church, ☎ (068) 22590, June-Sept. The amazing plaster decorations on the façades of some of the buildings fronting Listowel's great square were the work of a local artist in plaster, Patrick McAuliffe, who died in 1921. St John's former Church of Ireland in the centre of the square, has been turned into a literary, arts and heritage centre. Open daily, all year, ☎ (068) 22566. The North Kerry literary tradition, commemorated here, has one of its finest exponents in close proximity. John B. Keane, the writer, has his pub just nearby.

Writers Week in early summer is great fun for anyone with literary aspirations or inclinations and a thirst to match! On the Ballybunion road, just outside Listowel, is a graveyard from the mid-19th c. famine. Nearby, at *Finuge, 5 km (3 miles) SW of Listowel, Teach Siamsa* has Irish folklore displays and entertainment in summer.

At *Fitzgerald's Pet Farm, Abbeyfeale, 12 km (7 miles) SE of Listowel,* open daily, all year, ☎ (068) 31217, you can see the farm animals and old machinery as well as exploring a nature trail.

Fisherman at evening, Inch Beach

Lixnaw *9 km (6 miles) SW of Listowel.* The *Agricultural Museum,* open 10am-6pm Mon-Sat, 2pm-6pm Sun, June-Sept, ☎ (066) 32202 has collection of old farm implements.

Magharee Islands *8 km (5 miles) N of Castlegregory.* Off the N tip of the flat, sandy peninsula that divides Tralee Bay from Brandon Bay, this group of small islands is isolated and uninhabited. Boatmen from the small harbour at the N point of the peninsula will take you across in calm weather.

Smerwick Harbour *12 km (8 miles) NW of Dingle.* Good walks along both shores of this vast landlocked harbour, which turns into mudflats at low tide. There is a spectacular drive from the E shoreline of the bay to Ballyferriter and back to Dingle, by the Slea Head road.

Tarbert *16 km (10 miles) NE of Listowel.* The *Tarbert Bridewell,* open 10am-6pm daily, Apr-Oct, ☎ (068) 36500, is a recently restored 1830 courthouse, including cells and an exercise yard. Coffee and gift shop. *Tarbert House,* open 10am-4pm daily, May-Aug, ☎ (068) 36198. Built in the late 17th c., the house has exquisite Georgian interiors and furniture, also many family portraits. *Tarbert-Killimer car ferry,* regular crossings of the Shannon, daily, all year, ☎ (065) 53124.

Tralee *300 km (187 miles) SW of Dublin.* Pop.17,000. TIO, Ashe Hall, ☎ (066) 21288, all year. A lively and attractively set out business centre geared towards catering for tourists - the town is the gateway to the Dingle Peninsula. In recent years, some outstanding new tourist attractions have been added.

Kerry the Kingdom and Treasures of the Kingdom, Ashe Memorial Hall, Denny Street, Tralee town centre, open daily, Mar-Dec, ☎ (066) 27777. Kerry the Kingdom is a spectacular visual show. Geraldine Tralee uses a "time car" to recreate life in Tralee as it was in 1450, complete with sounds and smells. Treasures of the Kingdom displays the county history, from the Stone Age to the present and includes priceless archaeological treasures.

Aqua Dome, open 10am-10pm Mon-Fri, 10am-7pm, Sat, Sun, all year, ☎ (066) 28899 is a water-based leisure centre. *Siamsa Tire* is Ireland's lively national folk theatre, with regular shows from May to September; ☎ (066) 23055. *St John's Church (C)* was built in 1870 and has a 1959 statue of the locally-born St Brendan the Navigator. *Holy Cross Church (C), Princes Street,* was designed by the ubiquitous Pugin in the 19th c.

Ventry *10 km (6 miles) W of Dingle.* Formerly a major port, Ventry boasts a good natural harbour and sandy beach, with the imposing Mount Eagle in the background.

LIMERICK CITY AND COUNTY

Adare *16 km (10 miles) SW of Limerick.* TIO, Heritage Centre, Main Street, ☎ (061) 396255, Mar-Nov. With its Main Street lined with thatched cottages, Adare claims, with good reason, to be the best looking small town in Ireland. The **Adare Heritage Centre,** *Main Street,* open daily, all year, ☎ (061) 396666 has a multimedia presentation on its history, including the influence of the Dunraven family in the 19th and early 20th c. A model depicts Adare in 1500. Restaurant, shop. See ruins of 15th c. Franciscan friary and the 14th c. Desmond castle. Non-residents can explore the ground floor and demesne of **Adare Manor,** now a luxury hotel complete with golf course.

The Church of the **Most Holy Trinity (C)** and **Adare Parish Church** are both worth exploring as are Stacpoole's recently enlarged antiques shop and Carol's Antiques, also with a fine selection, both on the Main Street. Adare is also excellent for dining out.

Ballingarry *12 km (7 miles) SW of Adare.* **Knockfierna famine park** has restored pre-famine houses, ancient Mass Rock. Open daily, summer.

Ballyhoura Country Farm Trail *Kilfinane, 9 km (5 miles) SE of Kilmallock.* Open daily, all year, ☎ (063) 91300. A series of working farms open to visitors. They include cheese, deer, honey and trout farms.

Ballyneety *8 km (5 miles) N of Kilmallock, between Lough Gur and Kilmallock.* Ornamental **pheasant farm,** open 10am-9pm daily, ☎ (061) 351607. Has 30 varieties on show.

Bruree *6 km (4 miles) NW of Kilmallock.* **De Valera museum and heritage centre** tells the story of this great political leader (1882-1975), who went to school in this village. Open Tues-Sun, all year, ☎ (063) 91300. Three 13th c. de Lacy castles, waterwheel at the mill by River Maigue.

Bunratty *13 km (8 miles) W of Limerick.* **Bunratty Castle,** open 9.30am-5pm daily, all year. Built in 1460, the castle has been fully restored and now houses one of the finest collections of 14th-17th c. furniture and furnishings in Ireland. **Bunratty Folk Park,** open 9.30am-7pm daily, July, Aug, 9.30am-5.30pm daily, Sept-June. ☎ (061) 360788. This world renowned park has examples of

houses from every part of the region, plus a reconstructed 19th c. village street. Mac's pub and restaurant. Craft demonstrations, including basket weaving, bread and candle making and farriery. Bunratty Courtyard has a display of old farm implements.

The intriguing **Bunratty Winery,** open 9.30am-5.30pm daily, all year, ☎ (061) 362222 makes mead and poteen legally and has a small museum.

Durty Nelly's pub, adjacent to the folk park, is world famous and although rather small, is packed with atmosphere.

Castleconnell, *13 km (8 miles) NE of Limerick.* Walks along both banks of the River Shannon in this famous fishing village. **Pink Cottage** has locally made arts and crafts.

Bunratty Folk Park

Thatched Cottages, Adare

Celtic Theme Park and Garden

Kilcornan, 8 km (5 miles) NW of Adare.
Open 9am-7pm daily, Mar-Nov,
☎ (061) 394243.Recreations of many
fascinating buildings and sites from Ireland's
Celtic past. Celtic theme garden, coffee shop,
tea rooms.

Cratloe *11 km (7 miles) W of Limerick.*
Extensive woodland walks. The 17th c.
Cratloe Woods House open 2pm-6pm Mon-
Sat, June-Sept, ☎ (061) 327028.

Craggaunowen *13 km (8 miles) NE of
Shannon airport. Near Sixmilebridge.*
Open daily, Mar-Oct, ☎ (061) 367178.
Fascinating creation of Ireland's ancient
history. Highlights include a ring fort,
man-made islands (crannogs) and the replica
of the leather-hulled boat in which
St Brendan reputedly discovered America.

Going over the deep place,
O God of patience, take them
 by the hand
In case of a blow from a
 strong wave.
O Mary, look out for them
And don't leave them.

An extract from *Irish Blessings*
published by Appletree Press

Croom *11 km (7 miles) SE of Adare.*
Pleasant town on the banks of the
River Maigue. *The Mill,* open 10am-6pm
Mon-Thurs, 10am-9pm Fri-Sun, all year.
☎ (061) 397130. Restored as a heritage
project and includes a five storey granary.
Exhibition section. Visitors can grind their
own corn. *Buttercup Farm:* working farm
with exotic birds, traditional farm machinery.
Open daily, all year, ☎ (061) 397556.

Curraghchase *18 km (11 miles) W of
Limerick.* Open 9am-9pm daily, all year.
The estate of 19th c. poet and author Aubrey
de Vere is now a national park. The big house,
together with its priceless works of
art, was destroyed in an accidental fire in
1941. See the tombstones of de Vere's pets
and the earth mound where he sat to write.
Gardens, arboretum.

Drumcollogher *40 km (25 miles) SW of
Limerick. Irish Dresden* factory, open
9am-5pm Mon-Fri, all year. ☎ (063) 83030.
Fine porcelain products and Dresden
figurines. *Dairy Co-op Museum,* open
10am-6pm daily, all year, ☎ (063) 83113
details the history of Ireland's first
co-operative creamery. Also *Springfield
Castle deer farm and visitor centre,* daily,
all year, ☎ (063) 83162.

Foynes *37 km (23 miles) W of Limerick.*
Flying Boat Museum, open 10am-6pm daily,
end Mar-end Oct, ☎ (069) 65416 has
fascinating displays on the intriguing story
of the flying boats on the Shannon estuary
during World War Two. A small 1940s style
cinema shows newsreels from the period,
while the cafe is also decorated in period style.

Glenstal Abbey *14 km (9 miles) W of
Limerick.* Open all year, by arr,
☎ (061) 386103. This Benedictine college
has attractive grounds and chapel. The monks
work at a variety of crafts, including

bee-keeping, sculpture, silversmithing and
stone cutting. Scenic walks through nearby
Clare Glens.

Kilmallock *34 km (21 miles) S of Limerick.*
A monastery town founded in the 7th c.,
many of its medieval structures still survive,
including two town gates, part of the town
wall and the early 14th c. Dominican friary.
Kilmallock Museum, open 1.30pm-5.30pm
Mon-Fri, 1pm-5pm Sat, Sun, all year.
☎ (063) 91300. The museum reflects farm,
social and shop life in the 19th and earlier
20th c.

Limerick *198 km (123 miles) SW of
Dublin.* Pop.52,000. TIO, Arthur's Quay,
☎ (061) 317522, all year. The fourth largest
city in Ireland and an important market
and manufacturing centre, Limerick has
made substantial progress in recent years in
preserving its historical heritage. Many new
facilities have been developed for visitors,
including excellent new hotels and restaurants.

King John's Castle, beside the River Shannon,
open 9.30am-5.30pm daily, Apr- Oct, 12 noon-
4pm Sat, Sun, Nov-Mar. ☎ (061) 360788.
Built in the 13th c., the castle has been
extensively restored. It now houses a large
scale historical exhibition and audio-visual
show on the city and county. The latest
development here is *Castle Lane,* which
recreates a late 17th/ early 18th c. streetscape
in very vivid detail. Directly across the river
from the castle is the *Treaty Stone,* the place
where the Treaty of Limerick was said
to have been signed in 1691.

St Mary's Cathedral (CI) was built in the
late 12th c. by Donal O'Brien, the last king
 of Munster. The interior has been extensively
restored and the many interesting monuments
and 15th c. choir stalls should not be missed.
The Bishop's Palace is an 18th c. building
that was once home to the Protestant bishops
of Limerick. It's been well restored.
Open daily, all year.

Nearby, at Rutland Street, is the very fine
18th c. *Custom House,* which has been
extensively and superbly restored to house
the *Hunt Museum.* Housed here is the Hunt
Collection of 2,000 original works of art
and antiquity. There are works by Picasso,
Renoir and Jack B. Yeats and a Greek coin
revered since the Middle Ages as one of
the thirty pieces of silver. It also has priceless
archaeological collections from Ireland and
ancient Egypt, Greece and Rome as well as
religious works of art. Exhibitions, restaurant,
gift shop. Open 10am-5pm Tues-Sat, 2pm-
5pm Sun, all year. ☎ (061) 312833.

Portions of Limerick's medieval walls remain
near *St John's Cathedral (C),* a 19th c.
Gothic building with the tallest spire in
Ireland. Ask at the Presbytery to see the
15th c. mitre and cross. *The Dominican
Church (C), Baker Place, Pery Street,*

Croom monasterial Abbey, Limerick

has an impressive 17th c. statue of Our Lady of Limerick, while the modern ***Church of the Holy Rosary (C)***, *Ennis Road*, has Stations of the Cross made by the craftsmen of Oberammergau in Bavaria.

Limerick City Museum, *John's Square*, open 10am-5pm Tues-Sat, all year, ☎ (061) 417826. The museum has much material on local events and personalities, including archaeological finds, trade history and details of the Limerick Soviet declared in 1919. The houses and church in the surrounding square have been restored. ***The National Portrait Self-Collection*** can be seen at the University of Limerick, 9am-5pm Mon-Fri, all year, ☎ (061) 333644. ***Limerick City Art Gallery,*** *Pery Square*, open daily, except Sun, all year, ☎ (061) 310633. On the edge of the city's Georgian district, where much restoration work is under way, the gallery has works by many Irish artists, including Percy French, Charles Lamb, Walter Osborne and Camille Souter. Frequent exhibitions. The ***Belltable Arts Centre,*** *69 O'Connell Street*, open daily except Sun, ☎ (061) 319866. Frequent exhibitions, other cultural events, theatre, with plans for expansion, Coffee shop. Limerick lace is an age-old tradition and can be seen detailed at the ***Good Shepherd Convent,*** *Dublin Road*, open 10am-4pm Mon-Fri, all year. Extensive plans are under way to preserve and present this remarkable part of Limerick tradition.

Lough Gur *16 km (10 miles) SE of Limerick*. Remarkable series of prehistoric remains, including dolmens. The stone circle

is the largest in Ireland. Ruins of two medieval Desmond castles. Walks by lakeside. ***Interpretative Centre,*** open 10am-6pm daily, May-Sept, ☎ (061) 360788.

Newcastle West *42 km (26 miles) SW of Limerick*. Bustling market town with a 12th c. Desmond castle in the town square. See also tower house of ***Glenquin Castle,*** 15th c. Enjoyable walks in the demesne.

Pallas Grean *16 km (10 miles) SE of Limerick, off N24*. ***Ryan's honey farm,*** daily, Apr-Sept, ☎ (062) 57147.

Pallaskenny Agricultural College
8 km (5 miles) NE of Askeaton. College run by Salesian Order includes dairy farm, antique farm machinery. Daily, all year, by arr., ☎ (061) 393100.

Rathkeale *29 km (18 miles) SW of Limerick*. ***Castle Matrix,*** open 12 noon-5pm Mon, Tues, Sat, Sun, May-Sept, ☎ (069) 64284. The castle dates back to 15th c. and now has a vast library with many rare editions, fine furnishings, objets d'art, historic documents. Home of Irish International Art Centre. ***Irish Palatine Museum,*** open daily, Easter-Oct, ☎ (069) 64397 details the early 18th c. German settlers who came to this part of Ireland. Many moved on subsequently, to America. Exhibitions.

Shannon Airport *24 km (15 miles) W of Limerick*. Aviation hall of fame, shops, bars, restaurant. Nearby Ballycasey Craft Centre has a variety of craft workshops, including jewellery and pottery.

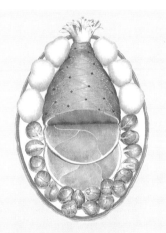

BAKED LIMERICK HAM

3-5 lb/1$^{1}/_{2}$ kg ham, cider to cover, $^{1}/_{2}$ Cup brown sugar, 1 tsp mustard, 20 whole cloves

Cover the ham with cold water and bring slowly to the boil. Throw out the water and replace with cider. Bring this just to the boil and lower the heat, keeping the liquid barely simmering for 20 minutes to the 1 lb/$^{1}/_{2}$ kg. Remove from the heat and allow to stand in the liquid for 30 minutes. Take out the ham, skin it and score the fat with a sharp knife in a diamond pattern. Stud with whole cloves. Mix the sugar and mustard and rub well into the surface of the ham. Bake in a pre-heated oven for a further 10 minutes to the 1lb/ $^{1}/_{2}$ kg at gas mark 6, 400°F, 200°C.

An extract from *A Little Irish Cook Book* published by Appletree Press

THE WEST

The West of Ireland conjures up images of great heather-clad boglands, mountain peaks, small seaside villages and the sandy beaches of Connemara. Clifden the 'capital' of Connemara, has tweed weaving, turf-smoke in the air and turf coloured water. Islands off the coast, like Inishbofin and the three, mainly Irish-speaking, Aran Islands, offer a relaxing and traditional way of life. Further north, spectacular landscapes continue to unravel: the cliffs and beaches of Mayo and Sligo, the great Slieve League cliffs in south Donegal, reputedly the highest in Europe, and Ireland's most remote island, Tory. Travel south from Connemara and Galway and another of Ireland's botanical mysteries comes into view, the Burren, with its lunar limestone landscape and exotic flora. Caves, too, at Ailwee. The man-made sits sympathetically with these primitive landscapes: Kylemore Abbey in Connemara, W B Yeats' castle near Gort, Co Galway, Galway city itself, buzzing with western culture and 'craic', and the stately town of Westport.

The Burren, Co. Clare.

BURREN AND CLIFFS OF MOHER

Ailwee Caves *3 km (2 miles) SE of Ballyvaughan.* Open 10am-6pm daily, Mar-June, 10am-7pm daily, July-Aug, 10am-6pm daily, Sept-Nov. ☎ (065) 77036. This strange subterranean landscape includes stalactites and stalagmites, all dazzlingly lit. The cave centre at the entrance is shaped like a Stone Age cairn and contains a restaurant and craft shop.

Ballyvaughan *16 km (10 miles) NE of Lisdoonvarna.* Pleasant seaside village with pier, facing Galway Bay. Fine drive to Lisdoonvarna and Corkscrew Hill. Good views over Galway Bay, especially when the sun's going down.

Burren *N of Corofin, E of Lisdoonvarna.* Huge limestone plateau covering a vast area of north Clare. Mile after mile of stark rock resembling a lunar landscape and full of history and prehistory, from huge dolmens and cairns to round towers and celtic crosses. Also an area of remarkable flora and fauna with artic, alpine and mediterranean plants growing together. Now a National Park, with

controversial interpretative centre under construction. *Burren Exposure:* new visitor centre; landscapes, history of the Burren, flora and fauna. Open daily, Apr-Oct. ☎ (065) 77277. *Newtown Castle:* 16th c. tower house, open 10am-6pm daily, Apr-Oct. ☎ (065) 77200. *Burren Perfumery,* floral centre and audio-visual on Burren flora. Open daily, all year, ☎ (065) 89102. *Burren Smokehouse,* see Atlantic salmon being smoked. Demonstrations in visitor centre, open daily, all year. ☎ (065) 74432.

Cliffs of Moher *10 km (6 miles) NW of Lahinch.* TIO, Apr-Oct. ☎ (065) 81171. Extending for 8 km (5 miles), these majestic cliffs are among the most outstanding natural features of the West of Ireland. Best seen from *O'Brien's Tower,* open 10am-6pm daily, Mar-Oct. *The Information Centre,* open 10am-6pm daily, all year, ☎ (065) 81171, also contains the TIO and has full details of the area. Craft shop, restaurant.

Corofin *15 km (8 miles) N of Ennis.* The *Clare Heritage Centre* in converted Church of Ireland church, open all year, 10am-7pm. ☎ (065) 37955. Has fine museum on 19th c. life in the county, besides genealogical records. Dysert O'Dea Castle has an *Archaeology Centre,* open 10am-7pm daily, May-Sept, ☎ (065) 37401, with an audio-visual show, local history exhibition and museum. Nearby is the *White Cross of Tola* and round tower.

Doolin *8 km (5 miles) SW of Lisdoonvarna.* Small fishing village on sandy bay, famous for its folk music. Trips to Aran Islands in fine weather. *Doolin Crafts Gallery,* open daily, all year ☎ (065) 74309.

Ennis *233 km (145 miles) SW of Dublin.* Pop. 14,000. TIO ☎ (065) 28366. An interesting town set on the banks of the River Fergus, with narrow, winding streets. Besides being the birthplace of Harriet Smithson, wife of the French composer Hector Berlioz,

O'Brien's Tower, Cliffs of Moher, Co. Clare

the town also saw such electoral firsts as the election of Daniel O'Connell in 1828 and Eamon de Valera in 1917. Ennis Friary, open 9.30am-6.30pm daily, June-Sept. This 13th c. Franciscan foundation was established by the O'Briens, Kings of Thomond. The ruins are well-preserved and the most outstanding features are a series of 15th and 16th c. sculptures. *De Valera Museum* and Library, open 11am-5.30pm Mon-Fri, all year, ☎ (065) 21616, has many historic relics of the district, including the spade with which Charles Stewart Parnell turned the first sod of the West Clare railway. *O'Connell Monument, town centre,* is on site of 1828 meeting at which Daniel O'Connell was nominated to stand for Clare. Also see new de Valera statue. Railway station has old locomotive from the long closed West Clare Railway.

Ennistymon *3 km (2 miles) E of Lahinch.* Delightfully set in wooded valley beside the River Cullenagh cascade. The Falls Hotel, overlooking the waterfalls, generates its own electricity from water power. The Main Street has interesting old-style shop facades, some with their names in traditional Irish lettering.

Inagh *9km (6 miles) W of Ennis, on Ennis-Ennistymon Road. Biddy Early's Brewery:* microbrewery named after 19th c. Co Clare woman with mystic powers. Open daily, all year, ☎ (065) 36742.

Kilbaha From its tiny harbour, road climbs west, very unevenly, for 5 km (3 miles) to Loop Head lighthouse. Superb views.

Kilfenora *11 km (7 miles) SE of Lisdoonvarna. Burren Display Centre* open 10am-6pm daily, Mar-May, 10am-7pm daily, June-Aug, 10am-6pm daily, Sept-Oct. ☎ (065) 88030. A fine introduction to the Burren, with its models of species and landscapes, historical detail and library. Staff will suggest scenic routes across the Burren for drivers, cyclists and walkers. Craft shop. Almost adjacent is *St Fachnan's Cathedral (CI).* The nave is used as a church, but the rest of the building is roofless.

Kilkee *65 km (35 miles) SW of Ennis.* TIO ☎ (065) 56112, June-Sept. Popular seaside resort with long, safe sandy beach stretchingfor 1.5 km (1 mile). Children's amusement park. The Duggerna Rocks, beyond the beach, form a striking natural amphitheatre that is used for bathing and sometimes outdoor concerts. Nearby Lookout Hill gives excellent views. *Heritage Centre,* open 11am-5pm Mon-Fri, July-Aug, ☎ (065) 56169, has artefacts and photographs of the area. *Kilkee Waterworld:* new water-based leisure centre. Open daily, Apr-Oct ☎ (065) 56855.

Kilrush *43 km (27 miles) SW of Ennis.* TIO ☎ (065) 51577, May-Sept. This striking market town, enlivened by weekly horse fairs,

has seen recent tourism developments, including a large marina. Scattery Island Information Centre, Merchant's Quay, open 9.30am-6.30pm daily, June-Sept. ☎ (065) 52139/52144. Gives details of the monastery founded on Scattery Island in the 6th c. by St Ciaran of Clonmacnoise. Also details of the area's wildlife. The *Kilrush Heritage Centre, Town Hall,* open 9.30am-5.30pm daily, June-Sept, ☎ (065) 51577/51597, depicts the town's history, including the Vandaleur family and their part in its 18th c. development. *Scattery Island Cruises,* daily in summer ☎ (065) 51327.

Knappogue Castle *10 km (6 miles) SE of Ennis.* Open 9.30am-5pm daily, May-Oct, ☎ (061) 360788. Built in the late 15th c. and the seat of the McNamara family until 1815. Restored in recent years to its medieval splendour, including a forge, orchard and gardens. Medieval banquets nightly during summer.

Lahinch *25 km (16 miles) NW of Ennis.* Popular resort with 1.5 km (1 mile) long beach. Promenade, sea-water swimming pool. Merriman Summer School, held in Aug, commemorates the author of the "Midnight Court", a bawdy 18th c. Irish language epic. *Lahinch Seaworld and leisure centre:* new water-based leisure facility, open daily, all year ☎ (065) 81900.

Lemanea Castle *7 km (4 miles) E of Kilfenora.* Amalgam of 1480 residential tower and early 17th c. fortified house, making striking ruins, which can only be seen from the road. Interior closed, as building is in a dangerous condition.

Lisdoonvarna *37 km (23 miles) NW of Ennis.* A leading spa town. The *Spa Wells*

Ruins on Lough Kee, Roscommom

Health Centre has a sulphurous spring, with pump house and baths, an excellent way of removing late night impurities from the system. Open daily, June-Oct, ☎ (065) 74023. *Lisdoonvarna Fair,* Sept, brings together bachelors in search of spouses. An interesting 3 km (2 miles) circular walk along the 'Bog' road via the Spectacle Bridge to SW of the town.

Milltown Malbay *32 km (20 miles) W of Ennis.* A former resort in an area of cliffs and sandy beaches, the town now hosts the annual Willie Clancy Summer School in July, a must for traditional musicians worldwide. To the west, Spanish Point marks the wreck of Armada warships. The top of Slieve Callan, to the east, offers fine views of the surrounding countryside.

Quin Abbey *10 km (6 miles) E of Ennis.* Well preserved and extensive ruins of early 15th c. Franciscan friary. Remains of a Norman castle were used to build the friary and three of its towers still stand.

Scattery Island *3 km (2 miles) offshore from Cappagh Pier.* Boat service and guided tours, summer only, details, Kilrush TIO. The island's monastic settlement includes five churches and one round tower.

SHANNONSIDE

Arigna Islands *W of Lough Allen.* A scenic route through the mountains is clearly signposted. Superb views of Leitrim countryside.

Athlone *125 km (78 miles) W of Dublin.* TIO Athlone Castle, ☎ (0902) 94630/92856, May - mid-Oct. This historic town, set halfway on the Shannon river system, also marks the boundaries between the provinces of Connacht and Leinster. The castle was built in the 13th c. and was extensively renovated in 1991, the 300th anniversary of its siege. The *Museum,* open 10am-4.30pm daily, May-Sept. ☎ (0902) 94630/72107, houses artefacts related to Athlone's colourful history and is linked to an interpretative centre, which depicts the Battle of Athlone in 1691, the flora and fauna of the Shannon and the life of the town's most famous son, Count John McCormack, the tenor, who was born just across the river from the castle. An extension to the museum and also a military museum are planned. Also on the west bank of the River Shannon, near the castle, the church of Saints Peter and Paul, is marked by twin spires and dome. Trips on the Shannon, aboard the MV Ross, are run daily in the summer from the marina. ☎ (0902) 72892. On-board bar and coffee shop. *Athlone Crystal, Pearse Street.* Factory tours, visitor shop. Open 10am-6pm Mon-Sat, all year ☎ (0902) 92867.

River Shannon at Athlone

mid-Sept, ☎ (0907) 20014. The ancestral seat of the O'Connor Don clan, the present house was built in the late 19th c. to an Italianate-Victorian style. The drawing room, library, bedrooms and chapel are some of the interior highlights. The billiard room has many archives, besides Carolan's harp.

Clonmacnoise *6 km (4 miles) N of Shannonbridge.* Open 10am-5.30pm daily, Nov mid-Mar, 10am-6pm daily, mid-Mar - mid-May, Sept-Oct, 9am-7pm daily, mid-May-early Sept. ☎ (0905) 74195. This 6th c. monastic site, beside the River Shannon, has cathedral, churches, round tower and high crosses. Visitor centre has the original high crosses and graveslabs. Audio-visual show, exhibitions.

Clonmacnoise & West Offaly Railway *Near Shannonbridge.* Open 10am-5pm daily, Apr-Oct. ☎ (0905) 74114. Narrow gauge railway trundles through the bogland for 8 km (5.5 miles) in fascinating hour-long trip, with plenty of sights of flora, fauna and distant mountains beyond the flat bogland.

Dromod *19 km (12 miles) SE of Carrick-on-Shannon.* It's part of the former Cavan/Leitrim railway. Steam trains are operational daily in summer. Also railway memorabilia, including many fascinating photographs in the former station house. Collection of railway carriages.

Drumshanbo *12 km (9 miles) N of Carrick-on-Shannon.* This small town at the south end of Lough Allen is a noted fishing centre. *Heritage centre* features iron and coal-mining in the vicinity, Leitrim lakes and other historical material. Open 10am-6pm Mon-Sat, 2pm-6pm Sun, Easter-Sept ☎ (078) 41522.

Elphin *13 km (8 miles) SW of Carrick-on-Shannon.* Small, but lively, cathedral town. The nearby Smith Hill is held to be the birthplace of Oliver Goldsmith.

Erne-Shannon Waterway
Tourist information, Mrs E. Smyth, High Street, Ballinamore, Mrs E. Mooney, Carrick Road, Drumshanbo. Stretching for 56 km (35 miles), it connects the Shannon and the Erne systems and opens up whole new boating and cruising vistas in a previously neglected but attractive part of the country. Boats can now sail from Killaloe right into the heart of the Lough Erne lakeland. In the £30 million project to restore the canal, 34 bridges were rebuilt and 16 locks reconstructed. Smart cards, like phone cards, are used to open them.

Frenchpark *13 km (8 miles) SW of Boyle.* Douglas Hyde, the Protestant founder of the Gaelic League, was the first President of Ireland. He was born at Ratra House, near here, which is now ruined and he is buried in the old graveyard at Frenchpark.

Boyle *14 km (9 miles) W of Carrick-on-Shannon.* TIO ☎ (079) 62145, May-Sept. Boyle Abbey, open 9.30am-6.30pm daily, June-Sept.This 12th c. Cistercian monastery is one of the most impressive foundations of its kind in Ireland. King House, 10am-6pm, May-Oct, is a museum with audio-visual presentation on local clan and military history. *Lough Key Forest Park, 3 km (2 miles) NE of Boyle* has many amenities, including cruising and forest walks, shop, restaurant. *Frybrook House,* an 18th c. house completes the Boyle triumvirate of historic buildings. Open 2pm-6pm daily, June-Sept, ☎ (079) 62170.

Carrick-on-Shannon *48 km (30 miles) SE of Sligo.* TIO The Marina, ☎ (078) 20170, Apr-Sept. The town is a renowned cruising base for the upper reaches of the River Shannon. The Costello Chapel, Bridge Street, open daily, all year, is considered to be the second smallest in the world.

Carrigallen *24 km (15 miles) NE of Mohill.* This tiny Co. Leitrim village has two outstanding attractions, the *Teach Duchais folk museum,* open 10am-1pm Mon-Fri, 2pm-5pm Sun, all year, ☎ (049) 33055. *Corn Mill theatre and arts centre,* details, ☎ (049) 39612.

Centre of Ireland There are several contenders for this title including a tower-like structure on a hill, 3 km (2 miles) north-east of Glasson and a stone pillar on an island off the western shore of Lough Ree, 6 km (4 miles) north-east Athlone, directly opposite Hodson Bay Hotel.

Clonalis House *0.8 km (0.5 mile) W of Castlerea.* Open 11am-5pm Tues-Sun, June-

Stone house doorway.

Douglas Hyde Interpretative Centre is open daily, May-Sept.

Hill of Rathcroghan *10 km (6 miles) SE of Frenchpark.* The ancient palace of the Kings of Connacht once stood here. A short distance from the central mound is an enclosure called Roilig na Ri (Burial Place of the Kings), where legend has it that the three Tuatha De Danaan queens, Eire, Fodhla and Banba are buried. They gave their names to prehistoric Ireland. Nearby is the grave of Dathi, the last pagan monarch of Ireland. His burial place is a smaller enclosure with a tumulus and extraordinary red pillar.

Killaloe *21 km (13 miles) NE of Limerick.* TIO Heritage Centre, ☎ (061) 376866, June-Sept. The old, narrow 13 arch bridge across the River Shannon from the small village of Ballina marks the southern limit of navigation on the Shannon system. ***St Flannan's cathedral (CI),*** built late 12th c. has various interior attractions, including an ogham stone and an oratory in the grounds. St Molua's oratory is in the grounds of ***St Flannan's cathedral (C), in the heights of the town.*** It was moved here in 1929 from Friar's Island in Shannon prior to flooding for the hydro-electric scheme. The new ***Lough Derg Heritage Centre,*** open 10am-6pm daily, June - mid-Sept, ☎ (061) 376866, traces the history of Ireland's inland waterways, including the Shannon, and details the ESB hydro-electric power station at Ardnacrushna, downstream from Killaloe. Derg Line, ☎ (061) 376364, has cruisers for hire and runs daily boat trips on Lough Derg. The Arra mountains are on the east side of Lough Derg and the road between Ballina and Portroe gives good views of the lake. The Graves of the Leinstermen, on slopes of Touninna, the highest mountain in the range, are a long line of vast prehistoric slate slabs.

Lough Derg Vast lake on River Shannon, stretching 32 km (20 miles) NE from Killaloe to Portumna. Holy Island, off W shore of lake, 26 km(16 miles) N of Killaloe, has round tower and extensive remains of 7th c. monastery. Boats from Mountshannon, Tuamgraney, June-Sept, ☎ (061) 921351.

Lough Ree Extends for 19 km (13 miles) north from Athlone to near Lanesborough. Two good viewing points are Ballykeeran - a hill overlooking Killinure Lough in the south-east corner of the lake, and the Hill of Ardagh, 6 km (4 miles) SW of Edgeworthstown. The country between Auburn and Ballymahon on the east shores of the lake is Goldsmith's Place; so named because Oliver Goldsmith, the 18th c. poet and playwright, spent his boyhood here.

Lough Rynn *11 km (7 miles) NE of Roosky.* Open 10am-7pm daily, May mid-Sept, ☎ (078)31427. Fine estate includes three walled gardens, arboretum, dairy yard, coach yard, farm yard. Craft shop, restaurant.

Manorhamilton *32km (20 miles) N of Carrick-on-Shannon.* Heritage centre tells the story of Sir Frederick Hamilton, who built the castle in the 17th century. Herb garden, coffee shop. Open daily, summer.

Mountshannon *8 km (5 miles) NE of Scariff.* An attractive, lakeside village. A plaque on the post office wall commemorates Ireland's last manually operated telephone exchange which was closed in 1987.

Portumna *N end of Lough Derg.* Portumna Castle is a great semi-fortified house built before 1618, with formal and geometrically laid out gardens in the Jacobean style. Exhibitions in castle and gate house.

Roscommon *43 km (27 miles) S of Carrick-on-Shannon.* TIO ☎ (0903) 26342, June-Sept. Attractive market town. At the top of the main street, in the square, see the facade of the old town jail, which once had a hangwoman, "Lady Betty", the last of her ilk in Ireland. Ruins of 13th c. Dominican friary just south of town.

Shannonbridge *8km (5 miles) SW of Clonmacnoise. Ashbrook Farm* has many farm animals, birds and much old farm machinery, Open daily, Apr-Oct. ☎ (0905) 74166.

Shannon Harbour *32 km (20 miles) W of Tullamore.* At the junction of Grand Canal and the River Shannon, the harbour is used for mooring cruisers. The place is now something of a ghost town with ruins of hotels, deserted quaysides and empty warehouses - sad reminders of its former glory as a major commercial centre.

Source of the Shannon From Dowra, near NE corner of Lough Allen, take the R207 N for about 6 km (4 miles), following the signposts, continuing down track for a further 3 km (2 miles), then climb for 0.8 km (0.5 mile).

Holy island on Lough Derg near Mount Shannon

Strokestown *19 km (12 miles) S of Carrick-on-Shannon.* An attractive village, said to have Ireland's widest main street, designed to match the Ringstrasse in Vienna for width. At the top of the main street is the St John's Heritage Centre in a former Church of Ireland church, open 9am-5pm Tues-Fri, 2pm-6pm Sat-Sun, May-Sept, ☎ (078) 33380.

A growing moon and a flowing tide are lucky times to marry in.

❖

Men may meet but mountains never greet.

❖

A gentle answer quenches anger.

An extract from *A Little Book of Irish Sayings* published by Appletree Press

Genealogical research, audio-visual presentations, exhibitions. At the other end of the main street, a long driveway leads through the estate grounds to **Strokestown Park House,** a fine 1730s edifice built in the Palladian style. Much restoration work has been carried out in recent years. Reception rooms, upstairs school room and nursery room, restaurant in old kitchens. Museum, open 11am-5.30pm Tues-Sun, Easter-Oct ☎ (078) 33013, has been built in the old stables and explores the many aspects of the great famine of the late 1840s, using a variety of presentation methods.

Tuamgraney *34 km (21 miles) N of Killaloe.* The small church (CI) in the village, with western parts dating back to the late 10th c., is believed to be oldest in Ireland still used for worship. Heritage Centre, open 10am-6pm Mon-Sat, 1pm-5pm Sun, Easter-mid-Sept ☎ (061) 921351. Displays on local history, video presentation on the village. Folk Museum displays include old household items, old newspapers.

Tulsk *12km (7 miles) W of Strokestown.* **Cruachain Ai heritage centre** is new and details the Celtic themes of the area. Shadow puppet theatre. Open 10am-6pm daily, Apr-Oct, or by arr. ☎ (078) 39268.

GALWAY'S CLADDAGH AND CORRIB

Aran Islands *16 km (10 miles) S of the Connemara coast.* TIO Kilronan, Inishmore, ☎ (099) 61263, May-Sept. Ferry services, ☎ TIO, and daily air services link the mainland and each of the islands. Three islands set in the Atlantic, the best time to visit the islands is in May or early June, when the Burren-like flora can be seen to its best advantage. During July and August the bulk of the islands' annual visitors, over 100,000, arrive making them feel distinctly over-crowded. Inishmore, the largest island, with a population of about 900, has a new Interpretative Centre at Kilronan, open 11am-5pm Apr-May, 10am-7pm daily, June-Oct. The centre gives a good view of the islands' culture and history. Daily showings of Robert Flaherty's 1934 film Man of Aran, ☎ (099) 61355. On the road out of Kilronan, you will see the many small fields divided by dry stone walls. On the western side of the island, Inishmore's biggest attraction is Dun Aengus prehistoric fort, set on the edge of a cliff. A new visitor centre

is due to open in 1998, near the hsitoric fort. Half the site, consisting of three concentric enclosures, has fallen into the sea, but what's left makes a fascinating sight. Inishmaan, the middle island, is where the traditional Aran lifestyle is most apparent. Conor Fort is a smaller version of Dun Aengus. John Millington Synge's Cottage, open Mon-Fri, June-Sept. The cottage has a fascinating collection of memorabilia. The island has fine cliff walks. Inisheer, by far the smallest of the islands, can be explored in an afternoon, but the sheer tranquillity of the place may tempt you to stay longer.

Athenry *24 km (15 miles) E of Galway.* The Norman walls are among the best preserved in Ireland, with five of the original six wall towers surviving. However, only one of the five medieval entrances to the town still exists the North Gate. The three-storey **Athenry Castle,** completed about 1250. Recent restoration work has been completed. See also the ruins of the Dominican friary, dating from 13th c. beside Clarinbridge River, on east side of the town. **Athenry Heritage Centre** in refurbished 19thc former church (CI) in the Square relates the town's medieval history. Open 10am-6pm Mon-Sat, 2pm-6pm Sun, June-Sept. ☎ (091) 844085.

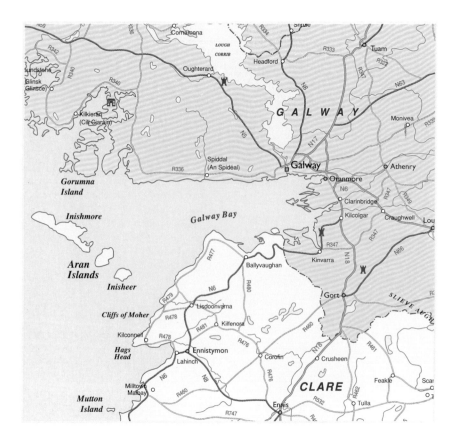

Aughrim *9 km (6 miles) SW of Ballinasloe.*
TIO ☎ (0905) 73939, Apr-Oct. *Interpretative Centre,* open 10am-6pm Mon-Sat, Easter-May, 10am-6pm, Mon-Sat, 12 noon-6pm, Sun, June-Oct. ☎ (0905) 73939. Has a good deal of information on the Battle of Aughrim, 1691, between the armies of James II and William, an important date in European history. Also prehistoric relics from the area and old household utensils. Audio-visual presentation.

Ballinasloe *64 km (40 miles) E of Galway.*
TIO ☎ (0905) 42131, July-Aug. Best-known for its annual horse fair in October - an eight day carnival that's one of the largest and liveliest events of its kind in Europe. *St Michael's Church (C)* is l9th c. and has stained-glass by Harry Clarke. Ruins of 14th c. Ballinasloe Castle, overlooking the River Suck.

Clarinbridge *13 km (8 miles) S of Galway.*
This small village is renowned for its oysters.

Clonfert Cathedral *24 km (15 miles) NE of Portumna.* The original monastery founded by St Brendan the Navigator in 563 was destroyed six times before becoming an Augustinian priory. The late 12th c. doorway is finest example of Romanesque style in Ireland.

Coole Demesne *3 km (2 miles) N of Gort.*
Open 10am-5.30pm daily, May, Sept, 10am-6.30pm daily, June, 9.30am-6.30pm daily, July-Aug. ☎ (091) 631804. The house where Lady Gregory once held literary court is long since gone, but visitors can enjoy walks through the demesne to Coole Lake, which

still has its swans. The "autograph tree" where her writer guests carved their initials can still be seen. Audio-visual show in the visitor centre, tea-rooms. *Kiltartan Gregory Museum* in old schoolhouse has memorabilia of early 20th c. Irish literary revival. Open 11am-6.30pm daily, June-Sept, 1.30-5pm Sun, May, Oct ☎ (091) 632346. *Heritage Centre in Gort Town Hall* details history of Gort as a market town. Open 9am-6pm daily, summer, ☎ (091) 631022.

Galway *217 km (135 miles) W of Dublin.*
Pop 50,000. TIO Victoria Place, Eyre Square, ☎ (091)583081, all year. The West's major town, Galway is set at the mouth of the River Corrib, near the Western Gaeltacht (Irish-speaking areas). The city grew rich on fishing and trade and its merchant class commissioned many fine buildings in the city. It is long since recovered from the vicissitudes of the mid-19th c. famine and isnow a prosperous city, well-endowed with facilities for visitors. Cultural traditions and activities are very strong in this city which is keenly aware of its Irish identity. The two main events in Galway's social calendar, both very lively indeed, demanding much stamina, are the *Galway Races* on the August bank holiday and the *Oyster Festival* at the end of September. Eyre Square in the centre of Galway has a memorial garden to the late John F. Kennedy, who as President of the US, visited the city in June, 1963. Other monuments include a sculpture of Padraic O Conaire, a noted early 20th c. Irish language writer. The Bank of Ireland, 19 Eyre Square, has some fine Irish silverwork, including a 1710 Mace. The Great Southern Hotel, facing the square, has

photographs and other relics of old Galway. Nearby, at the corner of Shop Street, a branch of Allied Irish Bank is housed in Lynch's Castle, late 15th c., one of Ireland's finest surviving town castles. Inside, explanatory photographs and text. The *Collegiate Church of St Nicholas (CI)* was built in early 14th c. and later enlarged, it houses many fine carvings and relics. Open daily, all year.

In the centre of Galway, doorways and windows from 17th and 18th c. merchants' houses can be seen in Abbeygate Street, Middle Street, Shop Street and St Augustine Street. The Spanish Arch was built in 1594 to protect the quay where Spanish ships unloaded their wares; four centuries ago, the city had a thriving trade with mainland Europe. Just past the arch, *Galway Museum,* open 10am-lpm daily, all year, has many fascinating relics, including photographs of the old tramway system that once ran between Galway and Salthill. ☎ (091) 564648. James Joyce's wife, Nora Barnacle, was brought up in the tiny house at 8, Bowling Green, which has been authentically restored. Open 10am-5pm Mon-Sat, mid-May - mid-Sept, Sheila Gallagher on ☎ (091) 584743.

The *Taibhdhearc na Gaillimhe* in Middle Street, stages regular Irish language performances and popular presentations of song, music and dance in summer, ☎ (091) 52024. The Druid Theatre, Chapel Lane, ☎ (091) 588617 is Galway's other theatrical institution, with regular lunchtime and evening performances. The Jesuit Hall, Sea Road, has plays and entertainment in English. *Nun's Island Arts Centre,* ☎ (091) 585886. Has regular performances and exhibitions. The *Town Hall Theatre* is a well-equipped performance venue. ☎ (091) 569777.

Galway is an excellent shopping city with many long-established outlets as McCambridges in Shop Street, which is an outstanding delicatessen and wine shop. As befits its cultural tradition, Galway is well-stocked with bookshops, including the venerable *Kenny's Bookshop and Art Gallery in High Street,* ☎ (091) 582739 / 581014 / 581021, which has a very large selection of Irish interest material, new and antiquarian. It also specialises in bookbinding. The *Sheela-na-Gig bookshop in Middle Street* deserves browsing time. *Galway Irish Crystal, Merlin Park,* open 9am-8pm Mon-Fri, 9am-6pm Sat-Sun, all year, ☎ (091) 757311. *Royal Tara China, Tara Hall, Mervue,* makes fine bone china, decorated and gilded. Factory tours, 11am-3pm Mon-Fri, all year. Shop open 9am-9pm daily, all year.

There are many pleasant walks in Galway. A stroll from the city centre to the salmon weir, will give you a good view of the salmon making their way upstream to Lough Corrib during mid-Apr-July. The busy harbour area

Kinvara village, Co. Galway

makes for some interesting walks, down to the seaward end of Nimmo's Pier, or on the opposite side, by the Long Walk. Alternatively walk along Upper Canal Road to Lower Canal Road via Dominick Street to The Claddagh. This area was an Irish-speaking fishing district, which retained its own strong identity until early this century. Its traditional thatched cottages were levelled in the 1930s to make way for more comfortable but infinitely less appealing local authority housing. Sadly all that's left of the area's traditions today is the Claddagh ring also known as the Galway wedding ring. The design depicts two hands clasped in friendship, around a crowned heart, symbolising the sentiment "let love and friendship reign". Reproduction pieces are popular souvenirs.

Kinvarra *SE Galway Bay.* This attractive fishing village makes an ideal base for exploring the Gort area and the Burren. Traught Strand is a fine sandy beach stretching for 7 km (4 miles). *Dungaire Castle,* open 9.30am-5.30pm daily, May-Oct. Nightly entertainment during the summer. ☎ (091)37108. This striking 16th c. castle is set overlooking Galway Bay and has been well restored.

Lough Corrib The second largest lake in Ireland and dotted with numerous small islands which vary in size from the truly minute to larger islands like Inchagoill, which once had a monastery.

Loughrea *32 km (20 miles) E of Galway.* Delightfully set on the north shore of Lough Rea. St Brendan's Cathedral (C) has fine examples of modern Irish ecclesiastical art.

Oughterard 27 km (17 miles) NW of Galway. TIO ☎ (091) 82808, all year. Fine village beside the western shores of

Lough Corrib, which is often described as the gateway to Connemara. Popular fishing spot. The 16 km (10 mile) drive from here to Maam Cross has amazing variety of scenery, from bog, lake and moorland to mountains. Sections of the old Galway-Clifden railway line are suitable for walking. In Oughterard, the V'Soske-Joyce factory, which makes exquisite carpets, rugs and wallhangings by hand can be seen by arr, ☎ (091) 82113/82140. *Aughnanure Castle,* open 9.30am-6.30pm daily, mid-June - mid-Sept, ☎ (091) 552214 was built by the O'Flahertys about 1500. The four-storey tower house is idyllically set beside Lough Corrib.

Salthill *6 km (4 miles) SE of Galway city centre.* This western suburb of Galway city is one of Ireland's leading seaside resorts, with excellent walks along the breezy promenade. *Leisureland* open daily, ☎ (091) 590455, has a full range of indoor activities, including a swimming pool.

Spiddal *19 km (12 miles) W of Galway.* Connemara village on north shore of Galway Bay. *Craft Village/Animal Farm* open daily in summer, ☎ (091) 83372, has thatched cottage and traditional farm implements.

Thoor Ballylee *6 km (4 miles) NE of Gort.* Open 10am-6pm daily, May-Sept. ☎ (091) 631436. W B Yeats bought this Norman tower in 1916, as a ruin, for £35. After restoring it, he and his wife George, lived there occasionally until 1928. Now fully-restored, with Interpretative Centre on Yeats' life and work. Bookshop, tea-room, riverside walk.

Tuam *24 km (15 miles) NW of Galway.* Small market town that was once a major ecclesiastical centre. The *Cathedral of the Assumption (C)* was built in the 1830s and

has many fine carvings. *St Mary's Cathedral (CI)* dates from the 1860s and incorporates 12th c. and 14th c. features. *St Jarlath's churchyard, west of the town centre,* has yews growing among the gravestones and surrounds the ruins of a 13th c. parish church. See also the 12th c. cross in the town square and the Mill Museum, west of the North Bridge, open 10am-6pm Mon-Sat, 2pm-6pm Sun, June - mid-Sept, ☎ (093) 25486. This converted 17th c. corn mill now houses a milling museum, with three sets of mill wheels and audio-visual presentation on locality's history. Tuam Arts Centre has regular functions. Railway station has a steam locomotive dating from 1875, rebuilt and in use, plus other engines. cc. steam rides.

Turoe Stone *5 km (3 miles) W of Loughrea.* Open 10am-8pm Mon-Fri, May-Sept, 10am-5pm Mon-Fri, Oct-Apr, 10am-5pm Sat-Sun and bank holidays. ☎ (091) 41580. Prehistoric pillar stone, decorated with Celtic inscriptions, one of the most significant monuments of its kind in Ireland. The *Pet Farm and Leisure Park, near the stone,* has rare animals and birds, duck pond, old farm machinery.

CONNEMARA

Cashel *22 km (14 miles) SE of Clifden.* Attractive fishing and shooting centre at the head of Cashel Bay.

Clifden *79 km (49 miles) W of Galway.* Pop 1,900. TIO ☎ (095) 21163 May-Sept. The capital of Connemara, Clifden has a wonderfully rangy, spacious feel to it, full of fresh air and turf smoke. The journey from Galway, which can take about two hours by bus or car, is an excellent introduction to the scenic glories of this part of Ireland. A highlight in the Clifden social calendar is the *Connemara Pony Show* in

Delightful is the season's splendour,
Rough winter has gone:
Every fruitful wood shines white,
A joyous peace is summer.

An extract from *A Little Book of Celtic Wisdom* published by Appletree Press

August. Clifden has two churches, the Church of Ireland one built in 1820, five years after Clifden was founded, and the striking Catholic edifice built 10 years later. The best way to see the seashore is to walk along the quay road, through the grounds of the ruined *Clifden Castle*, built by John D'Arcy, the founder of the town. To savour Clifden's alpine air, take the well-named *Sky Road out of Clifden for 5 km (3 miles)* to get excellent views of Clifden Bay. See the railway station; the line from Clifden to Galway was in use between 1885 and 1935. Millar's shop in the Main Street gives fine insights into the makings of local tweeds. *Derrygimlagh Bog, 6 km (4 miles) S of Clifden.* Foundations and some relics of the Marconi radio station destroyed during the civil war. Nearby is the site where Alcock and Brown landed after making the first trans-Atlantic flight in June, 1919. A cairn shaped like a plane is 3 km (2 miles) away. *Dan O'Hara's farm:* heritage and history centre includes prehistoric reconstructions, pre-famine farm. Audio-visual presentation. Open 10am-6pm daily, Mar-Oct ☎ (095) 21246.

Connemara National Park Open 10am-5.30pm daily, Apr, May, Sept, 10am-6.30pm daily, June, 9.30am-6.30pm July-Aug. ☎ (095)41054. Near Letterfrack, the park covers a vast area of Connemara, including the slopes of the Twelve Bens. Attractions include exhibitions, nature trails, audio-visual show, tearooms.

Coral Strand *6 km (4 miles) SW of Clifden.* One of the many fine strands in Mannin Bay.

Derryclare Lough Breathtaking drive from Ballynahinch Lake, east of the Twelve Bens. Continue past Lough Inagh and Kylemore. Mountains rise up on both side of the valley.

Inishbofin Island *19 km (12 miles) NW of Clifden.* Regular sailings daily, all year, from Cleggan harbour on the mainland. ☎ (095) 45806. Tremendous seascapes, safe beaches and plenty of very fresh air, straight from the

Atlantic. Many varieties of wild flowers. Ideal for water sports and walking. Hotel accommodation for visitors. See ruins of Cromwell's 17th c. barracks and ruins of St Colman's church and monastery.

Killary Harbour *24 km (15 miles) NE of Clifden.* Long, deep fjord-like inlet stretching inland for 16 km (10 miles). The road on the south side of harbour, through Leenane, gives tremendous views. *Leenane Cultural Centre,* open 10am-6pm daily, Apr-Sept, ☎ (095) 42323/42231, details the history of wool and sheep, with video presentations. Visitors can feed the lambs, or if they're really plucky, try their hand at sheep shearing.

Kylemore Abbey Between the Twelve Bens and the Dorraugh Mountains. Open 9.30am-6pm daily, all year ☎ (095) 41146. The abbey was built as a private home in 1864, later becoming a Benedictine convent. The nuns runs a girls' boarding school here. The grounds are freely accessible. Also craftshop, pottery and restaurant. Exhibitions in the visitor centre. Walled gardens.

Leenane *15km (9 miles) NE of Clifden. Cultural centre* details history of sheep industry in this area and general local history. Audio-visual presentation. Open daily, Mar-Oct ☎ (095) 42323.

Letterfrack *13 km (8 miles) NE of Clifden.* Founded in 19th c by Quakers as a mission settlement. excellent bathing strands at nearby Barnaderg Bay. *Diamond Hill, just E of Letterfrack,* offers marvellous views of the Connemara coast from its summit (445 m (1,460 ft) high).

Mweenish Island *Near Kilkieran.* Sandy beaches. Connected to the mainland by a bridge.

Omey Island *9 km (6 miles) SW of Cleggan.* Can be reached on foot at low tide. Fine beaches. Ruins of 7th c. religious buildings can be seen in the sandhills on the north side of the island.

Renvyle Peninsula *NW of Letterfrack. Renvyle House Hotel* was run for many years by Oliver St John Gogarty, writer, wit and contemporary of James Joyce. Excellent beaches nearby, views from Renvyle Hill. *Ocean's Alive* visitor centre has aquarium and maritime museum. Audio-visual presentation. Open 9.30am-7pm daily May-Sept, 10am-4.30pm Oct-Apr ☎ (095) 43473.

Rosmuck *32 km (20 miles) SE of Clifden.* See the cottage where Patrick Pearse, 1916 leader, stayed to improve his Irish. He also wrote most of his work here. Now the *Pearse Museum,* it houses mementoes and exhibitions, open 9.30am-6.30pm daily, mid-June mid-Sept. ☎ (091)74292.

Roundstone *22 km (14 miles) SE of Clifden.* Quiet fishing village built in the early l9th c. by Alexander Nimmo, a Scottish engineer who worked for years in the West of Ireland. *Dog's Bay* and *Gurteen Bay, 3 km (2 miles) SW of Roundstone,* offer fine, sandy beaches. *Roundstone Musical Instruments:* bodhran making with traditional material, Irish goatskin. Based in local craft centre. Open daily, all year, ☎ (095) 35808.

MAYO'S MOUNTAINS AND ISLANDS

Aasleagh Waterfall *32 km (20 miles) SW of Westport.* Peat-stained falls on the Erriff River, flanked by masses of rhododendrons.

Achill Island *West Mayo.* Connected to the mainland by a bridge, Achill is the largest island in Ireland, natural and unspoiled, mainly mountain, bog and heather. In fine summer weather, the place is a joy to visit, but when it's wet, it can be miserable, since so much of its enjoyment is based on outdoor activity. The main road runs to Keel, which has a 3 km (2 mile) long beach. The amazing cliff formations are like natural cathedrals carved by nature from the rock. The longer *Atlantic Drive* also gives good vistas of the island. On the seaward side of *Croghaun mountain, near Keem,* the cliff falls nearly 600 m (2,000 ft) to the sea. Keem Strand is a popular bathing place; sometimes, basking sharks come close to shore. *Slievemore village, 2.5 km (1.5 miles) north of Keel* is a ruin of this once thriving village which lost its population at the time of the mid-19th c. famine.

Sunset over Achill Island, Co. Mayo

Ballina *65 km (41 miles) NE of Westport.*
TIO ☎ (096)70848, May-Sept. The centre
of Ballina is straggling and uninspiring, but
the quayside walks beside the River Moy are
pleasant. The cathedral of *St Muiredach (C)*
on the east bank dates from the l9th c. *Dolmen*
of the Four Maols near the railway station.

Ballintubber Abbey *13 km (8 miles)*
S of Castlebar. Open daily. A 13th c.
foundation, it was largely destroyed by
Cromwellians in 1653. The abbey church
was marvellously restored in the early 1960s.
Interpretative centre, farm museum. Nearby
are ruins of *Moore Hall,* birthplace of George
Moore, noted late l9th/ early 20th c. writer.

Ballycastle *26 km (16 miles) NW of*
Ballina. Pleasant village in the Ballinglen
valley, with attractive coastal scenery and
good beaches and walking nearby.

Bellacorick *17 km (11 miles) W of*
Crossmolina, on the road to Bangor Erris.
You can play a tune on the *Musical Bridge*
by rubbing a stone along the north parapet.
However, don't attempt to cross bridge.
According to proven local legend, a sudden
end awaits anyone who tries. At the *Bord na*
Mona works, a tourist train takes visitors
around a narrow guage railway network
through the boglands, which provide fuel
for the nearby power station. Visitors can also
see the nearby *Wind Farm,* ☎ (096) 53002,
with 21 wind turbines, it is the only one of
its kind in Ireland.

Belmullet *63 km (39 miles) W of Ballina.*
This small town, enchantingly set, is the

entrance to the Mullet peninsula, a desolate
but beautiful place. The road runs south from
Belmullet to Blacksod Point, at the southern
end of the peninsula. The *Danish Cellar,*
8 km (5 miles) north of Belmullet, is a fine
looking bay fringed with cliffs. *Elly Bay*
on the east side of the peninsula has a
magnificent strand. *Doonamo Point,* *8 km*
(5 miles) north-west of Belmullet, has the
ruins of a prehistoric fort situated on the cliff
edge. Stupendous views out to *Eagle Island*
with its lighthouse.

Benwee Head This north-western tip
of Co Mayo has outstanding cliffscapes
and views out to the *Stags of Broad Haven,*
a cluster of rocks 3 km (2 miles) out to sea.

Castlebar *18 km (11 miles) E of Westport.*
TIO ☎ (094) 21207, Apr-Sept. A much
improved town in recent years. The green
sward of the Mall was once the cricket pitch
of the l9th c. Lord Lucan. A plaque in the
Mall commemorates Margaret Burke-Sheridan,
the internationally famous prima donna who
was born here, while one in the Main Street
marks the birthplace of Louis Brennan,
who invented the torpedo and the monorail.
The exhibition centre in the Town Hall has
regular exhibitions, arts and crafts events.

Ceide Fields *8 km (5 miles) W of*
Ballycastle. A spectacular setting on the north
Mayo coast for the equally striking pyramid-
shaped Visitor Centre and tea-room, open
10am-5pm daily, Tue-Sun, June-Sept,
☎ (096) 43325. Details the surrounding
Stone Age settlement, said to be the largest
of its kind in the world. The flora of the bog

is equally important, and the centre has
displays, exhibitions and video presentations.

Clare Island The largest island in Clew
Bay (there are said to be 365 in total - one
for each day of the year!), Clare Island has
a hotel and offers peace, solitude and walks
around the 15th c. Clare Abbey. Fine views
of Clew Bay and Connemara and Mayo
mountains. Boats from Roonagh Quay, near
Louisburgh. Aine O'Malley ☎ (098) 21129.

Cong *9 km (6 miles) SW of Ballinrobe.*
The legendary Maureen O'Hara/ John Wayne
film The Quiet Man, was partly made on
location here. *Heritage Cottage* has material
on the making of the film and on the history
of locality. Open daily, Mar-Nov
☎ (092) 46089. The 19th c. *Ashford Castle,*
now a luxury hotel with interesting historical
material, is open to non-residents. It was
originally occupied by members of the
Guinness family.

Croagh Patrick *8 km (5 miles)*
W of Westport. Ireland's holy mountain is
a steep but rewarding climb at any time,
but if you're really devout and want to do
it the hard way, try the annual pilgrimage
on the last Sunday in July. Views from the
summit are heavenly.

Crossmolina *13 km (8 miles) W of Ballina.*
Beautifully set on River Deel in the shadow
of Nephin Mountains, less than 2 km (1 mile)
from Lough Conn, in the heart of fabulous
salmon and brown trout fishing country.
North Mayo Heritage Centre. Open daily.
☎ (096) 31809. Old artefacts and farm
implements on display, genealogical research.
Crossmolina village is pleasantly set on banks
of River Deel.

Dromore West *27 km (18 miles) NE of*
Ballina on N59 to Sligo. Culkins Emigration
Museum is a purpose-built museum showing
details of local emigration, as well as old
artefacts and an old style shop. Open 10am-
5pm Mon-Sat, 1pm-5pm Sun, June-Sept.
☎ (096) 47152.

Foxford *16 km (10 miles) S of Ballina.*
The century-old *Foxford Woollen Mills,*
open 10am-5pm Mon-Sat, 12 noon-5.30pm
Sun, Apr-Oct, 10am-5.30pm Mon-Sat, 2pm-
5.30pm Sun, Nov-Apr. ☎ (094) 56756.
Has an outstanding and absorbing
presentation on its history and the effects
of the famine on the locality. Products
from the mills, other local crafts, on sale.
Art exhibitions. Also see the birthplace
in the town of Admiral Brown, founder
of the Argentinian Navy in early l9th c.

Inishturk *13 km (8 miles) SW of Roonagh*
Quay. Small but interesting and inhabited
island, measuring just 5 x 2.5 km (3 x 1.5
miles). Boats from Roonagh Quay. Details
on island life on display at the Inishturk Post
Office. ☎ (098) 68640.

Donegal Bay looking towards Sligo and Ben Bulben

Killala *11 km (7 miles) NW of Ballina.*
The small cathedral (CI) has fine paintings
and many historical records. Also a round
tower. Excellent walks on quayside and pier.
Boats to the secluded Bartragh island at
mouth of River Moy.

Kiltimagh *24 km (15 miles) E of Castlebar.*
Many 19th c. buildings in the town have
been restored, along with blacksmith's forge.
The goods store in the railway station is
now a museum of old farm implements
and household utensils. Exhibitions staged
in *Station Master's House,* open daily
12 noon-6pm June-Sept ☎ (094) 81494.

Knock *11 km (7 miles) NE of Claremorris.*
TIO ☎ (098) 88193, May-Sept. Knock is
a major pilgrimage centre, attracting over
2 million people a year. Magnificent new
basilica next the old church where the famous
apparition was seen in 1879. *Our Lady's
Domain* is finely landscaped parkland, with
trees, shrubs, roses. *Folk Museum,* open
10am-7pm daily, May-Oct, ☎ (094) 88100.
Has many relics of old-style life in Co Mayo.

Louisburgh *19 km (12 miles) W of
Westport.* Delightful small village near south-
west corner of Clew Bay and good, sandy
beaches. *Granuaile Centre,* open daily,
May-Sept, ☎ (098) 66195. Set in the former
St Catherine's Church details the life of this
western queen of the sea.

Mulrany *29 km (18 miles) NW of Westport.*
Attractive village between Clew Bay and
Blacksod Bay. Mild climate encourages giant

fuchsias and rare plants such as
Mediterranean heather. Good bathing beach.

Murrisk Abbey *8 km (5 miles) W of
Westport.* Ruins of 15th c. abbey, in fine
setting overlooking Clew Bay.

Newport *12 km (8 miles) N of Westport.*
Fronted by Clew Bay and sheltered to N by
Nephin Beg mountain range. *St Patrick's
Church* has Harry Clarke windows showing
the Last Judgement. An abandoned seven
arch railway bridge, once part of the old
Westport-Achill Island railway, spans the
river and is now part of a linear park. *Salmon
World Visitor Centre,* open daily, June-Aug.
☎ (098) 41107.This salmon research centre
has audio-visual presentation on the salmon,
together with a photographic record of the
centre's work.

Sheeffry Hills *22 km (14 miles) SW of
Westport.* The two main peaks are worth
climbing for the views from the top.

Straide *9 km (6 miles) S of Foxford.*
Michael Davitt Museum, open 2pm-6pm
Tues-Sat. Nancy Smyth ☎ (094) 31022.
Has archive material, including photographs
and documents, on the founder of the Land
League and founding patron of the Gaelic
Athletic Association.

Swinford *24 km (15 miles) NE of
Castlebar. Hennigan's Heritage:* heritage
centre with thatched cottage, theme farm.
Open 10.30am-8pm Mon-Sat, 2pm-8pm Sun,
Apr-Sept. ☎ (094) 52505.

Westport *260 km (162 miles) NW of Dublin.*
Pop 3,700. TIO ☎ (098) 21711 all year.
The most attractive town in Co Mayo,
Westport was planned by an 18th c. architect,
James Wyatt, who had been employed to
finish Westport House. The result is a town
planned with natural symmetry, divided by
the Mall that runs along both banks of the
rushing Carrowbeg River, spanned by a
hump-backed bridge. The atmospheric
Olde *Railway Hotel on the Mall* has many
interesting mementoes of the town and well-
known people who have visited Westport over
the years.

From the river, the streets rise up to the
Octagon, the focus of the town's commercial
centre. Westport has an intriguing mix of old-
style shops, modern emporia and continental-
style cafes. A traditional farmers' market is
held in the Octagon every Thursday morning.
Down by the harbour is the *Museum* which
details local history and maritime matters.

Westport House, 2.5 km (1.5 miles) W of
Westport. Open 2pm-5pm Sat, Sun, May,
2pm-6pm daily, June, 10.30am-6pm Mon-Sat,
2pm-6pm Sun, July, Aug, 2pm-5pm daily
Sept. ☎ (098) 21430. Stately home built
in late 18th c., with fine late Georgian and
Victorian furnishings. The dungeons have
video games to keep younger members of
the family happy, while many attractions
have been devised for the surrounding
parkland, including a children's zoo and a
narrow gauge steam railway. Visitors can
miss the bustle of children by coming early
in the day.

YEATS COUNTRY

Ballymote *22 km (14 miles) S of Sligo.* Michael Devlin ☎ (071) 83211. *Ballymote Castle* by Richard de Burgh, Red Earl of Ulster, extensive ruins flanked by six towers. Remains of Franciscan friary. Remains of the house of the 14th c. Knights of St John can be seen on the shores of *Templehouse Lough,* 3 km (2 miles) SW of village. *Irish Falconry Centre,* Michael Devlin ☎ (071) 83211. The medieval sport of falconry has been revived here.

Ben Bulben *N of Sligo.* This dramatic mountain, which dominates the surrounding countryside, features prominently in Irish mythology and also offers some decent walking.

Bricklieve Mountains *10 km (6 miles) SE of Ballymote.* A whole day can be spent exploring these remote mountain tops and the prehistoric burial cairns dating back to 2,000 BC.

Carrowmore *9km (4 miles) N of Sligo.* Largest megalithic tomb cemetery in Ireland. It's also the oldest, predating New Grange by some 700 years. Small exhibition. Open 9.30am-6.30pm daily, May-Sept.

Creevykeel Court Cairn *24 km (15 miles) N of Sligo, near Cliffony.* Some of the best megalithic remains in Ireland. The cairn is impressively sited, with mountains to the south and east.

Drumcliffe *6 km (4 miles) N of Sligo.* WB Yeats is buried in the churchyard (CI), beneath Ben Bulben. Yeats died at Roquebrune in the South of France in 1939, but his remains were not brought home until 1948. On his tombstone are carved the immortal words:

>Cast a cold eye
>On Life, on Death,
>Horseman, pass by!

Enniscrone *55 km (34 miles) W of Sligo.* Popular resort with 5 km (3 miles) long sandy beach, seaweed baths (very therapeutic), fine walks.

Glencar Lake *11 km (7 miles) NE of Sligo.* Scenic lough in a tranquil landscape with impressive waterfalls - the highest is an unbroken fall of over fifty foot, and pleasant walking.

Gleniff Horseshoe *Near Cliffony, midway between Sligo and Bundoran.* The route along the glen forms one of the most spectacular tours in the north-west.

Innisfree To find the island that Yeats immortalised, take the R287 through Dromahair, along the south side of Lough Gill. It is signposted.

Innismurray Island *6 km (4 miles) offshore from Streedagh Point.* 2 km (1 mile) from end to end, this low lying island has substantial early Christian monastic remains. The island's 50 inhabitants left in Oct 1947. Boats from Mullaghmore, Rosses Point, Streedagh.

Knocknarea *6 km (4 miles) SW of Sligo.* This cone-shaped limestone mountain dominates the surrounding area. From the summit you can enjoy tremendous views. The south eastern side of the mountain presents an easy climb. Carrowmore Megaliths, 3 km (2 miles)SW of Sligo. Open 9.30am-6.30pm daily, May-Sept. ☎ (071) 61534. Over 60 Bronze Age tombs are set at the foot of Knocknarea, making the site the largest such concentration in Ireland and one of the largest in Europe. A restored cottage has a small exhibition detailing the site.

Lissadell House *6 km (4 miles) NW of Drumcliffe.* Open 10.30am-4.15pm Mon-Sat, June-Sept. ☎ (071) 63150. This 1834 aristocratic mansion has been in the Gore-Booth family since it was built. It was the childhood home of Countess Markievicz, a leader in the 1916 Easter Rising and her sister Eva Gore-Booth. W. B. Yeats had many links with the family and the house and regularly slept in the bedroom above the porch. Tours of the house include the fine dining and music rooms. Impressive gardens, full of daffodils in spring. The woods on the estate are now a forestry and wildlife reserve.

Lough Arrow *32 km (20 miles) SW of Sligo.* Peaceful and picturesque lough dotted with islets. Nearby *Curlew Hill* offers some good walking and great views.

Lough Gill *3 km (2 miles) E of Sligo.* This wonderfully situated lake with its 22 islands rivals Killarney's lake district. Daily cruises in summer, George McGoldrick ☎ (071) 62000. Also *Wild Rose Waterbus* service, ☎ (071) 64266.

Mullaghmore *16 km (10 miles) N of Sligo.* Pleasant town with tranquil harbour and good beach in the shadow of

Classiebawn Castle. Annie's bar is over 200 years old and the pint here is drawn slowly.

Parke's Castle *On Sligo-Dromahair R286 road, NE of Lough Gill.* Open 10am-5pm Tues-Sun, Apr-May, Oct, 9.30am-6.30pm daily, June-Sept. ☎ (071) 64149. Restored early 17th c. plantation castle and courtyard. Exhibitions, audio-visual show, tearooms.

Rosses Point *8 km (5 miles) NW of Sligo.* Small but attractive seaside resort on north side of Sligo Bay, with two excellent beaches.

Sligo *217 km (135 miles) NW of Dublin.* Pop 17,500. TIO Temple Street, ☎ (071) 61201, all year. This old, flourishing town on the Garavogue River, with Ben Bulben to the north and a fine coastline nearby, deserves exploration. Its many Yeatsian links add strong cultural qualities. The *County Library and Museum, Stephen Street,* library open 10am-5pm Tues-Sat, also 7pm-9pm on Tues and Thurs, museum open 10.30am-4.30pm Tues-Sat, June-Sept. ☎ (071) 42212. Has special W B Yeats section, including first editions, his 1923 Nobel Prize for Literature and the Irish tricolour flag that draped his coffin. The art gallery section has Ireland's largest collection of works by Jack B Yeats, W B's brother. *Yeats Memorial Building,* at Hyde Bridge, open 10.30am-5pm Mon-Fri, all year. ☎ (071) 42693. This is the centre for the Yeats annual international summer school held in August. Audio-visual shows on the great poet's life and times. As a boy, Yeats spent many a happy hour in the *Watch Tower* on the corner of Adelaide Street and Wine Street, where his grandfather had kept sight of his sailing ships entering and leaving Sligo harbour. Also houses *Sligo Art Gallery. Hawk's Well Theatre* has frequent performances, ☎ (071) 61518/ 61526. *Sligo Abbey* dates from 13th c. and has almost perfect cloisters on three sides. Open 9.30am-6.30pm daily, June-Sept. Hargadon's Bar, O'Connell Street, has changed little over the century - all mirrors and mahogany. Guided walking tours of Sligo town, daily during the summer.

Malin Bay south of Glencolmcille, Co. Donegal

Strandhill *6 km (4 miles) W of Sligo.* Another pleasant seaside resort, this time on the southern shores of Sligo Bay. When the tide is out, you can follow the pillars from here to Coney Island, in the middle of the bay. The island has a fine sandy setting, with excellent sea views.

Streedagh *3 km (2 miles) W of Grange.* During low water at spring tide, you can sometimes see the wrecks of three Spanish Armada galleons, which sank here in 1588. Only one sailor survived.

Woodville Farm *3km (2 miles) W of Sligo, off Strandhill Road.* Farm animals, poultry, *old farm machinery museum.* Open 2pm-5pm, Sat, Sun, BH, June, 2pm-5pm Wed-Mon, July, Aug, or by arr, ☎ (071) 62741.

To go to Rome-
Is little profit, endless pain.
The master you seek in Rome
You find at home or seek in vain

An extract from *A Little Book of Celtic Wisdom* published by Appletree Press

DONEGAL HIGHLANDS AND ISLANDS

Ardara *39 km (24 miles) NW of Donegal.* One of Donegal's main tweed weaving centres, which is reflected in the *Ardara Heritage Centre,* open daily, ☎ (075) 41262. The Church of the Holy Family (C) has an Evie Hone stained-glass window in western nave, depicting the Word of God.

Arranmore Island *5 km (3 miles) offshore from Burtonport.* Largest island off the west coast of Donegal, with just over 700 inhabitants. Magnificent caves, cliffs and strands, including *Aphort,* on the south of the island, which is Arranmore's largest beach. Striking little villages, like Illion, where houses rise up from the chapel on the strand. Lough Shure, in the north of island, is Ireland's only rainbow trout lake. Regular daily sailings from Burtonport; the trip is an excitement in itself, Tom Gallagher ☎ (075) 20521.

Ballyshannon *24 km (15 miles) SW of Donegal.* The steep, narrow streets of this 17th c. town impart a fine historic atmosphere. The poet William Allingham was born at a house in The Mall in 1824. He died in 1889 and is buried in *St Anne's Churchyard, off the Main Street. Donegal Parian China,* open 9am-6pm Mon-Fri, all year, 9am-5.30pm Sat, May-Sept, 2pm-6pm Sun, June-Sept ☎ (072) 51826. Delicate china and porcelain. Video, factory tour, showroom.

Bloody Foreland *NW Donegal.* One of the best vantage points in the county, with views out to Tory Island. *Teach Mhuiris* is a traditional thatched cottage heritage centre and tea shop.

Bunbeg *15 km (10 miles) N of Dungloe.* Tiny restful fishing village with pretty harbour and extensive sandy beach to the north.

Buncrana *National Knitting Centre,* open daily, May-Sept, Mon-Fri, Oct-Apr. *Dunree Military Museum,* open 10am-6pm Mon-Sat, 12.30pm-6pm Sun, BH, June-Sept, ☎ (074) 61817.

Bundoran *30 km (19 miles) S of Donegal.* Premier holiday resort in the north-west, with a fine strand backed by a promenade. *Waterworld Centre,* open daily, ☎ (072) 41172, has range of water-based leisure activities, incorporating the existing swimming pool on the front. The headlands and cliffs near the town give fine walks and views.

Burtonport *8 km (5 miles) NW of Dungloe.* Small fishing village noted for its lobster and salmon.

Carrigart *23 km (15 miles) N of Letterkenny.* Quiet resort with good fishing and beach at base of the wonderful Rosguill peninsula.

Church Hill *16 km (10 miles) W of Letterkenny.* Angling centre near beautiful shores of Gartan Lough. ***Colmcille Heritage Centre,*** open 10.30am-6.30pm Mon-Sat, 1pm-6.30pm Sun, May, Sept, ☎ (074) 37306. Interpretative centre on life and times of St Colmcille (Columba of Iona), who was born in nearby Gartan in 521. Details of manuscript production.

Creeslough *10 km (6 miles) S of Dunfanaghy.* Attractive village on high ground overlooking an inlet from Sheephaven Bay.

Cruit Island *6 km (4 miles) N of Burtonport.* Small island with wild bog and reed beds makes for a memorable visit. Connected to the mainland by a bridge. Outstanding views, especially south to Arranmore island.

Donegal Town *30 km (19 miles) NE of Bundoran.* TIO, The Quay ☎ (073) 21148 Easter-Sept. ***Magee Tweed Factory,*** open Mon-Fri, all year, ☎ (073) 21100, welcomes visitors, also restaurant. Craft Village houses some new craft shops. ***St Patrick's Church of the Four Masters (C)*** is strikingly modern, dating from 1935. ***Donegal Castle,*** built in the 15th c. has been restored.

Dunfanaghy *13 km (8 miles) NE of Falcarragh.* Popular resort near Horn Head, one of the most attractive locations anywhere in Co Donegal. Magnificent strands in vicinity. One of last places in Ireland where the corncrake can be heard in its natural environment. Famine museum is open 10.30am-6pm Mon-Sat, all year ☎ (074) 36540.

Dunlewy *11 km (7 miles) E of Gweedore.* Enviously placed on the shores of Lough Nacung and at the foot of Mount Errigal, Dunlewy is a good base from which to explore the fantastic Poisoned Glen and ***Derryveagh Mountains. Lakeside Centre,*** open 10.30am-6pm Mon-Sat, 11am-7pm Sun, Easter-Oct. ☎ (075) 31699. Museum based on the life of a local weaver, Manus Ferry. His house has been reconstructed as an interpretative centre giving the flavour of early 20th c. Donegal home life. Demonstrations of woollen trade skills. Boat trips on lake, tea room, craftshop.

Fahan *6 km (4 miles) S of Buncrana.* Attractive village by shores of Lough Swilly with delightful beach.

Falcarragh *35 km (22 miles) NW of Letterkenny.* Bi-lingual village near the east end of the north-west Donegal Gaeltacht. ***Oldphert House and Gardens, Ballyconnell Estate,*** are being developed as a visitor centre.

Fanad Peninsula, *N of Ramelton.* This peninsula offers some of the best scenery in north Donegal. Head north for Ramelton and take in the three-mile long stretch of

Glencolumbkille near Ardara, Co. Donegal.

perfect beach at Ballymastocker Bay, the slightly delapidated resort of Portsalon and the wonderfully-positioned lighthouse at Fanad Head.

Fintown *13 km (8 miles) NE of Glenties.* Reconstruction of short section of narrow gauge railway that was once part of Donegal's elaborate railway system. Take a 15 km (3 miles) return trip which run every 30 minutes. Open 11am-5pm daily, June-Sept ☎ (075) 46280.

Glencolumbkille *56 km (35 miles) NW of Donegal.* This fascinating self-help co-operative community was inspired by the late Fr James McDyer. As he said: "If you like wild, rugged scenery, uncluttered beaches, a secluded area where you can unwind from modern city life, then Glencolumbkille is for you". ***The Folk Village and Museum,*** open 10am-6pm Mon-Sat, 12 noon-6pm Sun, Easter-May ☎ (073) 30017, has a series of buildings that include a school, shebeen (pub), tea house and craft shop. Also a group of traditional thatched cottages.

Glengesh Pass Between Ardara and Glencolumbkille, it rises spectacularly to 274 m (900 ft) before plunging to the valley. Excellent views.

Glenties *30 km (19 miles) NW of Donegal.* Striking small town set amid woods where two glens meet. ***St Conal's Museum,*** open 10am-5pm Mon-Fri, 11am-2pm Sat, May-

Rossnowlagh Bay, Co. Donegal

Aug, ☎ (075) 51277. Has large collection of railway memorabilia.

Glenveagh National Park *W of Letterkenny.* Open 10am-6.30pm daily, Apr-May, 10am-6.30pm Mon-Sat, 10am-7.30pm Sun, June-Sept, 10am-6.30pm Sat-Thurs, Oct. ☎ (074) 37088. This vast area of mountains, glens, lakes and woods has its own herd of deer. *Visitor Centre.* The centre has audio-visual show on the park. *Glenveagh Castle,* built 1870-1873, is open, for daily tours between 10am-6.30pm, Apr-Nov. *The Glebe House and Gallery,* open 11am-6.30pm daily, Apr, 11am-6.30pm Sat-Thurs, May-Sept. ☎ (074) 37071. This Regency house, set in woodland gardens, is exquisitely decorated with over 300 modern works of art, including Picasso and Kokoschka, plus many Irish and Italian artists.

Greencastle *32 km (20 miles) N of Derry. Maritime Museum* has a wealth of models and memorabilia. Open 10am-6pm daily, June-Oct, or by arr ☎ (077) 81086.

Grianan of Aileach *11 km (7 miles) S of Fahan.* Remarkable circular stone fort, in almost perfect condition, dating from about 1,700 BC. Open daily. Excellent views from top. The visitor centre in the nearby village

of Burt tells its story. Restaurant. Open 10am-6pm daily, summer, 12 noon-6pm daily, winter. ☎ (077) 68512. See striking modern church at Burt.

Inch Island *8 km (5 miles) S of Buncrana.* Despite its name, the "island" is actually part of the mainland! *Inishowen Heritage and Genealogical Centre,* open daily, details local history.

Inishowen Peninsula This NE corner of Co Donegal provides many fine views and interesting places to visit. Buncrana has a *Vintage Car and Carriage Museum,* open 10am-8pm daily, during summer, daily by arrangement in winter, ☎ (077) 61130. A fine collection of old cars, Victorian bicycles, model cars and trains. *Tullyarvan Mill Interpretative Centre,* open 10am-6pm Mon-Sat, 12 noon-6pm Sun, Easter-Sept. ☎ (077) 61613. Details of 250 years of textile production in the area. Also local wildlife, craft and souvenir shop.

National Knitting Centre, open daily, Jan-Sept, Mon-Fri, Oct-Dec, ☎ (077) 62355. Details of Donegal's handknitting cottage industry. Fort Dunree Military Museum, open 10am-6pm Tues-Sat, 12 noon-6pm Sun and bank holidays, Easter-Sept, tel. (074) 21160.

Once a coastal fort with commanding views, the museum details military history going back to Napoleonic times. There are many fine strands on the peninsula, including Pollan Strand near Ballyliffen. *Leisureland, Redcastle, Moville,* open daily, Easter-Sept, ☎ (077) 82306, has fun and entertainment for children of all ages. The tiny town of Malin is most attractive. From here, the road leads to Malin Head, the most northerly point, not only of the Inishowen Peninsula, but of all Ireland. Boats cross from the small harbour to the deserted island of Inishtrahull, abandoned over 60 years ago.

Killybegs *27 km (17 miles) W of Donegal.* Arguably Ireland's most important fishing port, set on a fine natural harbour. The place buzzes when the fishing fleet returns and the air is thick with gulls. Major annual sea-angling festival in August. *Donegal Carpets* has been handmaking luxury carpets since 1878. Factory tour by arr ☎ (073) 31688.

Kilmacrennan *11 km (7 miles) N of Letterkenny.* Ruins of a 15th c Franciscan friary. Lough Slat, near the village, is a very scenic area. *Lurgyvale Thatched Cottage,* open 10am-7pm daily, Easter-Sept ☎ (074) 39216. This 150 year-old thatched cottage recreates simple lifestyle of the early

19th c. Displays of farm implements, nature walk along river bank, craft shop, tea room, traditional music sessions weekly in summer.

Letterkenny *34 km (21 miles) W of Derry.* TIO Derry Road, ☎ (074) 21160 all year. *Donegal County Museum* in former workhouse, open 11am-4.30pm Tues-Fri, lpm-4.30pm Sat, all year, ☎ (074) 24613. Exhibits ranging from Stone and Bronze Ages to early Christian era. *St Eunan's Cathedral (C)* is a modern building in the Gothic style with richly decorated ceilings and striking windows. Its spire is a landmark for miles around.

Lifford *24 km (15 miles) SW of Derry.* *Cavanacor House,* open Tues-Sun Easter-Sept ☎ (074) 41141, is one of Donegal's oldest inhabited houses, dating back 300 years. It was the ancestral home of James Knox Polk, US President 1845-1849. Apart from the house there is a museum, art gallery with contemporary paintings and sculptures, pottery, craft shop, tearoom. *Lifford Visitor Centre is located in the restored basement of courthouse* and is open daily, Easter-Sept. ☎ (074) 41733.

Lough Derg *16 km (10 miles) E of Donegal. St Patrick's Purgatory in the middle*

of the lake has been a place of pilgrimage since early Christian times. The octagonal church was built in 1921. Boat trips on the lake, Easter-Sept. ☎ (072) 61518/61550.

Lough Eske *8 km(5 miles) NW of Donegal.* The 15-mile drive round the shore of the beautiful lough offers views of some of Ireland's most seductive scenery.

Navin/Portnoo *13 km (8 miles) N of Ardara.* The chief attraction of these twin villages is Navin's wonderful mile-long beach. At low tide you can walk to the offshore island of Innisheel, where there are remains of 12th c. churches.

New Mills *5 km (3 miles) W of Letterkenny.* Open 10am-6.30pm daily, June-Sept ☎ (074) 25115. Old corn and flax mill, up to four centuries old, has been recently restored and is a fascinating piece of early industrial archaeology. The millrace and mill wheels have also been restored.

Ramelton *13 km (8 miles) N of Letterkenny.* The *Old Meeting House,* open 9am-5pm daily, July-Aug, ☎ (074) 51266. The house has been restored and contains a library and geneaological centre. Rev Francis Makemie, a rector here, emigrated to America in 1683 and founded the first Presbyterian Church in Virginia. The 'Pool' here is a famous cast for salmon on the River Lennon. Walks by the old quayside warehouses.

Rathmullan *24 km (15 miles) NE of Letterkenny.* Once an anchorage for the British fleet during World War I, the town's solid villas are a reminder of those far-off days. The *Flight of the Earls Interpretative Centre,* open 10am-6pm Mon-Sat, 12 noon-6.30pm Sun, mid-May - Sept. ☎ (074) 58178 /58131. It commemorates the last two great Celtic chieftains, Hugh O'Donnell and Hugh O'Neill, who departed from the harbour here in 1607, creating a great turning point in Irish history. Fine beach, pier.

Rossguill Peninsula *N of Carrigart.* This wonderfully scenic peninsula can be seen to best advantage by taking the Atlantic Drive. A truly spectacular road, it runs right round the peninsula, starting at Downings, and affords stunning coastal views.

Rossnowlagh *17 km (11 miles) SW of Donegal Town. Abbey Assaroe Mills and Waterwheels,* open daily in summer. Waterwheels and site restored to form interpretative centre with audio-visual presentation on Cistercian history. Franciscan friary has grounds that are ideal for strolling, while viewpoint at the west end of the grounds overlooks the great sweep of Rossnowlagh strand. *Donegal Historical Society's Museum,* open daily, all year, ☎ (072) 51342. A fine repository of local artefacts and historical detail.

Sheephaven Bay *N Donegal.* Attractions on west side of bay include the ruins of early 16th c. *Doe Castle,* now ruined, **Ards Forest Park,** the seaside villages of Portnablagh and Dunfanaghy and great stretches of sandy beach, including Marble Hill strand.

Slieve League *SW Donegal.* The majestic cliffs here are the highest sea cliffs in Europe and are a truly awesome sight. Provided suitable care is taken, the climb to the summit of Slieve League will be suitably rewarding. Nearby Killybegs, one of Ireland's busiest commercial fishing ports, will provide a bustling antidote.

St John's Point *S of Dunkineely.* This peninsula stretches for about 8 km (5 miles) into Donegal Bay. A road covers almost the entire distance. One of Donegal's finest beaches - and that's saying something!

Tory Island *11 km (7 miles) off the NW Donegal coast.* Eamonn Heaney (Co-op Manager) ☎ (075) 20521. Reached by regular ferry service from Magheraroarty on the mainland ☎ (075) 31991. The island is a haven of solitude, craft working, primitive painting and bird watching. Historic features on the island include a round tower and the ruins of two churches, probably once part of the 6th c. monastery founded by St Colmcille. Visitors can now stay in comfort on Tory Island at the new hotel. Art gallery.

Crinog (a Celtic Monk's Lament)

Crinog of melodious song,
    No longer young, but bashful-eyed,
As when we roved Niall's northern land,
    Hand-in-hand or side by side.

Peerless maid, whose looks brimmed o'er
    With the lovely lore of Heaven,
By whom I slept in dreamless joy,
    A gentle boy of summers seven.

We dwelt in Banva's broad domain,
    Without one stain of soul or sense;
While still mine eye flashed forth on thee
    Affection free of all offence.

An extract from *A Little Book of Celtic Verse* published by Appletree Press

NORTHERN IRELAND

Of all the spectacular natural formations in Ireland, nothing can excel the Giant's Causeway on the north Antrim coast, its octagonal basalt columns testimony to some unknown upheaval of the earth countless aeons ago. Northern Ireland abounds with such places of outstanding natural beauty and interest. Off the north coast of Antrim lies the island of Rathlin, remote but rewarding to the visitor who takes a boat across from the unspoiled peaceful town of Ballycastle. The Glens of Antrim are verdant and magnificent, while the other side of Northern Ireland, the endless waterways of the Erne system offer paradise to boating enthusiasts who may now also take the new canal that links the Erne system with the River Shannon. More waterborne delights can be found along the Co Down coast, with its yachting havens, Strangford Lough and Newcastle. The Mountains of Mourne, which dominate this area offer wonderful climbing and walking possibilities.

Entrance to a field

Northern Ireland is rich not just in unspoiled, natural landscapes, but in man-made places too. Armagh has its ecclesiastical and prehistoric history and the city of Derry has been revitalised in recent years, while Belfast is full of attractions and facilities for its many visitors. Great houses and gardens are preserved by the National Trust across the province, while many of the North's traditional ways of culture are preserved in the pioneering Ulster Folk and Transport Museum.

GREATER BELFAST AND LAGAN VALLEY

Belfast *Pop. 300,000. TIO St Anne's Court, 59 North Street, Belfast BT1 1NB,* ☎ *(01232) 231221, all year* The capital of Northern Ireland is attractively situated on the Lagan estuary, at the foot of the Antrim plateau. Despite its relative decline as an industrial centre and the toll taken by the

so-called "Troubles" since 1969, the city is still thriving. Facilities for visitors, places to shop, eat and visit have been expanded considerably, to keep up with the increasing numbers of tourists, both from the United Kingdom and further afield, who visit the city. Belfast is a vigorous, no-nonsense city and its people are famed for their wry humour and wit. Much of the city's wealth came from the linen industry in the 1800s and this is evident in the city buildings - it is very much a Victorian city with some impressive architecture, notably the stately City Hall in the centre of town. Guided tours of City Hall ☎ (01232) 320202 extn 2346. It also has a very fine cultural tradition; its art galleries and museums, including some recent arrivals, well repay closer inspection. Access to the city is easy whether you arrive by air at the Belfast International Airport at Aldergrove or Belfast Harbour Airport; by car on the clearly marked and easy to use motorway system; by ferry or Seacat at the docks; or by rail. Major annual festivals in Belfast include: Belfast Arts Festival, a three week long cultural extravaganza in November; the Royal Ulster Agricultural Society Show in May; Orange parades on 12 July; Ancient Order of Hiberian parades on 15 August.

CATHEDRALS AND CHURCHES

Over 70 churches were built in the latter half of the 19th c., as Belfast expanded dramatically. Among the most notable are **Fitzroy Presbyterian** built in 1872 and **St Mark's,** *Dundela* (1878). **St Malachy's (C)** *in Alfred Street,* has an excellent fan-vaulted ceiling, while **St Patrick's (C),** *Upper Donegall Street,* has a chapel decorated by the esteemed painter, Sir John Lavery. The **Unitarian Church,** *Rosemary Street,* also has fine plaster and woodwork. **St Anne's Cathedral (CI),** *Lower Donegall Street,* is a modern Romanesque building. The mosaic roof of the baptistery is made up of 150,000 pieces of glass, symbolising the Creation. The tomb of the Ulster Unionist leader, Lord Carson, is in the nave of the cathedral.

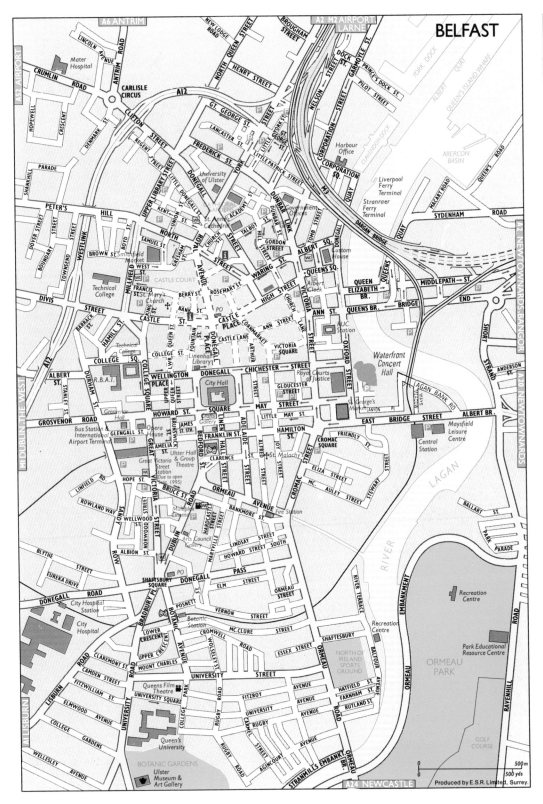

BELFAST

Lagan Valley

Lady Dixon Park

Cave Hill

NOTABLE BUILDINGS

City Hall *Donegall Square.*
Open (for guided tours only) 10.30am Wed.
☎ (01232) 320202, extn 2227.
Handsome structure with fine marble
interior, wall murals and excellent city
views from the dome.

Harbour Office *Corporation Square.*
Open by arr. ☎ (01232) 554422.
Recollections of Belfast's strong
maritime tradition.

Custom House *High Street.* Majestically
proportioned building. The writer Anthony
Trollope worked here as a surveyor's clerk
in 1841.

Royal Courts of Justice
Chichester Street. A substantial structure,
built in Portland stone which was a gift from
Westminster, the courts opened in 1933.

Queen's University of Belfast
University Road. Founded in 1849,
the university is a leading centre for many

branches of scientific research. The library
has over 750,000 books, many collections
and rare editions.

A Tyrone woman will
never buy a rabbit
without a head for
fear it's a cat.

An extract from *Irish Proverbs*
published by Appletree Press

91

MUSEUMS AND LIBRARIES

Ulster Museum and Art Gallery
Stranmillis Road. Open Mon-Fri, 10 a.m.-
5 p.m., Sat, 1 p.m.-5p.m., Sun, 2 p.m.-5 p.m.,
all year. ☎ (01232) 383000. Noted for its
Irish antiquities and art collections.
The Musuem houses treasures from the
Girona, a Spanish Armada galleon wrecked
off the north Antrim coast. Among the
distinguished Irish artists represented are
William Conor, Jack B. Yeats, Colin Middleton
and George Campbell. Sculptors represented
include Henry Moore, Barbara Hepworth and
F.E. McWilliam. Frequent visiting exhibitions.
Engineering hall has working examples of old
machinery. Shop, cafe.

Malone House *Barnett's Desmesne, Upper
Malone Road.* Open 10am-4.30pm Mon-Sat,
all year. ☎ (01232) 681246. This early 19th
c. building has a permanent exhibition on
Belfast parks.

Royal Ulster Rifles Museum
War Memorial Building, 5 Waring Street.
Open 10am-4pm Mon-Fri, all year.
☎ (01232) 232086. Relics of the regiment
and its predecessors.

Linen Hall Library *17 Donegall Square
North.* ☎ (01232) 321707. Established in
1788, the library has a fine collection of Irish
published material. Reading room, cafe.

Central Library *Royal Avenue.*
☎ (01232) 243233. Collection of early
Belfast printed books, photographs, maps,
exhibitions.

GALLERIES

Arts Council Gallery *56 Dublin Road.*
☎ (01232) 321402.

Arts Council Sculpture Park
185 Stranmillis Road. Works by noted local
sculptors in a garden setting.

Bell Gallery *13 Adelaide Park.*
☎ (01232) 662998. Dedicated to Irish artists.

Tom Caldwell Gallery *40 Bradbury
Place.* ☎ (01232) 323226. Exhibitions of
living Irish artists.

Cavehill Gallery *18 Old Cavehill Road.*
☎ (01232) 776784. Irish artists.

Eakin Gallery *237 Lisburn Road.*
☎ (01232) 668522. Irish artists.

Fendersky Gallery at Queens
Upper Crescent. ☎ (01232) 235245.
Contemporary art.

Crescent Arts Centre *2 University Road.*
☎ (01232) 242338. Contemporary work,
craft demonstrations.

Ormeau Baths *18A Ormeau Road.*
☎ (01232) 321402. As the name implies,
this is a conversion job, making a fine
contemporary art venue.

THEATRES AND CONCERT HALLS

Grand Opera House *Great Victoria
Street.* ☎ (01232) 241919. Grand style
Victorian theatre, presenting wide variety
of entertainment.

Arts Theatre *Botanic Avenue.*
☎ (01232) 324936. Popular productions.

Lyric Theatre *Ridgeway Street.*
☎ (01232) 381081. Performances of Irish
drama, including new works, international
theatre.

Group Theatre *Bedford Street.*
☎ (01232) 329685. Local amateur dramatics
society productions.

Old Museum *College Square.*
☎ (01232) 235053. New plays and
experimental theatre.

Ulster Hall *Bedford Street.*
☎ (01232) 323900. Everything from rock
bands to symphonies performed by the Ulster
Orchestra.

King's Hall *Lisburn Road.*
☎ (01232) 665225. Large exhibition and
concert venue.

Waterfront Hall *2 Lanyon Place.*
☎ (01232) 334455. Fine, ultra modern new
venue for concerts and other large scale
cultural events.

ROUND AND ABOUT

Bass Ireland Brewery
Glen Road. Open by written arrangement
only. Has audio-visual presentation on
brewery's history. Viewing of production
processes.

**Belfast Castle and Cave Hill Heritage
Centre** Daily, all year.

Belfast Zoo *Antrim Road.* Open 10am-5pm
daily, Apr-Sept, 10am-3.30pm daily, Oct-Mar.
☎ (01232) 776277. The zoo has new pens
allowing visitors to view sea lions and
penguins under the surface of the water.
Land-based species vary from bears and
gorillas to marmosets. Restaurant, tea house.
Hazelwood Park, beside the zoo, is a
delightful area, featuring a lake.

Belvoir Park *Newtownbreda,* 6 km
(4 miles) S of Belfast city centre. Extensive
parkland, with Norman motte and ruins of
the 14th c. Breda Old Church.

Botanic Gardens *University Road.*
Open 10am-5pm Mon-Fri, 2pm-5pm Sat-Sun
and bank holidays, Apr-Sept, 10am-4pm Mon-
Fri, 2pm-4pm Oct-Mar. ☎ (01232) 324902.
Dates back to 1828 and features rose garden
and herbaceous borders. The Palm House was
built in 1839 and has been restored, while the
Tropical Ravine, completed 1889, is a fine
example of horticultural Victoriana.

**Cave Hill Country Park and Belfast
Castle** Climb Cave Hill for panoramic
views from MacArt's Fort, where the United
Irishmen planned rebellion in 1795.
Belfast Castle, with its immaculate gardens,
has a new Heritage Centre, open 9am-6pm
daily, all year ☎ (01232) 776925. It tells the
story of this impressive baronial pile and the
even more historic Cave Hill. The park is
accessible at all times.

Colin Glen Forest Park *Stewartstown
Road, west Belfast.* ☎ (01232) 614115.
At the foot of the Black Mountain. The Park
has a waterfall, mill race, nature trails, wildlife
pond, restored aqueduct, heritage centre,
audio-visual presentation. Cafe.

Crown Liquor Saloon *Great Victoria
Street.* Open 11.30am-11pm Mon-Sat,
12.30pm -2.30pm, 7pm-10pm Sun, all year.
This magnificent high-Victorian pub, is richly
ornamented with fine woodwork, glass and tiles.

Belfast Castle

The Palm House in the Botanic Gardens, Belfast.

Falls Road / Shankill Road
The infamous Nationalist Falls and Unionist Shankill have considerable personality and are not without appeal.

Fernhill House
Glencairn Road, open daily, all year ☎ (01232) 715599. Known as the People's Museum, it tells the story of the greater Shankill area.

Giant's Ring
1.5 km (1 Mile) S of Shaw's Bridge, on S outskirts, Belfast. Freely accessible. Most impressive preshistoric earthwork over 200m (600ft) in diameter, with dolmen in centre. There are excellent views of Belfast from the nearby ancient earthwork on a hilltop.

Harland & Wolff Shipyard
Docks, town centre. Can be visited by written arrangement with the public relations department. This world reknowned shipyard was where the *Titanic* and *Canberra* were built, among many others. It now houses two of the world's largest cranes - 'Samson' and 'Goliath'.

Kelly's Cellars
Bank Place, off Royal Avenue. One of Belfast's oldest pubs, dating back 200 years.

Lagan Valley Regional Park
Comprises 16 km (10 miles) of towpath walks beside the River Lagan, starting at Stranmillis and ending in Lisburn. *The Lagan Lookout Visitor Centre,* open 11am-5pm Tues-Fri, 1pm-4.30pm Sat, 2pm-4.30pm Sun, Mar-Sept, 10am-5pm bank holidays. ☎ (01232) 315444. Extensive riverside developments under way beside the River Lagan will mean many new facilities for visitors.

Redburn Country Park
Old Holywood Road, E outskirts of Belfast. Woodland walks, fine views of Belfast hills and lough.

Sir Thomas & Lady Dixon Park
Upper Malone Road. Open dawn to dusk, daily, all year. ☎ (01232) 320202 extn 3441. Japanese garden. The City of Belfast International Rose Trials are held here. Restaurant.

Sport
Ravenhill Road is the main rugby venue in Belfast, while Windsor Park is Northern Ireland's premier football stadium. The city has nearly 20 leisure centres, four swimming baths and eight golf courses.

Crumlin
16 km (10 miles) W of Belfast. A pleasant village at the head of the wooded Crumlin Glen. Good walks beside the small Crumlin River, which forms cascades after the weir. *Talnotry Cottage Bird Garden, 2 Crumlin Road,* open daily, all year, ☎ (01849) 422900. This 200 year-old walled garden is a sanctuary for sick and injured birds. Former *US Air Force Base,* open 12 noon-6pm Sat-Sun, all year, ☎ (01849) 422128. Station 597 was a US 8th Army Air Force base in World War II. Memorabilia, audio-visual presentation. Shop, cafe.

Down Royal Racecourse
The Maze, near Lisburn. ☎ (01846) 621256. Regular horse races, including the Ulster Harp Derby in July.

NEAR BELFAST

Dundonald
8 km (5 miles) E of Belfast. *Dundonald Old Mill,* open 10am-5.15pm Mon-Sat, 11am-5.15pm Sun, all year. ☎ (01232) 480117, has Ireland's largest water wheel, which dates from 1752. Displays, craft shop, restaurant. *Streamvale Open Dairy Farm,* open 2pm-6pm Wed, Sat, Sun and bank holidays, Feb-May, Sept-Oct, 12 noon-6pm daily, June, 10.30am-6pm daily, July-Aug. ☎ (01232) 483244. *Dundonald Ice Bowl,* ☎ (01232) 482611. The centre offers ice-skating, ten-pin bowling and a children's adventure playground.

Hilden Brewery
Near Lisburn, on Belfast Road. Open 10am-5pm Mon-Sat, all year ☎ (01846) 663863. Fascinating small brewery in superb historical setting.

Hillsborough
5 km (3 miles) S of Lisburn. Charming village with steep main Street, an antiques and crafts centre. *Hillsborough Fort,* open 10am-7pm Tues-Sat, 2pm-7pm Sun, Apr-Sept, 10am-4pm Tues-Sat, 2pm-4pm Sun, Oct-Mar. ☎ (01846) 683285. *Shambles Arts Centre,* ☎ (01846) 682946: summer exhibitions. *Hillsborough Parish Church (CI)* dates from 1773, an imposing building with approaches to match. Sir Hamilton Harty, composer and conductor, is buried here.

Lisburn
13 km (8 miles) SW of Belfast. *Christchurch Cathedral (CI)* dates from early 18th c. and is a most interesting building. *Lisburn Museum* in the Assembly Rooms, Market Square, has much material on local history and archaeology, including railway items. Art gallery, exhibitions.

The major new development here is the *Irish Linen Centre,* open 10am-5pm Mon-Sat, 2pm-5pm Sun, all year, ☎ (01846) 663377. Details the history and heritage of what was once Ulster's greatest industry. Weaving workshop has hand looms. Audio-visual presentations. Shop, restaurant.

Moira
11 km (7 miles) SW of Lisburn. *St John's Parish Church (CI)* is situated at the head of an imposing avenue leading from the wooded park. Railway station is oldest

Strangford Lough, Co. Down

Bangor *21 km (13 miles) NE of Belfast.* TIO 34 Quay Street, June-Sept. ☎ (01247) 270069. *North Down Heritage Centre,* Castle Park Avenue. Open 10.30am-4.30pm Tues-Sat, 2pm-4.30pm Sun, Sept-June, 10.30am-5.30pm Mon-Sat, 2pm-5.30pm Sun, July-Aug. ☎ (01247) 271200. Set in the grounds of Bangor Castle, the Centre displays all kinds of memorabilia, including toys and railway memorabilia. Vintage film of Pickie Park, observation beehive in summer. *Bangor Abbey,* at entrance to town, just off the Belfast Road, has traces of the original monastery, but most was incorporated in the present church which was built in 1617. *Pickie Family Fun Park,* open 10am-sunset daily on the promenade has swan pedal boats, paddling pools, miniature train and cafe. *Bangor Marina* has some lovely walks along the promenade. *Ward Park,* open daily, all year, has a nature trail, children's zoo, bowls and putting green.

Castle Ward *1.5 km (1 mile) W of Strangford village.* Estate open dawn to dusk, daily, all year. House open 1pm-6pm Sat-Sun, all year. ☎ (01396) 881204. Vast country estate with woodlands, lake and seashore. The 18th c. house has façades in two different styles, one Classical, the other Gothic. Formal gardens, wildfowl collection, theatre in stable yard, cornmill used for exhibitions.

Comber *6 km (4 miles) SW of Newtownards.* Fine central square and village green. Some pubs may have a few precious bottles left of Comber whiskey, from the local distillery which closed down after World War II. *Castle Espie Centre,* open 10.30am-5pm Mon-Sat, 11.30am-6pm Sun, Mar-Oct, 11.30am-4pm Mon-Sat, 11.30am-5pm Sun, Nov-Feb. ☎ (01247) 874146. Ireland's largest collection of ducks, geese and swans, can be viewed from hides. Waterfowl gardens, woodland walks. Nature centre, shop, coffee room.

Copeland Islands *5 km (3 miles) N of Donaghadee.* Now deserted, but outstanding bird sanctuary. Boats from Donaghadee harbour.

Donaghadee *10 km (6 miles) SE of Bangor.* Most attractive seaside town, built around an imposing harbour. Grace Neill's bar, facing the harbour, dates from 1611. Peter the Great of Russia was entertained here in 1690s, while the poet Keats also paid a visit. Laneways in the town centre add atmosphere. *Summer cruises,* from harbour, ☎ (01247) 812215. Three hour cruises of Belfast Lough on former Scilly Isles lifeboat, ☎ (01247) 883403.

Downpatrick *14 km (9 miles) W of Strangford.* TIO 74 Market Street, ☎ (01396) 612233, all year. *Down County Museum,* open 11am-5pm Mon-Fri, 2pm-5pm Sat-Sun, June- mid-Sept, 11am-5pm Tues-Fri, 2pm-5pm Sat, mid-Sept - June. ☎ (01396) 615218. Located in a restored jail, the museum has Stone Age artefacts and

surviving railway building in Northern Ireland; it dates from 1841.

STRANGFORD AND NORTH DOWN

Ballycopeland Windmill *1.5 km (1 mile) W of Millisle.* Open 10am-7pm Tues-Sat, 2pm-7pm Sun, Easter-Sept, 10am-4pm Sat, 2pm-4pm Sun, Oct-Mar. ☎ (01247) 861413. The late 18th c. windmill was in use until 1915 and is still in working order.

The miller's house has been turned into a visitor centre, with an electrically-operated model of the mill.

Ballyhalbert *16 km (10 miles) S of Donaghadee.* Small fishing village on east coast of Ards peninsula, with small harbour and shore walk for 2 km (1.5 miles) to *Burr Point,* the most easterly point in Ireland.

Ballywalter *8 km (5 miles) S of Millisle.* Small fishing village with good beaches and harbour. The coastal road in vicinity offers good views.

Castle Ward near Strangford, Co. Down

Bronze Age gold found locally. St Patrick's
story is told in one of the gatehouses.
The saint is said to have been buried in the
grounds of the cathedral. *Saul Church* also
has an exhibition commemorating St. Patrick.

Downpatrick Steam Railway, Market Street,
☎ (01396) 615779 has trains on 1.5 km
(1 mile) of former branch line, restored signal
cabin, displays in station house. Walks in
Georgian mall. *Quoile Countryside Centre,*
open 11am-5pm daily, Apr-Sept, 1pm-5pm
Sat, Sun, Oct-Mar. ☎ (01396) 615520.
Inspect fish and wildlife in Quoile Pondage,
guided walks, trails, lectures, fishing jetty
and the ruins of a 16th c. castle. *St Patrick's
Heritage Centre* is planned.

Greyabbey *13 km (8 miles) SE of
Newtownards.* Open 10am-7pm Tues-Sat,
2pm-7pm Sun, Apr-Sept. Ruins of 12th c.
Cistercian abbey in fine parkland setting,
medieval 'physick' garden, visitor centre.
Greyabbey House, dating from 1760.
Open all year by arr. ☎ (012477) 88666.

Groomsport *5 km (3 miles) E of Bangor.*
Old-world village with beach, promenade
and summer displays of work by local artists.

Helen's Bay *5 km (3 miles) W of Bangor.*
Small resort on southern shore of Belfast
Lough. Pleasant walk from barmial-style
railway station to beach. At nearby
Crawfordsburn the country park offers
beaches and coastal and riverside walks.
The Crawfordsburn Inn dates from 1614.

Inch Abbey *1.5 km (1 mile) NW of
Downpatrick.* Open 10am-7pm Tues-Sat,
2pm-7pm Sun, Apr-Sept. The ruins of this
island monastery are reached by a causeway.
The abbey is Cistercian and was founded
in the late 12th c.

Killyleagh *Delightful village on W shore
of Strangford Lough, 24 km (15 miles) NW of
Downpatrick.* Pleasant walks around
Killyleagh's broad streets and up to gates
of the castle. Interesting harbour area.
*Delamont Country Park, 3 km (2 miles) S of
Killyleagh.* Open 9am-10pm daily, Apr-Sept,
9am-5pm Oct-Mar. ☎ (01396) 828333.
Restored walled garden, heronry, woodland

walks, fine views over Strangford Lough,
tea room.

Mount Stewart *8 km (5 miles) SE of
Newtownards.* House open 1pm-6pm Sat,
Sun, Apr, Oct. May-Sept. Garden open
10.30am-6pm daily, Apr-Sept. Temple of
the Winds, open 2pm-5pm daily, except
Tues, May-Sept. ☎ (012477) 88387/88487.
A fine 18th c. house with 19th c. additions.
Rooms include the blue themed "Rome"
bedroom. The Temple of the Winds overlooks
Strangford Lough. The gardens, with their
rare and unusual plants, formal and informal
vistas, are among the finest in these islands.
Shop, tea room.

Newtownards *10 km (6 miles) S of
Bangor. Ark Open Farm,* open 10am-5.30pm
Mon-Sat, 2pm-6pm Sun, Mar 17-Oct,
☎ (01247) 812672/820445, has many rare
breeds, including Vietnamese pot-bellied
pigs, Nigerian pygmy goats, llamas.
Ulster Flying Club, ☎ (01247) 813327,
pleasure flights from an airfield just outside
Newtownards. *Scrabo Country Park,* open
11am-6.30pm daily, except Fri, June-Sept,
☎ (01247) 811491. Woodland walks,
wildlife. Climb the 122 steps to the top
of *Scrabo Tower* for fine views of the
surrounding countryside.

Portaferry *40 km (25 miles) SE Belfast.*
Attractive seaside village facing Strangford
village across the lough. Long waterfront
has mix of Scots-style cottages and Georgian
houses. Boats leave from the quays for trips
around the lough. *Exploris* in Rope Walk,
Castle Street, open 10am-6pm daily Mon-Fri,
11am-6pm Sat, 1pm-6pm Sun, all year.
☎ (01247) 28062. This is a new high-tech
aquarium with impressive displays. Visitors
can sit in a cave beneath the open sea tank
and watch sharks and other giants of the deep.
See also the anemone tank.

Saintfield *16 km (10 miles) SE of Belfast.*
Rowallane: 21 ha (52 acres) of natural
gardens in National Trust care. Open
10.30am-6pm Mon-Fri, 2pm-6pm Sat, Sun,
Apr-Oct, 10.30am-5pm Mon-Fri, Nov-Mar
☎ (012328) 510131.

Seaforde *13 km (8 miles) SW of Downpatrick.*
Seaforde Gardens Butterfly House, open
10am-5pm Mon-Sat, 2pm-6pm Sun, Easter-
Sept. ☎ (01396) 811225. Has hundreds of
exotic butterflies, also reptiles and insects.
Maze with viewing tower, shop, tea room.

Somme Heritage Centre
Between Newtownards and Bangor.
Open 10am-6pm Mon-Thurs, 12 noon-6pm,
Sat, Sun, Apr-Sept, 10am-5pm Mon-Fri,
10am-4pm Sun, Oct-Mar, 10am-5pm
Mon-Fri 12 noon-5pm, Sat, Sun, July, Aug.
☎ (01247) 823202. Audio-visual recreation
of the Battle of the Somme, World War I.
Computerised information service, original
artefacts, lecture theatre, shop, restaurant.

Strangford *11 km (7 miles) W of
Downpatrick.* Attractively situated, facing
Portaferry across the mouth of Strangford
Lough (regular car-ferry crossings). A couple
of miles to the south, *Kilclief Castle* is one
of Ireland's earliest tower houses.

Struell Wells *2 km (1.5 miles) E of
Downpatrick.* 17th c. wells and bath houses,
on a site closely associated with St Patrick.

Ulster Folk & Transport Museum
Cultra, near Holywood. Open 9.30am-5pm
Mon-Fri, 10.30am-6pm Sat, 12 noon-6pm
Sun, Apr-June, Sept, 10.30am-6pm Mon-Sat,
12 noon-6pm Sun, July-Aug, 9.30am-4pm
Mon-Fri, 12.30pm-4.30pm Sat-Sun, Oct-Mar.
☎ (01232) 428428. This outstanding
museum provides a very full day out, in
search of Ulster's economic and social
history. A gallery houses displays of 19th c.
domestic objects, furniture, crafts,
photographs and William Conor paintings.
In the surrounding park, many buildings have
been reconstructed from their original sites,
including a weaver's house, a linen scutch
mill, a blacksmith's forge, even city streets
of old. In the transport section, all modes are
represented, from donkey creels to pony traps,
old aircraft to the Result schooner, built in
Carrickfergus in 1893. The railway collection
that once graced the Witham Street Museum
in east Belfast has been moved to Cultra.
The highlight is the Maeve, the largest steam
locomotive ever built in Ireland, for the old
Great Southern Railways. Horse and carriage
rides on the estate during high season
(Easter-Sept). Tea room.

MOUNTAINS OF MOURNE

Annalong *13 km (8 miles) S of Newcastle.*
The Mountains of Mourne really do "sweep
down to the sea" at this this agreeable fishing
village making a spectacular backdrop.
The harbour is often filled with fishing boats.
The Cornmill, open 2pm-6pm daily, Easter,
May-Aug, Oct ☎ (013967) 68736, built about
1830 and powered by a waterwheel, has flour-
making exhibition. Herb garden and cafe.

Ardglass *32 km (20 miles) NE of
Newcastle.* An important fishing port in
Co Down, with walks around both the inner
and outer harbours. Jordan's Castle, open
10am-7pm Tues-Sat, 2pm-7pm Sun, July-
Aug. The largest of a cluster of castles, this
is a well-preserved four storey tower house.

Bessbrook *5 km (3 miles) NW of Newry.*
Founded in 1845 by a Quaker linen
manufacturer, so it has no pub, though the
adjacent village of Camlough makes up for
this deficiency by having six! Walks around
the main College and Charlemont squares. See
the huge old mill, with dam, sluices and weirs.

Brontë Homeland Interpretative Centre *Drumballyroney, 5 km (3 miles) NE of Rathfriland.* Open 11am-5pm Tues-Fri, 2pm-6pm Sat-Sun, Mar-Oct. ☎ (018206) 31152/23322. Centre details life and times of Bronte family. School and church where Patrick Bronte, father of the novelist sisters, taught and preached, are preserved. His birthplace is one of many sights on the 13 km (8 miles) signposted drive which starts at the centre.

Castlewellan *8 km (5 miles) NW of Newcastle.* Pleasant market town with broad main street and two squares. *Forest Park,* open 10am-dusk daily, all year, ☎ (013967) 78664. Annesley Gardens: 18th c. walled garden, the arboretum was begun in 1740, old courtyards, tropical birds in glasshouses and a 5 km (3 mile) long sculpture trail around the lake. Visitor centre, cafe. Five good fishing lakes within 8 km (5 miles) radius of Castlewellan.

Cullyhanna *5 km (3 miles) N of Crossmaglen.* **Cardinal O Fiaich heritage centre** has material on locally born Cardinal, local history and archaeology. Open 9am-5pm Mon-Fri, 2pm-6pm Sun, 10am-6pm BH, all year, or by arr. ☎ (01693) 868757. Also **Hearty's folk cottage,** agricultural museum.

Dundrum *5 km (3 miles) N of Newcastle.* Small seaside village with the substantial ruins of the castle built by Normans in late 12th c. Views to sea and the Mountains of Mourne. **Dundrum Bay** has a sandy strand, while **Minerstown Beach** on the east side of the bay continues into the 6 km (4 miles) long **Tyrella strand,** where the sand is firm enough for driving. **Murlough Nature Reserve,** 3 km (2 miles) south of Dundrum, is rich in terms of botanic and wildlife interest. **Visitor Centre** open 10am-5pm daily, June - mid-Sept, ☎ (013967) 51467.

Greencastle *6 km (4 miles) SW of Kilkeel.* See the ruins of a **13th c. castle,** at the north entrance to Carlingford Lough, open 10am-7pm Tues-Sat, Apr-Sept, 10am-4pm Sat, 2pm-4pm Sun, Oct-Mar.

Hilltown *13 km (8 miles) N of Rostrevor.* Its numerous pubs are a reminder of the village's old days of brandy smuggling. Attractive tree-lined square. At "Bush Town", 5 km (3 miles) east of Hilltown on the B27, the fairy thorn tree at the junction of the Bryansford and Kilkeel Road, is the largest in the North of Ireland.

Katesbridge *Between Castlewellan and Banbridge.* Delightful little village on banks of Upper River Bann.

Kilkeel *16 km (10 miles) E of Rostevor.* The main fishing port of Co Down. Winding streets, stepped footpaths, many old houses of great character and an enjoyable harbour area all add-up to make Kilkeel an interesting

View of the Mourne Mountains from Castlewellan Forest

resting point for visitors. In addition, the water in the granite trough at 14th c. church ruins in town centre is said to cure warts!

Legananny Dolmen *7 km (4 miles) S of Dromara on the slopes of Cratlieve Mountain.* Widely considered to be the most graceful Stone Age monument in Northern Ireland.

Mountains of Mourne The mountains rise up in spectacular fashion from Newcastle and Annalong. Minor roads lead into the Mournes, but since none cross the centre of the range, you must walk to see the main peaks at close quarters. *Slieve Donard,* 850m (2,796 ft), the highest mountain, is well worth climbing for the spectacular views on a clear day, when you can see as far as Donegal and Wicklow in Ireland, the Isle of Man, north-west England and north Wales.

The climb takes about two hours from Newcastle. At the summit, you will see the remains of the 5th c. oratory built by St Domhanghort, who gave the mountain its name.

The *Mourne Coastal Path* runs south for 6 km (4 miles) along the seashore from Bloody Bridge, at the foot of Slieve Donard, while another path follows the course of Bloody River up into the mountains.

The *Silent Valley* and *Ben Crom* reservoirs supply water to Belfast and Co Down. Surrounding parkland, crafts shop, cafe and *Visitor Centre,* open 10am-6.30pm daily, Easter-Sept, 10am-4.30pm daily, Oct-Mar. ☎ (01232) 746581. On the western edges of the Mournes, near the *Spelga Dam,* 6 km (4 miles) west of Hilltown, you can experience a similar 'magnetic mile' effect to that in *Gortin Forest Park,* where your car appears to be going uphill when it's actually pointing downhill and vice versa! Besides the strange optical effects, the landscape views are quite stunning.

Newcastle *21 km (13 miles) SE of Downpatrick.* TIO Newcastle Centre, 10-14 Central Promenade, ☎ (013967) 22222, all year. One of Northern Ireland's top seaside resorts, magnificently situated, with its vast sandy beach backed to the immediate south by the towering Slieve Donard mountain, one of the Mountains of Mourne. In recent years, visitor facilities in the town have been much extended. *Newcastle Centre,* open daily, ☎ (013967) 25034, has an impressive range of indoor entertainments, including the Tropicana swimming pool, sports hall, lounge and cafe. It is ideal for occupying children during a spell of wet weather.

Mourne Countryside Centre, Central Promenade, open daily, summer, ☎ (013697) 24059, has displays, maps and other material detailing the Mournes. *Grant Gallery,* open 2pm-5pm Mon-Sat, ☎ (013697) 22349, has Irish and international paintings, sculptures. *Newcastle Art Gallery,* 18-22 Main Street, open daily, ☎ (013697) 23555. *Our Lady of the Assumption Church (C),* near the north end of Downs Park, is a modern, circular and striking building. The *Promenade Gardens* have a fountain commemorating Percy French, composer of the song The Mountains of Mourne. *Castle Park* has wide range of sporting activities, summer concerts, open-air entertainment. *Donard Park* rises up the lower slopes of Slieve Donard.

Newry *16 km (10 miles) NW of Rostrevor.* The town has many interesting features and good shopping. The Clanrye River and the canal bisect the town. The canal quaysides have some original 18th c. warehouses. *Cathedral of St Patrick and Colman (C)* in Hill Street, dates from 1825 and has unusual stained-glass windows and mosaics. *St Patrick's Church (CI),* Church Street, includes part of a 16th c. tower. *Newry Arts Centre,* Bank Parade, ☎ (01693) 61244, stages a variety of cultural events. *Newry Museum,* located in the arts centre, open 11am-5pm Mon-Fri, 10am-1pm Sat, all year, ☎ (01693) 66232. Has archaeological items, the table used by Nelson on HMS Victory and material on the "Gap of the North". A special feature of the museum is the restored 18th c. room with period furniture.

Rathfriland *6 km (4 miles) S of Katesbridge.* Small plantation town set on a hill. The steep streets rise to the square. Old buildings include a Quaker meeting house.

Rostrevor *14 km (9 miles) SE of Newry.* A small and delighfully nostalgic seaside town, where Victorian elegance still lingers.

Just behind the town, *Rostrevor Forest* offers gentle walking and more arduous mountain top climbing. *Kilbroney Park,* open daily, all year.

Scarva *6 km (4 miles) SW of Banbridge.* New *Interpretative Centre,* Main Street, open 11am-5pm Tues-Fri, 2pm-5pm Sat-Sun, Mar-Oct, ☎ (01762) 832163. Details the history and development of the Newry canal and also the history of Scarva, which developed because of the canal.

Silent Valley *8 km (5 miles) N of Kilkeel.* Parkland beside reservoirs, *information centre.* Open daily, all year.

Slieve Gullion Courtyard *8 km (5 miles) SW of Newry.* Early 19th c. courtyard in Slieve Gullion forest park. Walled gardens, breathtaking views. Open 9am-6pm Mon-Fri, all year, 12 noon-6pm Sat, Sun, Easter-Sept ☎ (01693) 848084. Tí Chulain cultural activities centre, due to open late 1998. ☎ (01693) 888828.

Tollymore Forest Park *3 km (2 miles) E of Newcastle.* Open 10am-dusk daily, all year. ☎ (013967) 22428. Numerous stone follies and bridges, sequoia tree in arboretum, wildlife and forestry exhibits. Pony trekking, fishing, walking, cafe.

Warrenpoint *5 km (3 miles) W of Rostrevor.* Spacious resort with fine square and tree-lined promenade. The two piers are ideal for fishing and walking. Summer boat excursions across Carlingford Lough to Omeath. The Burren Heritage Centre, Bridge Road, open 11am-6pm Mon-Fri, 2pm-6pm, all year ☎ (016937) 73378. Interprets the history of the Burren district of south Down from prehistory to 19th century. Video presentation. Craft shop, coffee shop.

ARMAGH'S ORCHARD COUNTRY

Ardress House *8 km (5 miles) E of Moy.* Open 2pm-6pm Sat-Sun and bank holidays, Apr-June, Sept, 2pm-6pm daily, July-Aug. Farmyard also open 12 noon-4pm weekdays May-June, Sept. ☎ (01762) 851236. 17th c. farmhouse with 18th c. additions in Neo-classical plasterwork in drawing room, good furniture and pictures. Farm implements, livestock, garden, woodland walks, playground.

Armagh *59 km (37 miles) SW of Belfast.* Pop 12, 700. TIO ☎ (01861) 521800. TIO Old Bank Building, 40 English Street, ☎ (01861) 527808, all year. For 1,500 years, Armagh has been the ecclesiastical capital of Ireland. Today, it retains much of its historic atmosphere, but many new visitor attractions

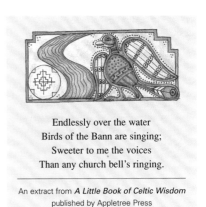

Endlessly over the water
Birds of the Bann are singing;
Sweeter to me the voices
Than any church bell's ringing.

An extract from *A Little Book of Celtic Wisdom*
published by Appletree Press

have been added. The Mall is a pleasant tree-lined oasis in the city centre. *St Patrick's Cathedral (C)* is set on a hilltop and is reached by a fine flight of steps, it is 19th c. Byzantine in style and has lavish interior decoration. Red cardinals' mitres hang from the ceiling of the Lady Chapel. *St Patrick's Cathedral (CI)* is largely an early 19th c. restoration of a 13th c. building. Tablet outside the north transept marks the reputed grave of Brian Boru.

St Patrick's Trian, open 10am-5.30pm Mon-Sat, 1pm-6pm Sun, Apr-Sept, 10am-5pm Mon-Sat, 2pm-5pm Sun, Oct-Mar. ☎ (01861) 521801, tells the story of Armagh's history and details Jonathan Swift's association with Armagh and the writing of Gulliver's Travels. Audio-visual theatre, exhibition, craft shop, cafe. *Palace Stables Heritage Centre,* open 10am-5.30pm Mon-Sat, 1pm-6pm Sun, Apr-Sept, 10am-5pm Mon-Sat, 2pm-5pm Sun, Oct-Mar. ☎ (01861) 529629. Shows how life was in Armagh in 1776. Visits to the archbishop's chapel, ice-house and walks in the demesne. County Museum, open 10am-5pm Mon-Fri, 10am-1pm 2pm-5pm Sat. ☎ (01861)523070. Material on history of the county, railway material and an art gallery. *The Royal Irish Fusiliers Regimental Museum,* open by arr. ☎ (01861) 522911, includes a 1943 Christmas card from Hitler. *Robinson Library,* open 10am-4pm Mon-Fri, all year, ☎ (01861) 523142, has books, manuscripts and registers going back to medieval times. *Armagh Planetarium.* Open 10am-4.45pm Mon-Fri, 1.15pm-4.45pm Sat-Sun, all year. ☎ (01861) 523689. Regular star shows. New attractions include the *AstroPark,* featuring a model solar system and a 17th c. telescope; the *Eartharium,* which shows the earth on three levels; and the interactive laser *Encyclopaedia Galactic.* Observatory grounds have sundial and audio-visual presentation of the work of the observatory. Navan Centre open 10am-6pm Mon-Sat, 11am-6pm Sun, Apr, June, Sept 10am-7pm Mon-Sat, 11am-7pm Sun, July, Aug 10am-5pm Mon-Fri, 11am-5pm Sat, 12 noon-5pm Sun Oct-Mar. ☎ (01861)525550. The exhibition details, in impressive style, the history and archaeology of one of Europe's most important Celtic sites. It was the seat of the ancient Kings of Ulster and the setting for the legends of Cuchulainn. Stunning visual and interactive displays.

Craigavon 60s architect's dream 'new town' yet to come true. Named after Northern Ireland's first Prime Minister. *Tannaghmore Gardens and Farm,* open daily. ☎ (01762) 343244. Victorian and rose gardens. Rare farm breeds, including Kerry cattle, Jacob and Soay sheep, saddleback pigs.

Fews Forest *15 km (9 miles) S of Armagh.* Great walking through forests and along moorland tracks. Fine views over counties Armagh and Down from some picnic sites.

Gosford Forest Park *Near Markethill.* Open daily. Walled garden, mock Norman castle, round tower built by German prisoners-of-war during World War II. Traditional poultry breeds, pigeons. Deer park, forest trail.

Keady *13 km (8 miles) S of Armagh.* Heritage Centre due to be completed in a restored mill in the town centre. It will include a history of local linen and other textile making.

Loughall *8 km (5 miles) NW of Armagh.* The centre of the county's apple growing district. *Orange Order Museum* recalls founding of the order here in 1795.

Lough Neagh Discovery Centre *Oxford Island, S shores of Lough Neagh.* Open 10am-7pm Apr-Sept 10am-5pm Wed-Sun, Oct-Mar. ☎ (01762) 322205. History of the lough, "working water" computer, wildlife exhibition. Birdwatching, walks, boat trips and cafe.

Mullaghbawn Folk Museum *Between Crossmaglen and Camlough, S Armagh.* Open 11am-7pm Mon-Sat, 2pm-7pm Sun, May-Sept, 2pm-7pm Sun, Oct-Apr. ☎ (01693) 888108. Thatched roadside museum in the style of a traditional farmhouse. Exhibitions, craft demonstrations and coffee shop.

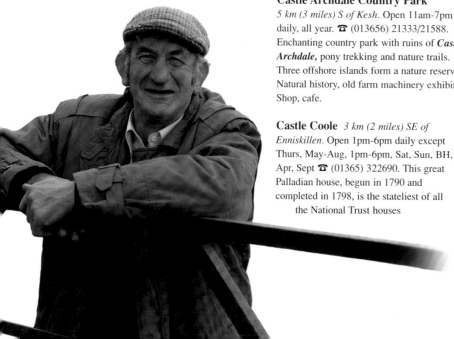

Portadown *43 km (27 miles) SW Belfast.* TIO ☎ (01762) 332499. Market town on the River Bann, and a major coarse fishing centre. *Swimming Pool:* indoor, heated. Learner and competitive pools. Portadown Golf club, 18 holes. ☎ (01762) 335356. *Moneypenny's Lock,* 3 km (2 miles) S of Portadown, open 2pm-5pm Sat-Sun, Easter-Sept. ☎ (01762) 322205. Restored lock-keeper's house and stables on the Newry canal. Exhibitions on the old lightermen, canal and lock, wildlife.

Slieve Gullion Forest Park *8 km (5 miles) SW of Newry.* Open 10am-dusk daily, Easter-Aug. ☎ (016937) 38284. Scenic 13 km (8 miles) drive around this well-wooded park. Mountain top trail gives excellent views to the Mountains of Mourne.

FERMANAGH LAKELANDS

Belleek Pottery *38 km (24 miles) NW of Enniskillen.* Open 9am-6pm Mon-Fri, 10am-6pm Sat, 2pm-6pm Sun, Mar-June, Sept, 9am-8pm Mon-Fri, 10am-6pm Sat, 11am-8pm Sun, July-Aug, 9am-5.30pm Mon-Fri, 10am-5.30pm Sat, 2pm-6pm Sun, Nov, 9am-5.30pm Mon-Fri, Nov-Feb. ☎ (01365) 658501. Visitors can see how this lustrous Parian ware is made. Production started here in 1857. Audio-visual presentation is followed by factory tour. Visitor centre has products for sale and a restaurant. ExplorErne exhibition tells story of Lough Erne. Open 10am-6pm daily, Mar-Nov ☎ (013656) 58866.

Boa Island *N side of Lower Lough Erne.* Joined to the mainland by a bridge. On the western side of the island, near the ancient cemetery, you can see two very strange old stone figures called "Janus statues" because they have a face on each side. Boats to *Lusty Beg Island,* a noted holiday spot, from the jetty on the eastern side.

Castle Archdale Country Park *5 km (3 miles) S of Kesh.* Open 11am-7pm daily, all year. ☎ (013656) 21333/21588. Enchanting country park with ruins of *Castle Archdale,* pony trekking and nature trails. Three offshore islands form a nature reserve. Natural history, old farm machinery exhibits. Shop, cafe.

Castle Coole *3 km (2 miles) SE of Enniskillen.* Open 1pm-6pm daily except Thurs, May-Aug, 1pm-6pm, Sat, Sun, BH, Apr, Sept ☎ (01365) 322690. This great Palladian house, begun in 1790 and completed in 1798, is the stateliest of all the National Trust houses

in Northern Ireland. Fine interior fittings and furnishings, include the State bedroom. Stables and coach house. Mature oak woodland, parkland running down to Lough Coole, with its flock of greylag geese. Shop and tearooms.

Crom Estate *5 km (3 miles)W of Newtownbutler.* Open 10am-6pm Mon-Sat, 12 noon-6pm Sun, Apr-Sept. ☎ (01365) 738118. Vast wood, farmland, loughs with rare plants and wildlife. Ruins of early 17th c. Crom Castle. Visitor centre. Nature trails, walks.

Derrin Lough *3 km (2 miles) NW of Tempo.* Shore walks, lake views. Nearby Topped Mountain has path to the summit and its Bronze Age cairn.

Devenish Island *5 km (3 miles) NW of Enniskillen.* Best-known of the 97 islands in Lower Lough Erne. The well-preserved round tower can be climbed by means of internal ladders. Early Christian religious ruins. Daily boats from Trory Point, Lower Lough Erne, Easter-Sept.

Enniskillen *138 km (86 miles) SW of Belfast.* Pop 10,500. TIO Wellington Road. Enniskillen, the county town of Fermanagh in the heart of Ulster's lakelands, is well set on an island between the two channels of the river linking Upper and Lower Lough Erne. *Enniskillen County Museum* is is devoted to the history and archaeology of Co Fermanagh, with models and dioramas. The story of the Maguire family, who had their headquarters here, is told in audio-visual form.

The Regimental Museum, open 10am-5pm Tues-Fri, 2pm-5pm Sat, 2pm-5pm Sun, May, June, Sept Tel. (01365) 325000, details the history of Royal Inniskilling Fusiliers.

Ardhowen Theatre and Arts Centre, Dublin Road, ☎ (01365) 325400. Theatre and other performance events plus exhibitions. *St MacCartan's Cathedral (CI),* Church Street, dates largely from the early 19th c. but has parts of the original 17th c. building. The old colours of Enniskillen regiments are laid up here. *Convent Chapel (C)* in Belmore Street has remarkable nave windows. The *Methodist Church* in Darling Street has some interesting features - the bulges in the balcony were designed to take crinolines! *Forthill Park,* on the east side of town, has good walks and views. Climb the 108 steps to the top of the *Cole Monument* for an excellent panorama of the town and surrounding lakelands. *Summer cruises* on Lough Erne, daily. ☎ TIO.

Florence Court *13 km (8 miles) SW of Enniskillen.* Open 1pm-6pm Sat-Sun and bank holidays, Apr, Sept, 1pm-6pm Wed-Mon, May-Aug. ☎ (01365) 348249. Three-storey 18th c. mansion linked to flanking pavilions by open arched corridors. The house has Rococo plasterwork and a collection of Irish

Near Carrickreagh, Co. Fermanagh

furniture. The grounds have a summer house, ice house, pleasure gardens and a water-powered sawmill. Many specimen trees in demesne including a yew tree that is said to have been the stock from which all Irish yews have been cultivated. Tea room and shop.

Inishmacsaint *W shore of Lower Lough Erne.* A place of great solitude, with High Cross and the remains of a 6th c. monastery. Boat from Killadeas.

Irvinestown *13 km (8 miles) N of Enniskillen.* **Irish Hammersley Pottery:** working pottery with audio-visual presentation. Open 9am-5pm Mon-Thurs, 9am-2.30pm Fri, Feb-Dec, ☎ (013656) 21934.

Lisnaskea *19 km (12 miles) SE of Enniskillen.* One of Fermanagh's few substantial towns. **Castle Balfour** is firmly Scottish in character. The town library has a small, but interesting, folklife display.

Lough Navar Forest Park
19 km (12 miles) NW of Enniskillen. Open 10am-dusk, all year. Vast expanse of woodland best approached from Derrygonnelly. Scenic drive concludes at summit viewpoint from which you get excellent views over Lower Lough Erne, most of south Donegal and north Sligo.

Marble Arch Caves *5 km (3 miles) W of Florence Court.* Open daily, mid-Mar - Sept, weather permitting. Tours 11am-4.30pm. ☎ (01365) 348855. Extensive caves open to the experts and general visitors alike. For the latter, the tour begins with an underground boat trip past the stalactites.

Monea Castle *10 km (7 miles) NW of Enniskillen.* Well-preserved, 17th c. castle, handsomely set at the end of a tree-lined lane. Like **Castle Balfour** in Lisnaskea, it is another plantation castle showing strong Scottish influences.

Rosslea *51 km (32 miles) SE of Enniskillen.* The Heritage Centre, open 9am-5pm Mon-Fri, 4pm-6pm Sat-Sun, Apr-Sept. ☎ (013657) 51750. Located in a late 19th c. schoolhouse, the centre has traditional farm implements, old crochet work. Genealogy service. Shop and tearoom.

White Island *16 km (10 miles) NW of Enniskillen.* This island set in Castle Archdale Bay, has eight inscrutable statues, not unlike those on Easter Island, and equally mysterious in their origins. Summer ferry service from Castle Archdale Marina.

MID-ULSTER

An Creagan Visitor Centre
20 km (12 miles) NE of Omagh, off A505. Details of 44 archaeological sites within 8 km (5 miles) radius. Open 11am-6.30pm daily Apr-Sept, 11am-4.30pm Mon-Fri, Oct-Mar ☎ (016627) 61112.

Ardboe Cross *W shores of Lough Neagh 16 km (10 miles) E of Cookstown.*

Well preserved 10th c. **High Cross** in remote setting. Ruins of old churches and a 6th c. abbey are nearby.

The Argory *6 km (4 miles) NE of Moy.* Open 2pm-6pm Sat-Sun and bank holidays, May-Sept 2pm-6pm daily, except Thurs, June-Aug. ☎ (01868) 784753. Fine early 19th c. house set in wooded countryside, overlooking the River Blackwater. The house has been little changed since early this century. Stable yard, sundial garden, extensive walks. Shop and tea room.

Beaghmore Stone Circles
22 km (14 miles) NW of Cookstown. Six stone circles and some cairns, dating back 4,000 years. Their origins and purpose are unclear.

Bellaghy *8 km (5 miles) NE of Magherafelt.* **Bellaghy Bawn** is 17th c. stronghold converted to heritage centre with material on archaeology, history and nature. Features the poetry, films and broadcasts of Seamus Heaney, the world-renowned Nobel Prize-winning Irish poet, who was born nearby in 1939. Open daily, except Mon, all year ☎ (01648) 386812.

Benburb *14 km (9 miles) S of Dungannon.* **Benburb Valley Heritage Centre,** open 10am-5pm Mon-Sat, 2pm-5pm Sun, Easter-Sept, Oct-Mar by arr. ☎ (01861) 549752, set in a former linen mill with much of the machinery intact, the centre tells the story of linen making here. **O'Neill Historical Centre,** Servite Priory, ☎ (01861) 548187. **Benburb Valley Park,** with walks beside the River Blackwater, overlooked by clifftop ruins of Benburb Castle.

Clogher *12 km (8 miles) SW of Ballygawley.* **Clogher Cathedral (CI)** was built on a hilltop in 18th c. and dominates the village. It claims to be the oldest bishopric in Ireland. The nearby village of Augher is set on a fine-looking stretch of the River Blackwater.

Coalisland *6 km (4 miles) NE of Dungannon.* An early centre of the industrial revolution in the North of Ireland. Coal has been mined here, on and off, for the past 200 years. The **Coalisland Corn Mill,** open 10am-8pm Mon-Fri, 11am-6pm Sat, 2pm-6pm Sun, June-Sept, 10am-6pm Mon-Fri, Oct-May. ☎ (01868) 748532. The mill details the town's industrial history with audio-visual techniques, old photographs and personal recollections. The nearby **Weaving Factory Museum** concentrates on this aspect of local industrial history.

Cookstown *74 km (46 miles) W of Belfast.* TIO, 48 Molesworth Street, ☎ (016487) 66727 June-Sept. A restored station is the setting for both the TIO and the **Museum** which details local heritage. Open 9am-5pm Mon-Fri, Easter-Sept, 9am-12pm Sat, July-Aug. ☎ (016487) 66727. The town has one of the longest and widest main streets in

Ireland and some agreeably old-fashioned pubs. *Killymoon Castle,* in the grounds of the golf club, and *Derryloran Parish Church (CI),* in the town, were both designed by John Nash, architect of Brighton Pavilion. The spire of the Catholic church in the town centre, is a landmark for miles around. *Kinturk Cultural Centre* has audio-visual presentation on the life of the eel and on local fishing history. Open daily, all year. ☎ (016487) 36512. *Drum Manor Forest Park:* shrub garden, butterfly garden. Open daily, all year.

Davagh Forest Park *13 km (8 miles) NW of Cookstown.* You can see most of Northern Ireland from the summit of *Beleevnamore Mountain* given a clear day.

Dungannon *69 km (43 miles) W of Belfast.* *Tyrone Crystal* began here in 1971, exactly 200 years after a previous crystal glass making factory had started production in the vicinity. Today, visitors can take a tour of the modern factory to see all stages of production. Guided tours, Mon-Thurs, Sat all year. ☎ (01868) 725335. *Peatlands Park,* open 2pm-6pm, daily all year ☎ (01762) 851102. Visitor centre details peatland ecology. Video, outdoor exhibits. Rail trip on narrow gauge railway formerly used in peat workings.

Donaghmore Heritage Centre, 6 km (4 miles) NW of Dungannon. Open 9am-5pm Mon-Thurs (4.30pm Fri), 11am-4pm Sat, May-Aug, all year. ☎ (01868) 767039. This converted late l9th c. national school has historical material on local industries. See also the high cross nearby. *Parkanur Forest Park,* 5 km (3 miles) W of Dungannon. Open daily, all year. Woodland trails and deer park. Farm buildings restored to original character.

Fivemiletown *32 km (20 miles) E of Enniskillen.*Two transport museum collections in the area. The *Blessingbourne Museum,* open daily, Easter-Sept. ☎ (013656) 21221. Has some coaches and carriages. Fivemiletown Library has a small display of local railway memorabilia.

Gortin Glen Forest Park *11 km (7 miles) N of Omagh.* Open 9am-dusk daily, all year. ☎ (016626) 48217. The 8 km (5 miles) forest drive has viewpoints, sika deer, wildfowl, a visitor centre and a cafe.

Moneymore *6 km (4 miles) NW of Cookstown.* Handsome plantation town with wide main street, reconstructed by the Draper's company in 1817. A number of nearby plantation towns are also of interest: Draperstown (also founded by the Drapers) and Magherafelt, granted to the Salters' Company by James I.

Omagh 54 km (34 miles) S of Derry. TIO, 1 Market Street, ☎ (01662) 247831/247832, all year. Quiet market town where the rivers Camowen and Drumragh meet. Hometown of noted author, Ben Kiely. The best view is

from the top of the steep, wide main street which leads to the courthouse. Riverside walks along the banks of the River Camowen.

Sion Mills *5 km (3 miles) S of Strabane.* Originally a model linen village, Sion Mills boasts an exceptionally wide main street, and still exudes much charm.

The Sperrins *S of Derry.* These wild remote mountains offer wonderful views from theri peaks and a fascinating array of wildlife. They also offer good walking, and the stunning Glenelly and Owenkillew river valleys attract both walkers and cyclists. In addition gold has recently been rediscovered in the mountains.

Sperrin Heritage Centre, 9 miles east of Plumbridge. Open 11am-6pm Mon-Fri, 11.30am-6pm Sat, 2pm-7pm Sun, Apr-Oct. ☎ (01662 648142). Features natural history and gold-mining exhibits plus other Sperrin treasures. Try your hand at panning for gold.

Springhill *8 km (5 miles) NE of Cookstown.* Open 2pm-6pm Sat-Sun and bank holidays, Apr-June, Sept, 2pm-6pm daily, except Thurs, July-Aug. ☎ (016487) 48210. 17th c. whitewashed house built for a settler's family, complete with family furniture, paintings, ornaments, curios, kitchen with old utensils. There is a large collection of costumes in the outbuildings, together with walled gardens, woodland walks, a shop and tearoom. Also one of Ulster's best authenticated ghosts!

Strabane *20 km (14 miles) SW of Derry.* TIO Abercorn Square, ☎ (01504) 883735, all year. *Gray's Printing Press* at 49 Main Street, open 2pm-5.30pm daily or by arr., except Thurs, Sun. ☎ (01504) 884094. See the display of 18th and l9th c. printing equipment. John Dunlap, who printed the first copies of the American Declaration of Independence in 1776, began his apprenticeship here. An audio-visual display tells the story of printing. Also see the ancestral home of Woodrow Wilson, US President 1913-1921, open daily, Apr-Sept, ☎ (01662) 243292.

Ulster-American Folk Park *5 km (3 miles) N of Omagh.* Open 11am-6.30pm Mon-Sat, 11.30am-7pm Sun, Easter-Sept, 10.30am-5pm Mon-Fri, Oct-Easter. ☎ (01662) 256320. This elaborate display tells the story of emigrant life in the 18th and 19th c. on both sides of the Atlantic. Among the many highlights are the emigration museum, the ship and dockside gallery, an American street, Pennsylvania log barn and farmhouse and a Victorian chemist's shop. Craft shop and cafe.

Ulster History Park *11 km (7 miles) N of Omagh.* Open 10.30am-6.30pm Mon-Sat, 11.30am-7pm Sun and bank holidays, Apr-Sept, 10.30am-5pm Mon-Fri, Oct-Mar. ☎ (01662) 648188. From the Stone Age to the end of 17th c., the park traces the story of settlement in Ireland. Audio-visual

presentations and exhibition gallery in the new visitor centre. Shop and cafe.

Wellbrook Beetling Mill *6 km (4 miles) W of Cookstown.* Open 2pm-6pm Sat-Sun and bank holidays, Apr-June, Sept, 2pm-6pm daily, except Tues, July-Aug. ☎ (01648) 751735. This water-powered hammer mill was used for the final stage in linen making; the machinery is still in working order. Walks by mill race and Ballinderry River.

DERRY CITY AND COUNTY

Castlerock *13 km (8 miles) NW of Coleraine.* Bracing seaside village just W of Bann estuary. Good beach. Open air swimming pool. *Castlerock Golf Club,* 18 holes.

Downhill Castle, *13 km (8 miles) NW of Coleraine.* Landscaped estate laid out in late 18th c. by Frederick Hervey, Earl of Bristol and Anglican Bishop of Derry. The ruins of the bishop's palatial house can still be seen. Also gardens, fish ponds, woodland, glen and cliff top walks. *Mussenden Temple* perched on the clifftop, open 12 noon-6pm Sat-Sun and bank holidays, Apr-June, Sept. ☎ (01265) 848728. Grounds open at all times.

Coleraine *50 km (31 miles) NE of Derry.* TIO Railway Road, ☎ (01265) 44723 open all year. Dating back to the 5th c., Coleraine is a Plantation town and boasts some fine Georgian houses and streets. It is now the location of the main campus of the University of Ulster. The *Riverside Gallery,* ☎ (01265) 44141, has regular exhibitions, while the *Riverside Theatre,* ☎ (01265) 51388, stages regular productions. The *Wilson Daffodil Gardens,* also on campus, have rare Irish-bred daffodils and narcisci. Best seen in April when the flowers are in full bloom.

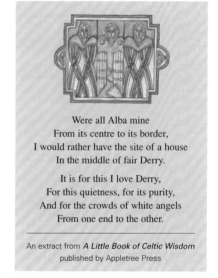

Were all Alba mine
From its centre to its border,
I would rather have the site of a house
In the middle of fair Derry.

It is for this I love Derry,
For this quietness, for its purity,
And for the crowds of white angels
From one end to the other.

An extract from *A Little Book of Celtic Wisdom* published by Appletree Press

Derry City at Dusk.

Derry *117 km (73 miles) W of Belfast.* Pop 95,000. TIO, 8 Bishop Street. ☎ (01504) 267284 open all year. Although its official title is Londonderry, this city set on both banks of the River Foyle is often called by the simpler, older title of Derry. Derry hit the world headlines with the famous civil rights march of October 1968. Then serious disturbances, starting in 1969, put the Bogside on the global agenda. A walk from the Guildhall, through William Street, to Free Derry Corner, with its internationally known legend, "You are now entering Free Derry", will give a vivid illustration of the historical turmoil of this intensely Irish city. The Bloody Sunday Memorial in Rossville Street commemorates the victims of one of the worst atrocities of the past 30 years of the Northern conflict, when 14 people on a civil rights march were shot dead by British paratroopers on 30 January 1972. In recent years, Derry's prosperity has improved and many new visitor amenities have been opened. The *Walls of Derry,* largely intact, but just 1.6 km (1 mile) in circumference, and complete with the Roaring Meg cannon, are the best place to start a city tour. *St Columb's Cathedral (CI),* built in 1628 and consecrated in 1634, has many relics of the 1688-89 siege, which was the political pivot of the city's history and development, until the events of 1968 onwards. The mortar shell which contained the surrender terms of the siege is preserved in the cathedral porch, while the *Chapter House* has relics of the siege and an audio-visual presentation. *Long Tower Church (C)* to the SW of St Columb's Cathedral, is the oldest Catholic church in the city, it dates from the 1780s, and it has an interesting Rococo interior. *St Eugene's Cathedral (C)* is much more recent, built in

the Gothic style in the late l9th c. and finally completed in 1903 with the addition of the cross on top of the spire.

At the very centre of Derry is the *Guildhall.* It was built in late Gothic style in 1890 and is the venue for arts events. Just round the corner from the Guildhall is the *Harbour Museum* in Harbour Square ☎ (01504) 377331, open 10am-1pm 2pm-4.30pm Mon-Fri all year, which has a replica of the craft St Columba used to sail to Iona, and many details of Derry's vital role as a port during World War II.

The *Tower Museum* tells Derry's story from prehistory to the present, including the 1689 siege, in an exciting presentation. See also the craft village. The *O'Doherty Tower,* above the museum, open 10am-5pm Mon-Sat, July, Aug, 10am-5pm Tues-Sat, Sept-June, ☎ (01504) 372411, has artefacts from the Spanish Armada ships wrecked off the Irish coast in 1588. *Ulster Science Centre,* Foyle Street, has interactive exhibitions. ☎ (01504) 370239. *Foyle Valley Railway Centre,* beside Craigavon Bridge, open 10am-5pm or by arr. Tues-Sat, May-Sept. ☎ (01504) 265234. Much material on the narrow gauge systems of Co Donegal and Londonderry & Lough Swilly railways, which have long since closed down. Also operational models, audio-visual presentations and trips on diesel railcars on track running through *Foyle Riverside Park,* (weekends only from May to Sept). Earhart Centre, Ballyarnet on the west bank of the Foyle, open 9am-4.30pm Mon-Thur, 9am-1pm Fri, all year. ☎ (01504) 354040. This is a cottage exhibition devoted to Amelia Earhart, the first woman to fly the Atlantic solo, who landed here in 1932. Adjoining *wildlife sanctuary* is open 9am-dusk Mon-Fri, 10am-6pm Sat-

Sun, ☎ (01504) 353202. *Fifth Province,* Butcher Street: audio-visual techniques telling the story of the Celts. Open 10am-8pm daily, Apr-Sept, 9am-4.30pm Mon-Fri, Oct-Mar. ☎ (01504) 373177. *Hilltop Open Farm,* Ballyarnet, open 1pm-6pm daily, Mar-Aug, lpm-6pm Sun, Sept-Feb. ☎ (01504) 354556. Has exotic game birds, poultry, rare breeeds of pigs, sheep and Highland cattle.

Gordon Gallery, 36 Ferryquay Street, open 11am-5.30pm Tues-Fri, 11am-lpm Sat, all year, ☎ (01504) 266261, has regular exhibitions by well-known Irish artists. *Orchard Gallery,* Orchard Street, open 10am-6pm Tues-Sat, all year, ☎ (01504) 269675, has regular exhibitions and lectures. *Magee College,* Northland Road, has occasional theatre, film and other cultural events as does the *Foyle Arts Centre,* Lawrence Hill, ☎ (01504) 363166. The *Heritage Library,* 14 Bishop Street, a reference library with reading room and genealogical research centre, also puts on exhibitions, ☎ (01504) 269792.

Draperstown *9 km (6 miles) SW of Maghera.* Named after the London Company of Drapers, which was part of the plantation of Derry city and county, this east Co Derry town is building a new heritage centre which will detail the often barbarous events of that plantation.

Dungiven *32 km (20 miles) SE of Derry.* See the ruins of the 12th c. Augustinian priory, on the banks of River Roe. The ruins of the early Christian *Banagher Church* are 5 km (3 miles) south of the town, while a similar distance to the north are the ruins of Bovevagh Church.

Eglinton *8 km (5 miles) NE of Derry.* This tree-lined village, near Derry airport, has a very English air. Enjoyable walks in the Muff Glen, just south of the village.

Garvagh *17 km (11 miles) S of Coleraine.* The *Folk Museum* has many artefacts on local history and is open 2pm-5pm Thurs, Sat, June-Aug. ☎ (012655) 58216.

Hezlett House *8 km (5 miles) W of Coleraine.* Open 1pm-5pm Sat-Sun and bank holidays, Apr-June, Sept, daily, July-Aug, except Tues. ☎ (01265) 848567. Not so much a house as a 17th c. thatched cottage furnished in Victorian style. Also a small museum of farm implements.

Knockcloghrim Windmill *11 km (7 miles) N of Magherafelt.* Open 9am-7pm Mon-Sat, Easter-Sept, 9am-5pm Mon-Sat, Oct-Mar. ☎ (01648) 44745. The *Heritage Centre* is located inside this restored windmill, which was in working order until the Great Wind of 1895 blew off its sails! Local history, viewing gallery, working scale model.

The coast Road, Co. Antrim

Limavady *27 km (17 miles) E of Derry.*
TIO council offices, Benevenagh Drive,
☎ (015047) 22226 all year. Market town
with plenty of Georgian style. The six-arched
Roe Bridge dates back to 1700. In 1851,
Jane Ross, a local resident, noted down a tune
played by a travelling fiddler which became
known later as the "Londonderry Air", and
later again as "Danny Boy".

Magilligan Strand *From near Eglinton
to Magilligan Point.* This vast sandy strand,
arguably the most impressive beach in Ireland,
stretches for some 24 km (15 miles) along
the east shores of Lough Foyle. Tremendous
views of the Inishowen Peninsula, across
the estuary.

Mountsandel Fort *1.5 km (1 mile)
SE of Coleraine.* A large oval mound,
dominating the River Bann. See the site
of the oldest house in Ireland, lived in
9,000 years ago close by. Riverside walks.

Ness Country Park *11 km (7 miles)
SE of Derry.* Broadleaved woodland walks.
Nature trail. Path from car park leads to the
highest waterfall in Northern Ireland, about
12 m (39 ft).

Portstewart *6 km (4 miles) SW of Portrush.*
TIO Town Hall, ☎ (0126583) 2286.
The main streets of this attractive Victorian-
style town form an Atlantic promenade,
winding round rocky bays, with shore paths
at each end. Magnificent 3 km (2 mile) long
strand between town and River Bann, backed
by dunes.

Roe Valley Country Park *1.5 km (1 mile)
S of Limavady.* Open 10am-5pm daily,
Easter-Sept, 10am-4pm daily Oct-Mar.
☎ (015047) 22074. The first domestic
hydro-electric power station in Northern
Ireland, built in 1896 has been preserved,
along with the water wheels used for linen
production. Museum, exhibitions, riverside
walks, cafe. Park always accessible.

ANTRIM COAST & GLENS

Antrim *27 km (17 miles) NW of Belfast.*
TIO 16 High Street ☎ (01849) 465156 all
year. TIO Pogue's Entry, Church Street.
☎ (01849) 428331, Easter-Sept.

Pogue's Entry was the childhood home of
Alexander Irvine, who became a missionary
in New York's Bowery and wrote My Lady
of the Chimney Corner about the lives of
Irish country folk. The *Irvine House* is open
10am-5pm Mon-Fri, 10am-2pm Sat, all year.
☎ (01849) 428331/463113, extn 230.
The round tower in *Steeple Park* is about
1,000 years old and is well-preserved and
freely accessible. *Massereene Demesne,*
☎ (01894) 428000, is a restored 17th c.
garden fashioned in the Anglo-Dutch style,
with wooded grove, ponds and walks.

Antrim Castle Grounds 17th c. Anglo-
Dutch water garden. Woodland walks.
Interpretative facilities in nearby *Clotworthy
Arts Centre,* a listed building. Open 9am-6pm
Mon-Fri, 10am-6pm Sat, 2pm-6pm, Sun
☎ (01849) 428000.

Ballintoy Harbour *8 km (5 miles) NE of
Ballycastle.* North Antrim cliff path runs for
18 km (11 miles) from here to Runkerry taking
in the *Giant's Causeway, Dunseverick Castle,
White Park Bay.* The village has a most
attractive harbour: white piers and a white
beach make fine a contrast with the black cliffs.
Parish church with beautiful resurrection
window. Youth Hostel. Cliff-top walks Boats
to the cave below *Kinbane Castle* ruins.

Ballycastle *108 km (67 miles) NW of
Belfast.* Pop 3,300. TIO Sheskburn House,
7 Mary Street, ☎ (012657) 62024, all year.
A most attractive seaside resort on the north
Antrim coast, completely unspoiled.
Ballycastle proper is 3 km (2 miles) inland
and is connected to the harbour area by a
broad tree-lined avenue. An ideal base for
exploring the many delights of the Antrim
coast and host to the lively two day *Oul'
Lammas Fair,* which dates back to 1606,
held on the last Monday and Tuesday in
August. Bargains and banter are plentiful,
as are the local delicacies of dulse (edible
seaweed) and yellowman (a sticky
honeycomb). Ballycastle is the departure
point for boats to *Rathlin Island,* which
beckons invitingly across the sound.
Ballycastle Museum open 2pm-6pm July -
mid-Sept, ☎ (012657) 62942, has folk and
social history of the Glens, set in 18th c.
schoolhouse. The *Marconi Memorial* on
the seafront, marks the spot from which
the inventor of wireless telegraphy made his
first successful transmission in 1898, between
Ballycastle and Rathlin Island. *Pans Rock,*
east end of Ballycastle beach, is an old salt
drying pan and is reached by a footbridge. In
the 18th c. extensive coal mining was carried
out at Ballycastle and remnants of this mining
can be seen along the coast and in the glens.
Pony trekking in the glens is popular, try the
Watertop Trekking Centre;Watertop Farm
188 Cushendall Road, Ballycastle, 9 km (6
miles) S of Ballycastle. Open 10am-5.30pm
daily, July-Aug. ☎ (012657) 62576/63785.
Museum, ornamental game birds, farm tours,
sheep shearing demonstrations (July-Aug),

pony trekking, boating and fishing. Farm tours and sheep shearing demonstrations.

Bonamargy Friary, *0.8 km (0.5 mile) E of Ballycastle.* Ruins of Franciscan friary built about 1500 on the banks of the River Margy.

Ballymena *18 km(11 miles) N of Antrim.* The largest town in this area, Ballymena is a prosperous market town with a strong Scottish influence and a reputation for meanness! *Morrow's Shop Museum,* Bridge Street: local history and artefacts. Open Mon-Sat, all year.

Ballymoney *12 km (8 miles) SE of Coleraine.* Two interesting churches: *Our Lady and St Patrick (C),* built of local basalt, fine stained glass windows and *Trinity Presbyterian Church,* built in 1884 by Home Rule advocate, Rev. J B Armour. *Leslie Hille Heritage Farm Park,* 1.5 km (1 mile) W of Ballymoney. Museum, rare breeds, deer, ornamental fowl, gardens, lakes, nature trails, horse-trap and donkey rides through 18th c. estate. Open 2pm-6pm Sun, BH, Apr, May, Sept, Sat, Sun, June, daily July, Aug. ☎ (012656) 66803.

Bushmills *5 km (3 miles) S of Giant's Causeway. Old Bushmills Whiskey Distillery,* open 9.30am-5.30pm Mon-Sat, 12 noon-5.30pm Sun, Apr-Oct, 10am-3.30pm Mon-Fri, Nov-Mar. ☎ (012657) 31521. Attractively set by St Columb's Rill, Bushmills has the world's oldest whiskey distilling licence, dating from 1609. Audio-visual presentation, tours, tasting, Distillery Kitchen. The Bushmills open-top bus travels the scenic route between Bushmills and Coleraine, taking in the Giant's Causeway, daily all year.

Carnlough *5 km (3 miles) NW of Glenarm.* Pretty Glens of Antrim village, at the head of Glencloy, constructed in the mid-19th c. by the Marquess of Londonderry.

Carrick-a-Rede *8 km (5 miles) W of Ballycastle.* ☎ (012657) 31159/62178. This swinging rope-bridge spans the chasm between the mainland and Carrick-a-Rede Island. Not for the faint-hearted, it is only in position in the salmon fishing season (May-Sept).

Carrickfergus *18 km (11 miles) NE of Belfast.* TIO Knight Ride, Antrim Street, ☎ (019603) 66455, all year. *Carrickfergus Castle,* open 10am-6pm Mon-Sat, 2pm-6pm Sun, Apr-Sept, 10am-4pm Mon-Sat, 2pm-4pm Sun, Oct-Mar. ☎ (01960) 351273. Built in 1180 by John de Courcy, the castle had a garrison until 1928. Exhibition on castle's history, including audio-visual presentation, shop and cafe. Last admission 30 mins before closing. *St Nicholas Church (CI),* off Market Place, dates from 12th c. and has interesting stained-glass windows. There is a small section of old town walls nearby.
Louis MacNiece plaque in North Road, marks where the distinguished poet lived from when

he was two years of age until he went up to Cambridge University. His father was rector of St Nicholas. *Carrickfergus Gasworks,* ☎ (01960) 366455 was one of the last coal-fired gas-making operations in Ireland when it closed down in 1964. Exhibition of machinery and also domestic equipment worked by gas. Audio-visual presentation. *Knight Ride and Heritage Plaza.* Open 10am-8pm Mon-Sat, 12 noon-6pm Sun, Apr-Sept, 10am-5pm Mon-Sat, 12 noon-5pm Sun, Oct-Mar. Last admission 30 mins before closing. ☎ (01960) 366455. This is a monorail ride through the history of Carrickfergus from 531. Shops and cafe.

The *Andrew Jackson Centre* at Boneybefore, open 10am-6pm Mon-Fri, 2pm-6pm Sat-Sun, Apr-Oct. ☎ (01960) 366455. The centre commemorates the 7th US President and has exhibition devoted to the 1st Battalion, US Rangers which were raised in Carrickfergus in 1942. Rowing boats can be hired in harbour and there are walks along the wide promenade and Marine Gardens.

Cushendall *27 km (17 miles) SE of Ballycastle.* The "capital" of the Glens of Antrim, this village is one of the most distinctively Irish parts of Northern Ireland. The village was largely created by a 19th c. landowner Francis Turnly. Boats for hire from *Red Bay Boats,* which also has boat building yard. ☎ (012667) 71331.

Cushendun *8 km (5 miles) N of Cushendall.* The most northerly of the Glens of Antrim. Some cottages designed by Clough Williams Ellis, famed for the village of Portmerion in north Wales. He also designed nearby "Glenmona" - the home of Lord Cushendun. Many delightful cliff walks in vicinity of Cushendun. *Loughareema Vanishing Lake,* beside road from Ballycastle to Cushendun. This lake can dry up very quickly, as if someone had pulled the plug! *Ossian's Grave,* 5 km (3 miles) S of

Cushendun. This megalithic tomb on the slopes of Tievebulliagh mountain is the burial place of the warrior-bard son of Finn McCool. Nearby, a modern bard is commemorated; the cairn in memory of John Hewitt, a renowned 20th c. Ulster poet.

Dunluce Castle *5 km (3 miles) E of Portrush.* Open 10am-7pm Mon-Sat, 2pm-7pm Sun, Apr-Sept, 10am-4pm Tues-Sat, 2pm-4pm Sun, Oct-Mar. Dramatic ruins set on a craggy cliff. The castle dated mostly from 16th and 17th c. In 1639, part fell into the sea, taking with it several unfortunate servants who were in the kitchens at the time. The ruins are among the largest and most spectacularly set of any castle ruins in Ireland. Visitor centre, audio-visual presentation.

Dunseverick Castle *E end of Giant's Causeway.* Some slight ruins of one of Ireland's oldest castles, built around 500, perched on a high crag.

Fair Head *6 km (4 miles) NE of Ballycastle.* One of the most rugged and desolate spots on the north coast, with wonderful views of Rathlin island and south-west Scotland in clear weather.

Giant's Causeway *3 km (2 miles) N of Bushmills.* TIO ☎ (012657) 31855 all year. Giant's Causeway accessible to visitors at all times. Visitor Centre open daily, 10am-7pm daily, summer, 10am-4pm winter.
The *Giant's Causeway,* with more than 40,000 hexagonal basalt columns, is a world heritage sight, and offers an extraordinary panorama. The *Visitor Centre* depicts the flora, fauna and geology of the area, together with a replica of the hydroelectric tram that ran between the Causeway and Portrush until 1951. Shop and tea room.

Causeway School Museum, next to Giant's Causeway Visitor Centre, open 11am-4.30pm daily, July-Aug. ☎ (012657) 31777.

DULSE AND YELLOWMAN...

Did you treat your Mary Ann to Dulse and yellowman At the Ould Lammas Fair at Ballycastle-o?

Dulce is a purple edible seaweed. It can be stewed and eaten as a vegetable or with oatcakes. Yellowman is a toothsome, honeycombed, sticky toffee, traditionally sold at the Ould Lammas Fair at the end of August.

1 lb / $^1/_2$ kg / 1$^1/_2$ cups golden or corn syrup, 8oz / 250g / 1 cup brown sugar. 1 tbsp butter (heaped), 2 tbsp vinegar, 1 tbsp baling soda.

In a large saucepan slowly melt together all the ingredients except the baking soda. Do not stir. Boil until a drop hardens in cold water (240°F, 190°C on a sugar thermometer). Stir in the baking soda. The toffee will immediately foam up as the vinegar releases the gas from the baking soda. Pour onto a greased slab and while just cool enough to handle fold the edges towards the centre and pull repeatedly until the whole is a pale yellow colour. Allow to cool and harden in a greased tin and break into chunks with a toffee hammer - or anything else that comes to hand.

An extract from *A Little Irish Cookbook* published by Appletree Press

Originally a National School, designed by Clough Williams Ellis, recreates the atmosphere of a 1920s classroom.

Glenariff Forest Park *Between Waterfoot and Ballymena.* Open 8am-dusk daily, all year. ☎ (012667) 58232. Spectacular glen walk with three waterfalls. Scenic path runs round the sheer sides of the gorge. Walks and trails to mountain viewpoints. Visitor centre, shop, restaurant.

Glenarm *16 km (10 miles) N of Larne.* Delightful village in southern Glens with park offering walks up the glen beside Glenarm river.

Glenavy *13 km (8 miles) NW of Lisburn.* Ballance House was the birthplace of John Ballance, prime minister of New Zealand from 1891 until 1893. The house has material showing the links between Ireland and New Zealand. Open 11am-5pm Tues-Fri. 2pm-5pm Sat, Sun, BH, or by arr. ☎ (01846) 648492.

Gracehill *3 km(2 miles) W of Ballymena.* Model settlement founded by Moravians in the 18th c . The original square survives as do the separate buildings for men and women. German Christmas customs are still observed in the village church.

Islandmagee *Peninsula near Larne,* stretching for 11 km (7 miles) and 3 km (2 miles) at its widest point. Fine cliffs on the eastern side and bathing at ***Brown's Bay*** and ***Ferris Bay. Ford Farm Park and Museum,*** open 2pm-6pm daily, all year, ☎ (01960) 353264. This small country museum features butter-making and sheep-shearing demonstrations.

Larne *34 km (21 miles) NE of Belfast.* TIO Narrow Gauge Road, ☎ (01574)260088, all year. Ferry terminal, ☎ (01574) 270517, all year. *Larne & District Historical Centre,* Old Carnegie Library, 2 Victoria Road, open 2pm-5pm Tues-Sat, all year. ☎ (01574) 279482. Exhibits include turn-of-the-century country kitchen, milk house, blacksmith's forge, family history material. ***Carnfunnock Country Park,*** 5.5 km (3.5 miles) N of Larne. Open 10am-dusk, daily, Easter-Oct. ☎ (01574) 270541/ 260088. Maze shaped like map of Northern Ireland, walled garden, adventure playground, golf, putting green and visitor centre. The ***Antrim Coast Road,*** which runs from Larne to Cushendun and on to Ballycastle, offers some of the most impressive coastal scenery in Ireland. The mountain roads leading off it, especially in the Cushendall area offer good views. Maud's Ice Cream, Glenlo village. ***Visitor centre,*** tours of ice cream making factory. Open 8am-4pm Mon-Fri, all year. ☎ (01574) 272387.

Murlough Bay *Just E of Fair Head.* Unspoiled bay in National Trust care. See monument to Sir Roger Casement on the way down to the shore.

Co. Antrim coast

Portballintrae *3 km (2 miles) SW of Giant's Causeway.* Pleasant, secluded seaside village with harbour and beach.

Port Braddan *W end of White Park Bay.* This tiny hamlet has Ireland's smallest church, a mere 3x2 m (11x6 ft).

Portglenone *13 km (8 miles) W of Ballymena.* Augustine Henry grove commemorates a forestry pioneer. Woodland walks beside the River Bann. Open 10am-sunset, daily all year. ☎ (01266) 821241.

Portrush *19 km (12 miles) N of Coleraine.* TIO Dunluce Centre, Sandhill Drive, ☎ (01265) 823333. ***Dunluce Centre*** is a virtual reality entertainment centre that includes the high-tech ***Turbo Theatre,*** the ***Earthquest*** interactive fun adventure, the ***Myths & Legends*** theatre, a viewing tower for superb views over Portrush and surrounding area, outdoor playpark for children. Shop and restaurant. ☎ (01265) 824444. ***Waterworld*** is a water-based leisure centre, ☎ (01265) 822001. ***Portrush Countryside Centre*** is open daily in summer, ☎ (01265) 823600. ***Town Hall Theatre,*** amusement arcades, seafront. Excellent beaches on east and west strands. Boat trips from harbour to caves at ***White Rock,*** and to ***The Skerries,*** offshore islands home to multitude of sea birds.

Rathlin Island *13 km (8 miles) offshore from Ballycastle.* Northern Ireland's only inhabited island, with a population of about 100, has plenty of natural attractions. Nearly all the coastline is formed by cliffs, but the island itself is flat, making for easy walking. Near the ***East Lighthouse*** are cement blocks with title "Lloyds" marked on them - the base of the wireless mast set up for Marconi's first radio tranmission in 1898.

Brockley has the remains of a Stone Age settlement, while ***Knockanas,*** between Brockley and the harbour, has traces of an early Christian settlement. ***Kebble National***

Nature Reserve, near the West Lighthouse, is home to colonies of kittiwakes, razorbills and guillemots. The island is an ideal base for deep sea fishing and scuba diving. During summer there are boats daily from Ballycastle, weather permitting. The mail boat runs three times a week, all year. ☎ (012657) 63934/ 63917.

Templepatrick *8 km (5 miles) SE of Antrim.* ***Patterson's Spade Mill,*** open 2pm-6pm Sat-Sun and bank hoidays, Apr-May, Sept, daily (except Tues) June-Aug, ☎ (01849) 433619. The last surviving water-driven spade mill in Ireland which was in operation until l990. All the original equipment has been restored and there are demonstrations of spade making.

Torr Head *E end of Murlough Bay.* Approached by narrow road from either Cushendun or Murlough Bay. Desolate spot affording excellent views over the North Channel. Scotland is only 19 km (12 miles) away.

Waterfoot *1.5 km (1 mile) S of Cushendall.* Modest village at mouth of Glenariff river. The main appeal here is Glenariff Glen, known as the "Queen of the Nine Glens". Steep mountains rise on both sides of the glen which narrows to a deep wooded gorge. A path winds along, and a further path runs from the head of the glen to Ballycastle.

Whitehead *8 km (5 miles) N of Carrickfergus.*Attractive seaside town with good walks along promenade. ***Whitehead Excursion Station*** has a unique collection of Irish standard gauge steam locomotives and coaches at the Headquarters of ***Railway Preservation Society of Ireland.*** Regular steam events. ☎ (01960) 353567.

White Park Bay *3 km (2 miles)W of Ballintoy.* The half-moon bay is one of the finest in the North, but it's not recommended for swimming because of the currents.

GAZETTEER INDEX

GUIDE & KEY TO ATLAS

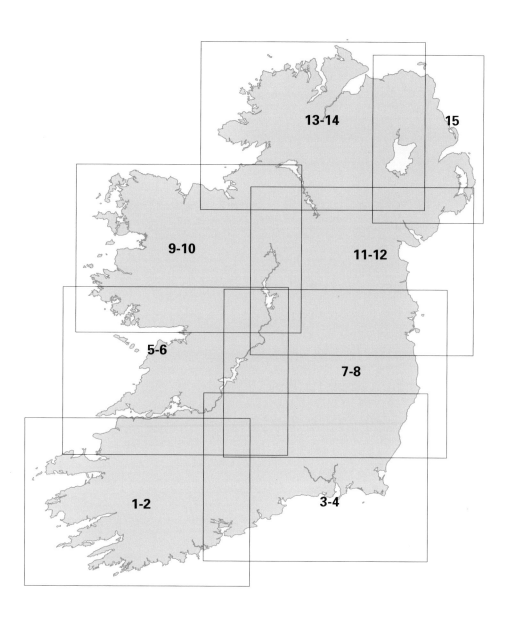

13-14

15

9-10

11-12

5-6

7-8

1-2

3-4

Key to Atlas

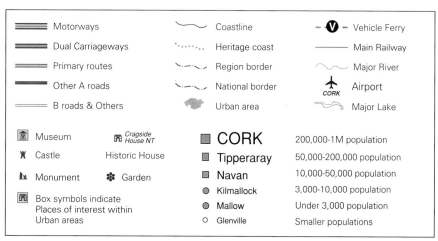

≡≡≡ Motorways	⌐⌐ Coastline	–**V**– Vehicle Ferry
▬▬▬ Dual Carriageways	·······. Heritage coast	—— Main Railway
▬▬▬ Primary routes	⌐·–·⌐ Region border	∿∿ Major River
▬▬▬ Other A roads	⌐·–·⌐ National border	✈ Airport CORK
≡≡≡ B roads & Others	▲ Urban area	∿ Major Lake

Ⓜ Museum	🏠 Cragside House NT	■ **CORK**	200,000-1M population
✗ Castle	Historic House	■ Tipperaray	50,000-200,000 population
⑂ Monument	❀ Garden	■ Navan	10,000-50,000 population
🏠 Box symbols indicate Places of interest within Urban areas		● Kilmallock	3,000-10,000 population
		● Mallow	Under 3,000 population
		○ Glenville	Smaller populations

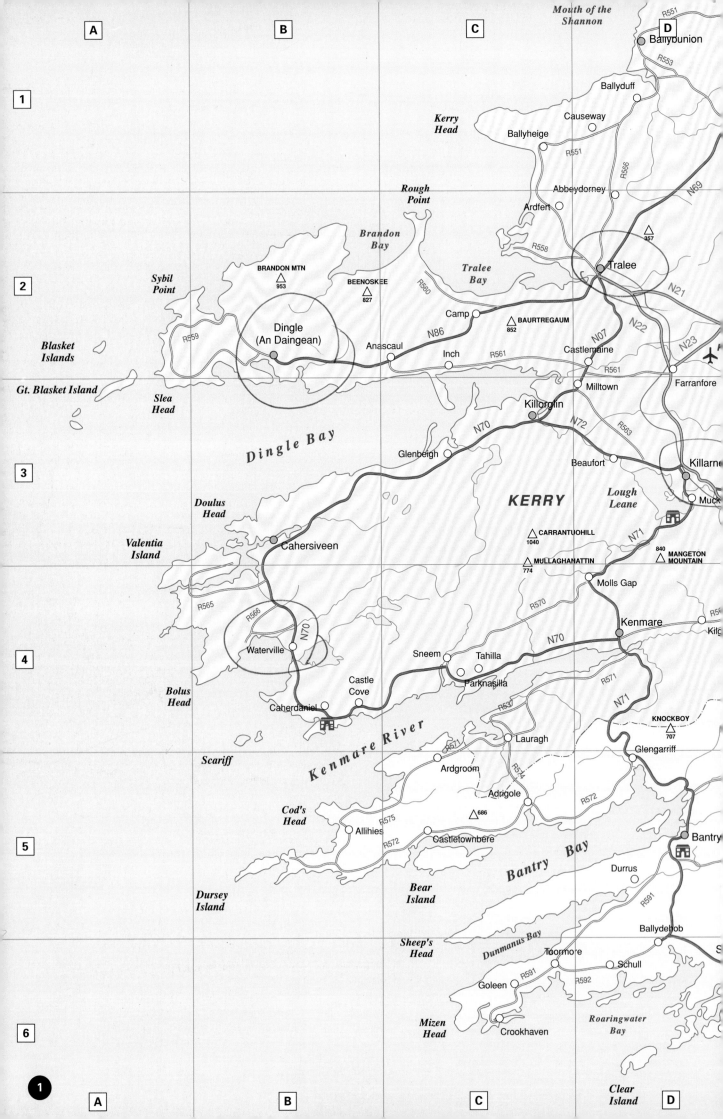

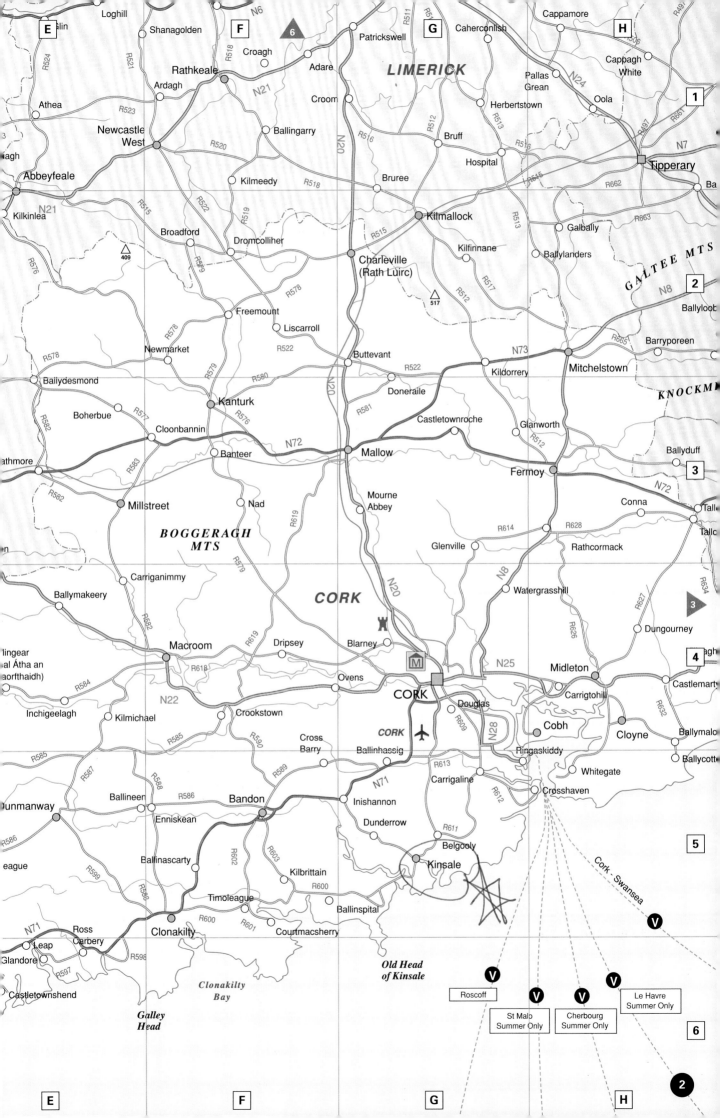

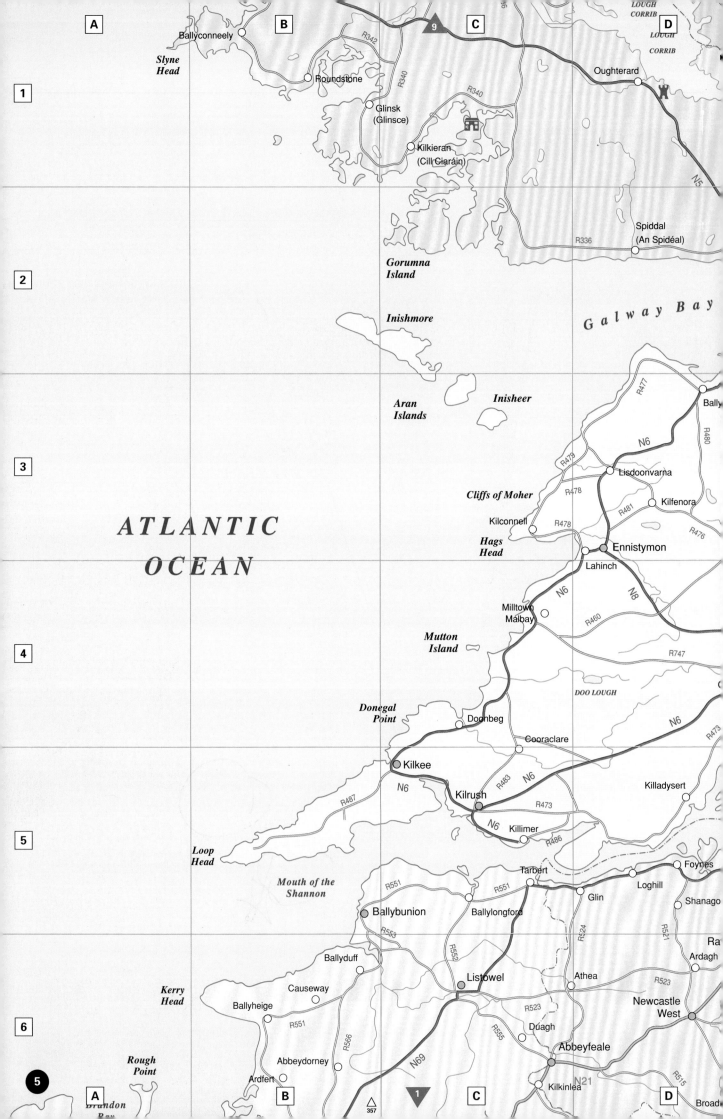

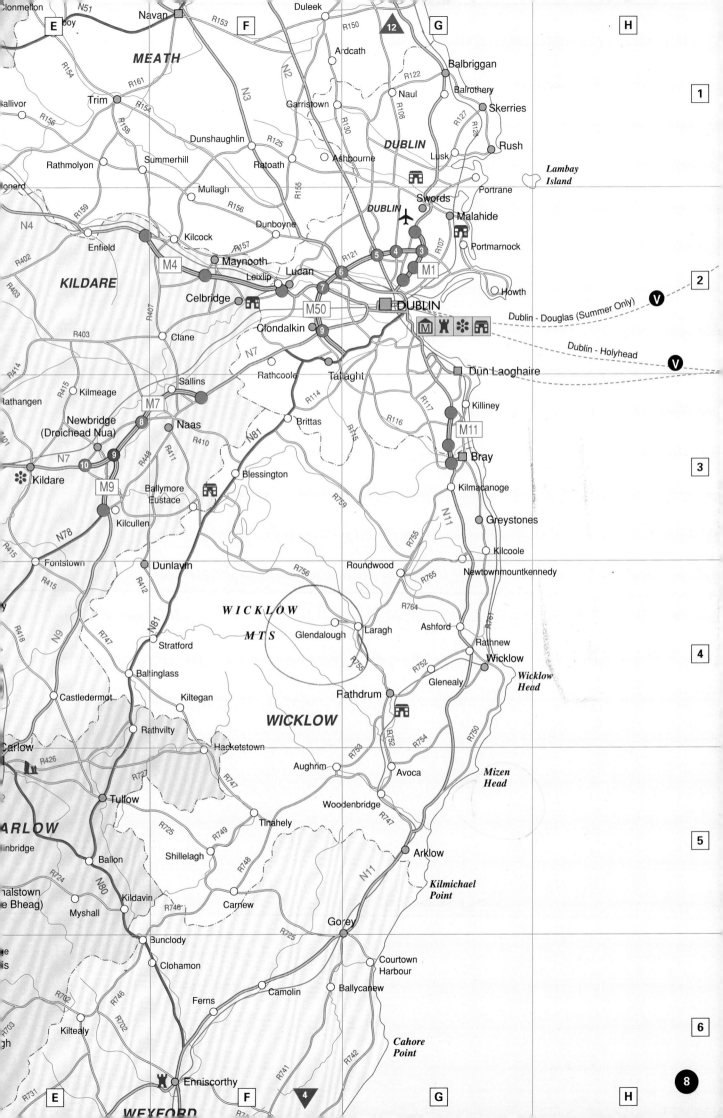

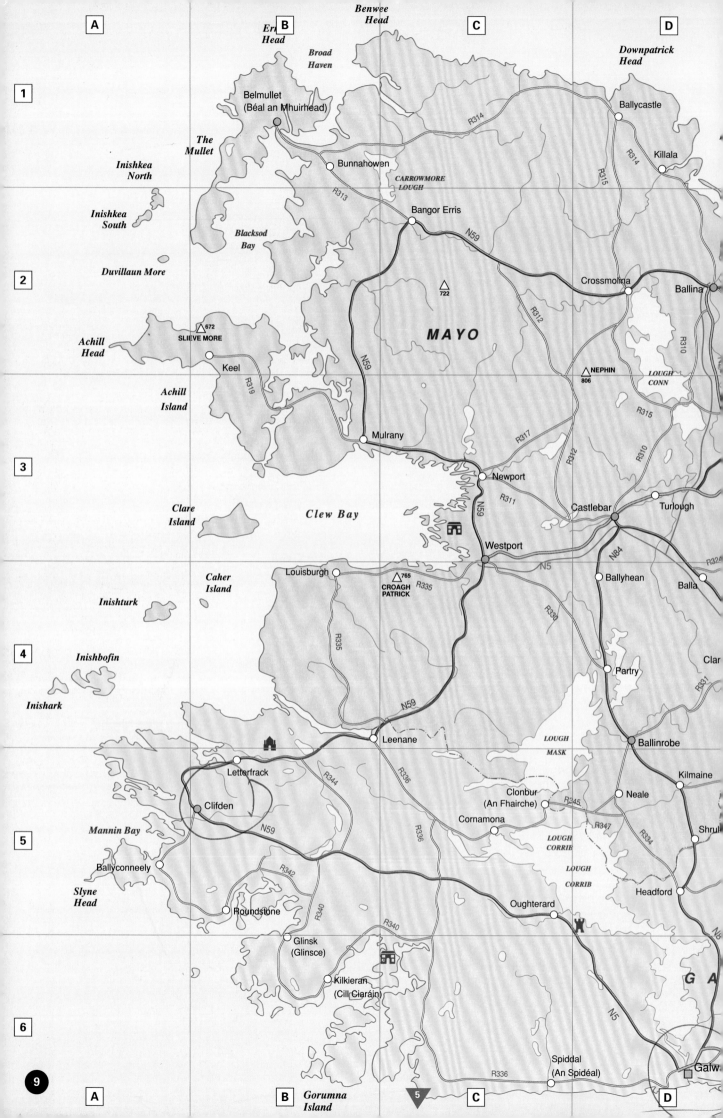

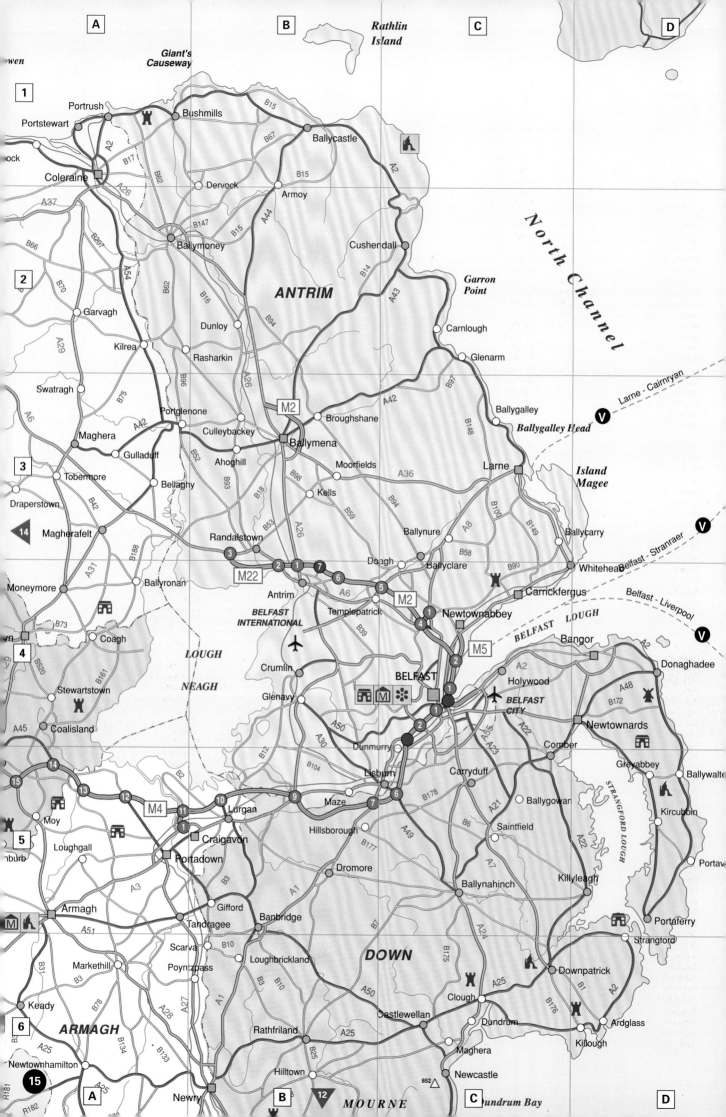

ATLAS INDEX